D1564441

A BIBLICAL PEOPLE
IN THE BIBLE BELT

A BIBLICAL PEOPLE IN THE BIBLE BELT

THE JEWISH COMMUNITY OF MEMPHIS, TENNESSEE, 1840S-1960S

Selma S. Lewis

MERCER UNIVERSITY PRESS
MACON, GEORGIA

ISBN 0-86554-602-9   MUP/H454

The paper used in this publication meets the minimum requirements
of American National Standard for Information Sciences— Permanence of
Paper for Printed Library Materials, ANSI Z39.48-1984.

Library of Congress Cataloging-in-Publication Data

Lewis, Selma S., 1921-
    A biblical people in the Bible belt: The Jewish community of Memphis,
Tennessee, 1840s-1960s / by Selma S. Lewis
        xvi + 279 pp.   6 x 9" (15 x 22 cm.)
    Includes bibliographical references and index.
    ISBN 0-86554-602-9 (alk. Paper).
    1. Jews—Tennessee—Memphis—History. 2. Memphis (Tenn.)—
Ethnic relations. I. Title.
    F444.M59J5   1998
    976.8'19—dc21   98-22299
                                                              CIP
Additional Information to be Provided

For my parents,
Rose and Harry Seligman

CONTENTS

PREFACE / IX

ACKNOWLEDGMENTS / XV

1. IN THE BEGINNING / 1

2. EARLY PROSPERITY / 13

3. THE CIVIL WAR YEARS / 31

4. THE YELLOW FEVER EPIDEMICS / 55

5. THE EASTERN EUROPEAN IMMIGRATION / 63

6. THE EARLY TWENTIETH CENTURY / 83

   A PHOTO ALBUM APPEARS AFTER PAGE 126

7. SURVIVING THE GREAT DEPRESSION / 127

8. THE HOLOCAUST AND THE BIRTH OF ISRAEL / 155

9. BETWEEN WARS AND SOCIAL UPHEAVAL: THE FIFTIES / 177

10. THE SIXTIES / 185

EPILOGUE / 205

SELECTED BIBLIOGRAPHY / 209

INDEX / 225

PREFACE

The Jewish community of Memphis, Tennessee has long been an integral part of the city's history. In a relationship begun less than twenty years after the city was founded in 1819, the Jews of Memphis have been key contributors to its life. Jews have participated fully in Memphis's development, shared its problems, enjoyed its successes, profited from its blessings, and furthered its welfare and culture. Never more than a small fraction of the total population, the Jewish community has nevertheless been a significant presence in the city.

Jews came to Memphis from within the United States and from beyond its borders. As the country began to expand to the west, Jews were among those who followed the national pattern. Although most chose to remain in the urban centers of the Eastern Seaboard, others were attracted to opportunities provided by the westward movement. Some of the Jews who ventured westward joined others from abroad to form the nucleus of the Memphis Jewish community.

The familiar story of the emigration of Jews from Europe to the United States is composed of as many facets as there are people to tell their tales. Unlike other groups who, in the words of President John F. Kennedy, settled this "nation of immigrants," Jews had "no single old country."[1] They came to our shores from all over the Old World, impelled to emigrate by difficult conditions that varied not only from country to country but also from year to year.

Since ancient times Jews have lived in many countries, often under adverse conditions. Between the fall of the second Temple in 70 C.E. and the establishment of Israel as the Jewish homeland in 1948, Jews existed in their adopted lands as a minority presence amid an often hostile majority. But life in the United States of America has been different.

Though still a distinct minority in the United States, Jews have lived in this country under the legal protection of a written constitution. In addition, they have lived under the psychological protection of what might be considered a social contract with the United States. In a remarkable

---

[1]David M. Brownstone and Irene M. Frank, editors, *America's Ethnic Heritage* series (New York and Oxford, England: Facts on File Publications, 1988), 7.

1790 letter President George Washington wrote to the Jewish congregation of Newport, Rhode Island:

> All possess alike a liberty of conscience and immunities of citizenship. It is now no more that toleration is spoken of as if it was by the indulgence of one class of people that another enjoyed the exercise of their inherent rights. For happily the government of the United States, which gives to bigotry no sanction, to persecution no assistance, requires only that they who live under its protection should demean themselves as good citizens in giving it on all occasions their effectual support.[2]

Laws may not alter feelings, but they do dictate actions. In the United States, anti-Semitism is not sanctioned by law. As a result, America has often served as a haven for Jews from all over the world.

This history of Jews in Memphis will record from what places they came, when they arrived, and where and how they lived. It will consider what institutions they developed, how they made their living, how they practiced their religion, and how they related to the dominant religious groups. It will examine how they adapted and changed, and what they retained of their old lives as they adjusted to their new circumstances. Author Salman Rushdie writes of the process of cultural adaptation:

> When people come halfway across the planet they don't just bring their suitcases. They bring everything. And even as they reinvent themselves in their new city—which is what they do—there remain these old selves, old traditions, erased in part, but not fully. So what you get are these fragmented, multifaceted, multicultural selves.[3]

This consideration of the formation and development of the Jewish community of Memphis will focus on the cultural, religious, and intellectual

---

[2]Cited in Frank J. Coppa and Thomas J. Curran, *The Immigrant Experience in America* (Boston: Twayne Publishers, 1976), 164.

[3]Salman Rushdie, interviewed by Gerald Mazerati, quoted in [Memphis] *Commercial Appeal*, February 26, 1989) B5.

selves the immigrants brought with them, and on what it has meant to be both Jewish and southern.

This book is not intended to be a compendium of names of members of the Jewish community, all of whom are important and have made their own contributions to the whole. That would be a useful record, but it would be a different book. Incorporated into this history, however, will be stories of individuals who either led exceptional lives, made significant contributions to the life of the city, or were themselves representative of general trends. Choice of these individuals is often dictated by the existence of records or by the possibility of interviewing descendants.

Jonathan Sarna has defined "Jewish community" as "the corporate dimensions of American Jewish life, embracing within it both the strictly religious and the not so clearly religious dimensions of Jewish existence, the ethnic ties of individual Jews, and the political striving of Jews as a group."[4] He believes that there is a sense of ongoing Jewish group identity that changes over time. This book will rely on Sarna's definition as it deals with the history of the Jewish community in Memphis. It will examine this history, not as an isolated account, but as part of the record of the growth and development of the city of Memphis.

Several themes emerge from the history of the Memphis Jewish community. One is that Memphis has been a favorable place for Jews to live. For reasons about which one can only speculate, little overt prejudice has been expressed. Perhaps it was because the Jews were too few in number to constitute a threat, or perhaps it was that the early Jews earned the respect of the larger community by being among the major builders of the city, contributing to its growth and welfare. Or perhaps it was because blacks have been the primary scapegoats, sparing the Jews the role they usually filled. Perhaps prejudice was blunted, too, by "Boss" Ed Crump, who ruled the city for almost fifty years and encouraged the acceptance of Jews and other religious minorities, and by the fact that Jews always took care of the needs of their own people as well as attending to those of the community as a whole. Jews have continually held leadership positions in the city's business, political, and institutional life. Much of the success of Memphis's

---

[4]Jonathan Sarna, "Jewish Community Histories: Recent Non-academic Contributions," *Journal of American Ethnic History*, 6(Fall 1986): 64.

commerce is due to Jewish business development in the city. Throughout the history of Memphis, Jews have been major supporters of cultural and philanthropic activities of the community. During the 1960s the Jewish community also greatly facilitated the integration at business and entertainment sites and at public facilities. These themes will recur throughout the book.

The writing of this book has been especially rewarding for me. This story of the Memphis Jewish community, while not my personal story, is sufficiently universal to the experience of Jews in this country that it has been almost autobiographical. Like so many others, I grew up hearing horror stories about the Russia of the czars from which both my parents came to this country. My father spoke seldom about his early life. Not so my mother; she sang the beautiful folk songs of her native land and told vivid tales of life in the village of Nicholaev, where her father had been a timber merchant and a man learned in the Talmud. She inscribed indelibly on my mind the stories of Cossacks on horses riding through her village, beating, injuring, sometimes killing Jews. The children were hidden away wherever possible, but safety was never assured. Easter, she recalled, was the worst time of all. The Easter bunny has never been my favorite symbol.

In the early days of 1900, the pogroms grew even more intense, as the czar needed more scapegoats on whom to blame the severe economic conditions that plagued the country. Finally, despairing that circumstances would ever improve for Jews in Russia, in 1903 my mother's parents decided to send her, aged sixteen, and her sister, Bessie, aged eighteen, to the promised land of America to join an uncle, a brother, and a sister who already lived there. My mother's description of the journey across, in the steerage class of an ocean liner, was both sad and funny. She had only one pair of shoes, and on the first day aboard the ship, someone stepped on the sole of one of them, tearing it off completely. Fortunately, from her point of view, her sister spent the eight days of the voyage in bed, seasick the entire time, so Mama had Aunt Bessie's shoes to wear.

My mother's description of her first sight of the Statue of Liberty in New York harbor was always told in awe-filled tones. Her first experience with Americans was to be offered a banana with which she was totally unfamiliar. She peeled it, threw away the white inside and tried to eat the peel. To add to her feeling of strangeness, on the streets of New York she saw the first black person she had ever seen. She followed him for several blocks to try to determine whether or not his color was the result of being terribly dirty.

Leaving New York with her sister, my mother went by train to Louisville, Kentucky, to visit their uncle, and then to Nashville, Tennessee, where their married sister welcomed them. It was a joyous reunion, tempered with the sorrow of having left behind their parents and other siblings.

Mama soon began to work as a sales clerk at Lebeck's, a department store in Nashville. She told of the first year in her new country when she cried every night because she could not speak the language. She attended night school to learn English and the requirements for naturalization. By the age of twenty-three, she had become literate in her new tongue, had attained citizenship in the United States, and had met and married my father.

The story of my mother's immigration to America is not at all unusual. It has been repeated so many times that it begins to seem quite ordinary. But it reflects the qualities of courage, determination, and burning desire for freedom and dignity that are, I believe, common to the experience of all immigrants who came to this country, regardless of their origins. When the Jewish Historical Society of Memphis and the Mid-South offered me the opportunity to write about this experience, I felt honored and grateful. To tell the story of such forebears is a responsibility and a privilege.

ACKNOWLEDGMENTS

The Jewish Historical Society of Memphis and the Mid-South recognized the urgency of capturing the past before it faded further. Its vision inspired the writing of this book, and its support has encouraged the project every step of the way. In particular I wish to acknowledge my debt to Harriet Stern and Leonid Saharovici whose contributions have been immeasurable.

Financial support has come from the Memphis Plough Community Foundation, the Memphis Jewish Federation and the Herman Bensdorf II Residuary Trust. The Southern Jewish Historical Society provided a grant for photographic equipment and supplies. The generosity of these benefactors supplied essential funds, and, by implication, a vote of confidence. I wish to thank them all.

Gifted photographer Jan Meyer graciously volunteered to provide photographs to illustrate the book and thanked me for the opportunity to be involved! Shirley Klass worked to gather information on the photographs used.

Several sources of material must be acknowledged. The staff of the Memphis Room of the Memphis Public Library and Information Service, especially Dr. Jim Johnson and Patricia La Pointe, have done a remarkable job of preserving documents, clippings, and photographs. I doubt that the book could have been written without their invaluable help in locating information. The staff of the Mississippi Valley Collection at The University of Memphis; Shirley Feibelman, organizer of the archives at Temple Israel; and Rosalyn Lit at the Temple Israel library have been cooperative and helpful. The Center for Southern Folklore and its director, Judy Pelser, have furnished excellent Holocaust interviews and stories of the "Pinch." The Goldbergers—Leo, Herman and Bobby—have opened the files of the *Hebrew Watchman* and answered many of my questions. I am grateful to all of these generous resources.

Several people have taken the time to read portions of this book and have given me the advantage of their counsel: Harriet Stern and Gloria Felsenthal, who have been supporters of this project from its inception; Marjean Kremer, whose collaboration has always been honest and wise; Jane Lettes, who generously and carefully corrected mistakes in grammar and punctuation; and Peggy West, who has always made her perspective and expertise available. Judith Daniels's and May Lynn Mansbach's suggestions and concern have guided me through the revisions that could have been painful but have instead only improved every aspect of this book. I am grateful to them and to Rabbi Micah Greenstein, who knew Ms. Daniels and suggested that I ask her to help. How lucky for me! While I alone am responsible for errors, the people who assisted me deserve any credit. Sincere appreciation is offered as well to all the people who have shared their memories and stories.

Historians are fortunate if they have predecessors on whose shoulders they can stand. I wish to acknowledge the work of Sam Shankman, both his published works and his unpublished manuscript of the history of Memphis Jews. Dr. Berkley Kalin has interviewed and written of many members of the Jewish community. Rabbi James Wax's "History of the Jews of Memphis, 1860-1865" gathered important information of the early Jews. Rabbis A. Mark Levin of Anshei Sphard-Beth El Emeth Synagogue, Raphael Grossman of Baron Hirsch Synagogue, and Harry Danziger of Temple Israel have been unfailingly helpful. Kim Henley not only typed the initial copy of this book, but read it as she typed, offering suggestions for which I thank her. Last, but far from least, I wish to express my thanks to my wonderful husband and best friend, Marshall.

1

IN THE BEGINNING

"America, you have it better than our old continent, you have no fallen castles, no stones . . . and are not inwardly torn by useless memories and old quarrels."

—Goethe

The history of the Jewish community of Memphis is a chapter in the larger history of Jews in the United States. It is also a part of the history of Jews in the South. It differs from other southern Jewish histories insofar as Memphis differs from her sister cities. Memphis is distinctive in its location on bluffs above the Mississippi River and in its boundaries that border Arkansas to the west and Mississippi to the south. In addition to its location on the river, Memphis enjoys other geographical advantages. It was founded 22 May 1819, in the heart of one of the richest cotton-growing regions and one of the most extensive hardwood lumber forests in the country. In the early 1820s, it was the largest city not only in Tennessee but in the entire Mid-South.

Memphis's position made it a logical distribution center for home-grown cotton, lumber, and products from the North and East. The town developed western characteristics; it built wide streets and emphasized trade as a result of its location on the river, but it was strongly southern because of the dominance of cotton and slavery.[1]

The nationwide Panic of 1819, followed by years of depression in Virginia and North Carolina, sped the flow of immigrants to Memphis, causing an early spurt in population.[2] At the same time, the rising price of cotton encouraged many to come in search of rich farm land in the newly opened area. Between 1820 and 1830, hundreds of settlers came into the

---

[1]Gerald Capers, *Biography of a Rivertown* (New Orleans: Tulane University Press, 1966), 76.

[2]Ibid., 30.

area from Virginia, North Carolina, east and middle Tennessee, Alabama, Kentucky, Mississippi, South Carolina, and Georgia. Some brought black slaves with them. As large plantations developed and the demand for slaves increased, blacks were brought from eastern plantations and sold in southwestern slave markets. Memphis became the largest such market in the area.

Life in Memphis in the 1820s was rude and rough, dominated by flatboats that plied the Mississippi River. The city had few of the tempering, conservative forces present in older, more organized communities. During its first two decades there were few signs of change. Houses were built of logs, more refined structures appearing only after sawmills appeared in the 1820s. Streets were so full of ruts and holes that travel was dangerous. It was reported that a team of oxen pulling a wagon on the main street in 1843 drowned in one of the holes.[3]

Religious activity in the 1820s was "as crude as the town itself." There were some small beginnings of organized religion in the period as Methodist circuit riders and itinerant Presbyterian preachers appeared on the scene. The first places of worship were private homes, warehouses, saloons, carpenter shops; in 1826 a meetinghouse was built in Court Square. The first church was built in the 1830s by the Methodists, followed quickly by churches built by the Episcopalians, Presbyterians, and Baptists. The first Catholic mass in the city was celebrated in 1839 at the home of Irish schoolmaster, Eugene Magevney.[4]

After the Civil War, the black population increased more than in any other major southern city. Its presence created a buffer for the Jews, who never comprised more than one percent of the total population. Prejudice against the Jewish minority was, to a great extent, displaced by this more visible and more threatening minority.

The Jewish community of Memphis began in the late 1830s but had its roots in the opening of Jewish immigration to the New World. Recent scholarship adds a new theory about the origins of the Jews in America, advanced by Cyrus Gordon, an expert in early Middle Eastern languages, who headed the Department of Mediterranean Studies at Brandeis University. Nine skeletons were found in 1889 in a burial mound at Bat Creek, Tennessee. At first they were believed to be Cherokee Indians

---

[3]Ibid., 62.
[4]Ibid., 62, 64, 119.

because an engraved stone found with other relics under one skull was thought to bear a Cherokee message. But when Gordon saw a photograph of the stone in 1970, he decided that the researchers had been viewing it upside down. He translated the message to read either "for the Judaeans" or "for Judaea." In addition, the script had a strong resemblance to that found on Hebrew coins of around 100 C.E.

Also, carbon-dating tests on wooden artifacts from the grave revealed that a mass burial occurred between 32 and 769 C.E. The soil had not been disturbed until that period. Another corroborating factor is that bracelets discovered in the grave were fashioned of a kind of brass produced by the Romans only between 40 B.C.E. and 200 C.E. Bat Creek is in the Tennessee River Valley, accessible via the Gulf of Mexico, through open country and on the river. Gordon paints the following possible scenario:

> You're a member of an oppressed minority. The Romans eliminated the Semitic commercial states, including the Judaeans, one by one. Your people are navigators and sailors. So, what do you do? You get as far away as possible from the long arm of Rome, even across the Atlantic.[5]

In the constant re-evaluation of history this interesting speculation may prove to have merit.

According to the more established theory, Jewish immigration to the New World began with one Jewish person in Columbus's crew when he landed on the shores of America in 1492. But the year 1492 was even more significant in the history of Jewish immigration to America because it is the year the Jews of Spain and Portugal, called Sephardim, were expelled from their homelands.[6]

Some of these Sephardim went from Spain and Portugal to a Dutch colony in Brazil. After the Portuguese reconquered Brazil in 1654, thirty-three of the Sephardim sailed for America.[7] They had no way of knowing that they were the first trickle of what was to become the largest flow of immigration in Jewish history. The Sephardim were wealthy, aristocratic

---

[5]Donald Dale Jackson, "Who the Heck Did Discover the New World?" *Smithsonian*, (September, 1991): 76.

[6]Alberta Eiseman, *From Many Lands* (New York: Athenaeum, 1970), 15.

[7]Eiseman, *From Many Lands*, 137.

Jews who brought with them an established culture created centuries before their expulsion.[8] The reception of the thirty-three Sephardim in New Amsterdam by Governor Peter Stuyvesant would hardly have led them to conclude that America would be a different, more permanent place of refuge than any that Jews had ever before experienced. Stuyvesant threw them in jail and threatened to expel them, but influential Jews in the Netherlands persuaded him to allow them to remain on the condition that "the poor among them shall not become a burden . . . but be supported by their own nation."[9]

This was not a novel idea to the Jews, who in Europe were accustomed to leading segregated lives and taking responsibility for their own. Stuyvesant's injunction and its acceptance by the thirty-three immigrants has had a lasting influence on the Jews of America. It is the cornerstone on which citizenship has been built, and it is trumpeted from pulpits and forums throughout the land, wherever Jews congregate. Jews in America have developed institutions and organizations to ensure that their needy would not be dependent on the state but would be provided for by fellow Jews. This ideal became an integral part of the development of Jewish communities throughout the country and is an enduring aspect of Jewish life in Memphis.

Who were the first Jews to come to Memphis? Why did they choose this new, raw, southern-western town with its frontier characteristics, far from their co-religionists? Why did they not, like their predecessors in the New World, elect to stay in the more developed coastal areas of the East, where Jewish communities already existed?

The founders of the Memphis Jewish community were drawn from the second wave of Jewish immigrants, who came to America between 1820 and 1880. They were predominantly Ashkenazim, Yiddish-speaking Jews from Germany and German-speaking parts of Eastern Europe. (Some Eastern European Jews came before 1880, but they were very few.) Of the 1,500,000 German immigrants who came during this period, about two to three percent were Jewish. In most of Europe, the hope engendered by the Enlightenment, with its ideals of reason and equality, proved to be illusory, leading to new problems and frustrations. In Italy the status of Jews

---

[8]Arthur Hertzberg, *The Jews in America: Four Centuries of an Uneasy Encounter: A History* (New York: Simon and Schuster, 1989), 26.

[9]Eiseman, *From Many Lands*, 15.

deteriorated under the anti-Semitic Pope Pius VI (1775-99) whose Edict on the Jews led to enforced baptisms and removal of children from Jewish homes. In Prussia, Frederick the Great, despite his declared personal support for principles of the Enlightenment, enacted a Jewish Law in 1750 that denied most Jews a hereditary right of residence. Jews had to pay "protection" taxes and fines in lieu of military services, from which they were excluded, and were compelled to purchase products of the state. The first genuine reforms in central Europe were introduced by Joseph II of Austria, from 1781 onwards, but even they were a mixed blessing. He abolished the special poll tax and yellow badge, the ban on Jews attending universities, and some trade restrictions. At the same time, however, he prohibited the use of Yiddish or Hebrew in business and public records, did away with the jurisdiction of rabbis, and introduced military service for Jews who had formerly not been allowed to serve. Jews remained under residence restrictions in Vienna and elsewhere, and their rights were often denied by hostile public officials.[10]

While all immigrants came to America seeking economic improvement, the Jews had other reasons for emigrating. The armies of Napoleon had imposed the principles of the French Revolution on the lands they conquered, including Jewish emancipation, granted by the National Assembly to the Jews of France in 1790 and 1791. But the defeat of Napoleon in 1815 brought an end to Jewish civil rights in France and in the countries conquered by France. In those countries, government policy toward the Jews became even more severe than it had been before the Napoleonic changes. The situation in Bavaria was especially hard. Bavarian Jews had not benefitted from the changes brought by Napoleon. The number of Jewish families in a particular locality was not allowed to grow; often only the eldest son, who had received his father's Schutzbrief (protective letter), would be allowed to marry and join the community. Younger sons had to wait for the childless possessor of a registration certificate to die before they could consider marriage. Large numbers of young, unmarried Jews began emigrating to avoid such an unpromising future.[11]

---

[10]Paul Johnson, *A History of the Jews* (New York: Harper and Row, 1987), 304.

[11]Judith A. Endelman, *The Jewish Community of Indianapolis: 1849 to the Present.* The Modern Jewish Experience Series, E. Paula Hyman and Deborah Dash Moore, (Bloomington: Indiana University Press, 1984), 11.

By coming to America, Jews of central and western Europe hoped to escape increasing anti-Semitism, the economic hardship and dislocation caused by early industrialization, and later, the political unrest, disorder, and disappointment that followed the revolutionary wars of 1848.[12] Combined with the hope of freedom and tolerance in the New World, these were powerful incentives to migration. In the time-honored manner of the first to arrive, the Sephardim already in this country looked down on the newcomers, the German "peddlers," and disdained their traditions as "unrefined."[13]

Fortunately for the western European immigrants, their arrival in America coincided with the vast territorial expansion that was taking place in the United States. While the Sephardim usually remained in the coastal cities of the East, many of the Ashkenazim were attracted to the hinterlands, where economic opportunity and adventure beckoned.[14] For the Sephardim, always small in number, all aspects of Jewish life—social, religious, and philanthropic—had been confined to the synagogue community. But the Germans began a process of secularization and factionalization that has characterized the modern era.[15] As they headed west, German Jews shed their orthodox traditions, often in direct proportion to the distance they traveled from other Jewish settlements.[16]

Since medieval times, Jews in Europe had been precluded from owning land and from practicing most professions. As a result, they became artisans or engaged in trade and finance. The Germans who came to America typically arrived with a trade: they were weavers, carpenters, masons, blacksmiths, and tailors.[17] Because they sometimes had family and friends already in America, many came with a sense of shared identity and trust, vital components of successful business relations.

---

[12]Leon A. Jick, *The Americanization of the Synagogue, 1920-1870* (Hanover, New Jersey: published for Brandeis University Press of New England, 1976), 3.

[13]Max Dimont, *The Jews of America: The Roots and Destiny* (New York: Simon and Schuster, 1978), 82; and Hertzberg, 147.

[14]Dimont, *Jews of America*, 82.

[15]Ibid.

[16]Steven Lowenstein, *The Jews of Oregon, 1850-1950* (Portland, Oregon: Jewish Historical Society of Oregon, 1987), 34.

[17]Frank J. Coppa and Thomas J. Curran, "From the Rhine to the Mississippi," in Coppa and Curran, eds., *The Immigrant Experience in America* (Boston: Twayne Publishers, 1976), 49.

Some of the new arrivals had developed banking and financial abilities in Europe where they were often forced by default to fill the function of moneylenders, an occupation forbidden to non-Jews by their religion. In America their skills in crafts and enterprise were distinct assets, valuable in the new, rapidly developing country.[18] They successfully transplanted many of their European occupational experiences, adapting them to their new situations.[19] In the South the immigrants discerned an opening in the economic spectrum and inserted themselves as mediators between the landed aristocracy and the poor farmers.

The first known Jewish settlers in Tennessee were probably peddlers who in the late 1830s and 1840s moved north from New Orleans and the river towns of Mississippi, south from St. Louis, and west from Cincinnati and Louisville.[20] A petition presented to the state legislature in 1819 contained one hundred thirty-eight signatures of persons desiring to reside in southwest Tennessee. It included no name that appears to be Jewish. The first census taken in Memphis on 31 December 1820 listed three hundred sixty-four persons, including heads of families, other family members, and slaves. No obviously Jewish name is among them.[21]

The first known Jewish resident of Memphis was David Hart, who emigrated from Germany in 1838.[22] He operated Hart's Inn and Saloon, on the north side of Adams, between Front and Main Streets. A newspaper announcement of 4 June 1843 stated that a Dr. Boynton would continue his "mesmeric exhibitions at the hall over Hart's saloon." Later, on 25 February 1849, another account indicated that

the ladies of Memphis entertained Mrs. Bowman, the wife of Captain A. H. Bowman of the United States Corps of Topographical Engineers, who had superintended construction of the road through the Arkansas swamp lands opposite Memphis at Hart's.

---

[18]David M. Brownstone. *The Jewish American Heritage*, vol. 2 of America's Ethnic Heritage series, David M. Brownstone and Irene M. Franck, general editors (New York: Facts on File Publications, 1988), 5.

[19]Henry J. Tobias. *The Jews in Oklahoma*, a vol. in Newcomers to a New Land series (Norman, Oklahoma: University of Oklahoma Press, 1980), 6.

[20]Bernard Postal and Lionel Koppman. *American Jewish Landmarks: A Travel Guide and History.* 3 volumes (N.Y.: Fleet Press Corp. 1954), vol. 2, 241.

[21]James Roper, *The Founding of Memphis*, 1818-1820 (Memphis: Memphis Sesquicentennial, Inc., 1970), 23.

[22]*American Jewish Historical Society Archives.*

The article further noted that "never before in Memphis was there such a gathering of dazzling beauty." David Hart married Fannie Rothschild and they had five children. They left Memphis in the 1850s or 1860s, moving to Lafayette, Indiana.[23]

The second Jewish name connected with Memphis is that of Joseph Andrews, who came to Memphis in 1840 from Charleston, South Carolina, with his wife Sally, the daughter of Revolutionary War supporter Haym Solomon. (Some scholars believe that Sally was Solomon's granddaughter.) Andrews became a successful merchant in the city, involved in cotton, banking, and brokerage businesses. He built the city's first three-story home, at the corner of Court and North Second Streets.[24] In addition to notable contributions he made to the growth of the Memphis Jewish community, Andrews served as one of the ten aldermen for the term of March 1847 to March 1848, the twenty-first corporate year of the city.[25]

During the Mexican American War, on 12 March 1847, a dinner was held at the Commercial Hotel to honor Lieutenant Commander William Hunter, the inventor of the submerged propeller, and the officers of his ship, the *Allegheny*. Andrews was a member of a Committee of Honor appointed to escort Hunter to the dining room to be greeted by three hundred admirers. Andrews was also a member of a committee charged with soliciting subscriptions for a dinner to honor volunteers returning from the war.[26]

Joseph Andrews is regarded as the founder of the Jewish community of Memphis, an event that can be dated from 1847 when Andrews's brother, Samuel E., died, and Andrews donated land for a cemetery for his burial. In so doing, Andrews followed the tradition of Jews everywhere who acquire a burial place as soon as their ranks are large enough to need one. Thus we conclude that sufficient numbers of Jews lived in Memphis when the cemetery was first established to consider them a community. The land that Andrews gave was the first Jewish cemetery in Tennessee. He bought the

---

[23]Ibid.

[24]Perre Magness, "Jews Came to Memphis in the 1840's", *The Commercial Appeal*, (April 7, 1988), 2.

[25]James D. Davies, *The History of the City of Memphis* (Memphis: Hite, Crumpton, and Kelly, 1873), 36.

[26]Turner J. Fakes, Jr., "Memphis and the Mexican War," *West Tennessee Historical Society Papers* 1(1948): 136-37.

plot of wilderness land on Bass Avenue, now Jefferson, from Marcus Winchester, mayor of the city and brother of founder James Winchester. It was reported that Andrews paid "one eagle," a colloquial term for a ten-dollar gold piece.[27]

Other Jewish immigrants from Germany who joined Andrews in the 1850s included his brother Samuel E., Henry Seessel, David Levy, A. Barinds, Moses Bamberger, Benjamin Emanuel, Henry Oppenheimer, Emanuel Levy, Jacob Bloom, and Samuel Schloss. Together with Andrews they formed a nucleus for a community. Once the cemetery was established, the group realized that an organization was needed to administer it. The Hebrew Benevolent Society was formed in 1850 to serve that function and, in the spirit of Stuyvesant's injunction, to perform acts of charity needed by Memphis's Jews "so they would not become a burden on the city." Benjamin Emanuel was elected president. Services were conducted under the group's auspices on the High Holy Days until Congregation B'nai Israel, later renamed Temple Israel, was organized in 1853.[28]

The fledgling congregation used a rented hall on Front Street as its first house of worship until its fortunes were enhanced in 1853 by a bequest of two thousand dollars from the estate of philanthropist Judah Touro of New Orleans. These funds enabled the congregation to lease the Merchants and Farmers Bank Building at Main and Exchange Streets and to convert it into a place of worship, with seats for one hundred fifty men and forty-six women. Isaac Mayer Wise, founder of American Reform Judaism, came from Cincinnati on 25 March 1858, to dedicate the new sanctuary. The congregation contracted for the property on 11 May 1860; by 1865 it owned it—entirely free of debt.[29]

In the beginning, cantors were the spiritual leaders of the congregation. Cantor Jonas Levy of Little Rock, Arkansas, delivered the first sermon. The first rabbi chosen by the congregation was the Rabbi Jacob J. Peres, who was

---

[27]Selma Lewis, *Temple Israel Cemetery History* (Memphis: Temple Israel, 1990.

[28]*American Jewish Spectator*, Memorial Number, 53; Perre Magness, "Jews Come to Memphis in the 1840's," *The Commercial Appeal*, 7 Ap. 1988, 2, and "The Congregation of the Children of Israel vs. Jacob J. Peres," in Thomas S. Caldwell, *Reports of Cases Argued and Determined in the Supreme Court of Tennessee*, 1865-66 (Nashville: S. C. Mercer, 1867); James A. Wax and Helen G. Wax, *Our First Century, 1854-1954* (Memphis: Temple Israel, 1954).

[29]James A. Wax, "The Jews of Memphis, 1860-1865," (Memphis: *West Tennessee Historical Society Papers*, III, 1949): 16.

engaged in December 1858, as "lecturer, leader, and teacher in English and German, and to lead the choir, at a salary of six hundred dollars a year."[30]

The story of the relationship of the congregation with its first rabbi is a curious one, reflecting the theological conflict within the congregation itself. Among the congregation's first members were some who were Orthodox and others who were attracted to moderate Reform. In their search for a rabbi in 1858, the congregants had consulted the foremost Orthodox leader of the time, Rabbi Isaac Leeser of Philadelphia. Leeser recommended Peres, a child prodigy who when he graduated from high school in the Netherlands was given a stipend by his king to attend the Netherlands Israelitish Seminary. Before he was eighteen, Peres had edited a Hebrew grammar and a book of proverbs in five languages. In addition to his rabbinical training, Peres was a scholar in the fields of language, literature, and mathematics. He came as an Orthodox rabbi, established a Hebrew school, and performed his other duties. He also studied law and founded the legal firm of Peres and Micou.[31]

Jacob Peres had a large family. He soon found his salary of fifty dollars a month, even when supplemented by tuition from the Hebrew school he established, insufficient to support his wife and four children. He started a grocery, produce, and commission business to "make ends meet" and kept it open on Saturdays to take advantage of the primary commercial day of the week. Some members of the congregation objected to this violation of Sabbath observance. At the congregation's quarterly meeting on 15 April 1860, charges were brought against Peres, alleging that he had engaged in secular labor on a holy day. In a formal trial held by the congregation, Peres was found guilty and dismissed. In response, Peres challenged the congregation's action and filed suit against it in the civil courts. He won the portion of the case involving salary due on the unexpired term of his contract but lost his libel suit against the congregation. In its decision in regard to the libel suit, which later became a precedent, the Tennessee State Supreme Court ruled that "a religious institution is sovereign; that its laws and regulations are supreme; and that its policies and practices may not be challenged by legal action in a court of law."[32]

---

[30]John Carruth, "Temple Israel's Children: History of the South's Second Largest Reform Jewish Congregation,: *The Commercial Appeal*, (6 Oct. 1953), 16.

[31]Sam Shankman, *The Peres Family* (Kingsport: Southern Publishing Co., 1938), 8.

[32]The Children of Israel vs. Peres,Ó 620 (see n. 31), quoted in Wax, *Our First Century*, 4.

The congregation's internal conflict was apparently resolved shortly thereafter by a split in membership. The Children of Israel (B'nai Israel) turned toward Reform Judaism, while some forty members, who preferred to remain Orthodox, withdrew, and with Peres as spiritual adviser, formed a new synagogue, called Beth El Emeth. Thus, the schism within Congregation B'nai Israel was healed only by becoming a real separation, a process that occurred frequently in other congregations throughout the country.

In looking for a new leader, Congregation B'nai Israel sought the advice of Rabbi Isaac Mayer Wise. *The Israelite*, a newspaper published by Wise, carried the following advertisement:

> Wanted by the Hebrew congregation of Memphis, Tn., a person that can officiate as Teacher, Preacher, and Reader. He must be qualified to instruct children in Hebrew, lecture once a week either in German or English and read the Prayers properly. The Congregation are in favor of Moderate Reform. Salary $1,000.00 per annum, including emoluments. Applicants must be recommended by Dr. I. M. Wise . . . . [33]

Although the tenure of Peres at Congregation B'nai Israel was brief, his ideals of service to the community provided a pattern that has been followed throughout the history of the congregation. In 1865 he was elected President of the Memphis School Board. In this position he made positive changes: three modern schools were built, physical education instituted, and the curriculum generally improved. Also, Peres wrote and lectured on the philosophy of language and translated Dutch literature into English.

Although Jacob Peres died in the yellow fever epidemic of 1879 at the age of forty-nine, followed shortly by his wife, his commitment to community welfare lived on in his surviving sons. Two of his sons, Hardwig and Israel, also served as Presidents of the Memphis School Board; each was prominently involved in fraternal, civic, charitable, and religious organizations.[34]

---

[33]Wax, *Our First Century*, 26.
[34]Shields McIlwaine, *Memphis Down in Dixie* (New York: E. P. Dutton Co., 1948), 27.

2

EARLY PROSPERITY

"Seek ye the welfare of the city to which I have carried you off, and pray to
the Lord for it."

—Jeremiah

The first Jews to come to Memphis arrived from western Europe
when the city was young. They chose Memphis because they were
enterprising, ambitious individuals, eager to better themselves economically.
In Memphis, they saw a strategically located town on the brink of expansion, a town where the skills they brought with them would be in demand.
Within a short period, their predictions that the city would grow and
become a center of commercial activity were fulfilled.

A New Orleans newspaper editor speculated in 1850 that Memphis
would soon be "the most important town in the South, after New Orleans."
At Memphis's newly constructed Adelphi Theater, a delighted capacity
crowd at five dollars and a standing room crowd at three dollars heard
soprano Jenny Lind, even though her performance took place at eleven
a.m.[1] The city offered a number of other cultural attractions, as performers
who traveled to Nashville included Memphis on their tours. During the
1850s minstrels were popular in the city, with a dozen groups, including
Christy's, giving public performances.

Memphis's growth in population was accompanied by an even greater
increase in wealth. A hall was built on Main Street by the Independent
Order of Odd Fellows. The Exchange Building built on Front Street in 1847
included a "most magnificent City Hall that was one hundred six by fifty-
two feet. The building was large enough to house Courts, Medical Hall,
Council Chambers, and the Mayor's Office."[2] A city school system, founded
in 1858, was patterned after Nashville's, which had been established six

---

[1]Robert A. Corlew, *Tennessee: A Short History* (Knoxville: University of Tennessee
Press, 1981,) 204.
[2]Memphis City Directory, 1849.

years earlier. Eleven new banks, organized between 1853 and 1858, were clear signs of increasing prosperity in a city that had only three banks before 1850.[3]

Memphis's location in the center of the South, on both the east-west and north-south trade routes, contributed to its growth. In addition to its good port on the Mississippi River, with its extensive water links, this location naturally led to the development of an early railroad terminus. The Memphis-Ohio Railroad was organized in 1853. But for the city the greatest event of the 1850s was completion of the Memphis and Charleston Railroad on 27 March 1857, a milestone that occasioned one of the most monumental celebrations in Memphis history. From that time on, cotton, hardwood, food, and manufactured goods passed through Memphis in large quantities. By 1891 Memphis was shipping a total of 60,000 bales of cotton annually. On one day in that year as many as a hundred and one flatboats were tied up at the wharf.[4]

As Memphis gained in importance as a river port, its economic structure became more complex. Its new, larger, and more diverse population included bankers, manufacturers, doctors, lawyers, newspaper editors, and railroad presidents. New factories and new industries were established. Mail coaches were running regularly by 1841, and a dozen new businesses were begun.[5]

Everywhere on the frontier, newly-arrived immigrants strapped on backpacks filled with items farmers needed and peddled their goods on foot from farmhouse to farmhouse. Jewish peddlers were usually well received by rural families, which typically saw few visitors. A circle was cleared in front of the fireplace, chairs and beds were pushed back, and the peddler took the place of honor in the middle of the floor. Removing the heavy leather fastenings from his pack, he rolled back the awning-striped cover to expose his wares. There were brightly colored clothes in his first bag; then, when his canvas roll was opened, there came a rush of smells: sachets, cheap perfumes, soaps, leather goods, and spices filled the room with tantalizing fragrances. "It was like bringing a country store right up to the most isolated

---

[3]Corlew, *Tennesssee*, 236; Capers, *Biography*, 102.

[4]W. T. Rainey and Co., *Memphis City Directory, 1855-1856*; Babette Becker, *Chronicle of the Congregation*, (Memphis: pamphlet, n.d.), 7; Capers, *Biography*, 102; John Carruth, "Israel's Children: History of the South's Second Largest Reform Jewish Congregation," *Commercial Appeal*, 6 September 1953, 16.

[5]Capers, Biography, 102, 102.

country hearth," wrote Thomas D. Clark. When peddlers were able to save enough money, they bought horses and buggies. As they gathered a little more capital, they stopped traveling and established small stores or became wholesale dealers for other retailers. A few successful or lucky ones eventually created large businesses from these small beginnings.[6]

As Memphis prospered, so did its Jewish citizens. One of the early immigrants was Abraham Boshwit, who arrived in 1850. Like many of the other German immigrants, he peddled, traveling from farm to farm by horse and wagon. His travels took him as far as Illinois, where his horse died. Undeterred, he bought another horse. But when he set out the next day, he realized that his new horse was blind. Boshwit returned to the seller to obtain a functioning horse, or a refund, but the seller refused to give him either. Still undeterred, he went to Springfield and consulted a lawyer named Abraham Lincoln, who sued the seller and gained satisfaction for Boshwit.[7]

When they could afford to do so, peddlers in Memphis, as in other parts of the United States, opened little stores. Among early local exemplars of this familiar pattern followed by immigrant German Jewish peddlers were the Lowenstein brothers—Benedict, Elias, Abraham, and Bernard. The first to come was Benedict, who arrived in New Orleans in 1854, totally friendless and without financial resources. He began his career with the proverbial pack on his back, offering many kinds of products to rural women who seldom were able to travel. His route included west Tennessee and Kentucky in the summer and Mississippi and south Arkansas in the winter. By 1855 he had enough money to open a small store in Memphis at Poplar and Front Streets.[8] By 1862 he had expanded into a twenty-five foot store located at 247 Main Street, on the east side, just above Court Square. As Benedict's business grew and his need for help increased, he sent for his brothers in Germany.

---

[6]Thomas D. Clark, "The Post-Civil War Economy in the South," in *Jews in the South*, ed. by Leonard Dinnerstein and Mary Jo Pahlson (Baton Rouge: Louisiana State University Press, 1973) 163; Steven Lowenstein, *The Jews of Oregon, 1850-1950* (Portland: Jewish Historical Society of Oregon, 1987) 45.

[7]Buck Boshwit personal interview, 1992.

[8]Paul R. Coppock, "Mid-South Memoirs: Bridging the Generations of Business Growth," *Commercial Appeal*, 28 November, 1976; [Memphis] *American Jewish Spectator*, 25 April 1919.

In these booming times in Memphis, B. Lowenstein and Brothers Company flourished, and soon occupied the entire building in which it had begun as a small tenant. The company bought the building in 1865, then purchased the adjacent building to the north, then the building north of that, and eventually added the building to the rear.[9] The Memphis *Daily Bulletin* of 1 April 1865, reported: "Lowenstein and Brothers have removed their large stock of dry goods, hosiery, boots, and shoes from the old stand under Odd Fellows' Hall to their splendid store, No. 242 Main Street, corner of Jefferson."

In 1883 Lowenstein and Brothers continued to expand, moving across the street to the Goodlett Building with its electric lights and fancy chandeliers. The spectacular success of the store was directed at first by its founding brother, Benedict. After Benedict's death, his brother Elias took over management of the business that under his leadership became one of the most highly regarded, heavily patronized stores in the city and was widely known for selling quality merchandise.

Lowenstein was active in the community as well. He was chairman of the General Trade Committee's Dry Goods Division of the Memphis Merchants Exchange. He served as a member of the Standing Committee of Trade for the Memphis Cotton Exchange. He was a director of the Pioneer Cotton Mill, a successful producer of cotton goods.

For many years Lowenstein's maintained a wholesale as well as a retail division, but the wholesale division was not re-established after it burned in 1910. Elias then bought out his brothers' interests in the store, and then continued to operate it himself. Elias Lowenstein died in 1919.[10]

Another German-born peddler who became a successful businessman was Henry Seessel. In *Memoirs of a Mexican Veteran*, published in 1891, Seessel described his experiences in the Mexican-American War of 1846-1848, and wrote as well of his early days on the road, before he moved to Memphis. Convinced that there were promising opportunities in the growing city, he brought his German-born wife to Memphis and went into the butchering business, surviving a bad partner to attain financial success. He opened a store of his own at the Poplar Street Market, and in October 1863 he began to advertise in the *Memphis Daily Appeal*.

---

[9] Ibid.

[10] J. M. Keating, *History of the City of Memphis and Shelby County, Tennessee, Vol. 1* (Syracuse, NY: D. Mason and Company), 18.

In 1874 Seessel made his son Albert a partner; in 1877 Albert opened his own store. Both father and son had a reputation of "catering to the carriage trade." Seessel's became and remained a chain of family-owned supermarkets until it was sold in 1996 to a larger corporation. In Memphis he opened a slaughterhouse, the beginning of what was to become a chain of grocery stores throughout the city. Having to start all over in business after each traumatic time, Seessel survived not only the Mexican-American War, but also the Civil War, and the yellow fever epidemics that later plagued the city.[11]

Of course, not all Jewish store owners began as peddlers. Solomon Halle and his brothers arrived in the United States with capital, and in 1859 opened Oak Hall, a men's clothing store at 251 Main Street. Today it is still operated by fifth-generation descendants of the original owners. In Halle, Denmark, now a part of Germany, where the family lived, Solomon Halle was named Solomon von Halle, a title of distinction. The title "von" was added to the family name in 1590 by the King of Denmark when the family moved to Hamburg. The Halle family was the only Jewish family in Hamburg and one of the few Jewish families in Europe to have been so honored.[12]

Two stores were founded by Jewish merchants in 1862. Menken and Brothers, on the corner of Court and Main Streets, was founded by J. S. Menken, who came to Memphis from Cincinnati where his father had owned a successful store, S. Menken and Sons. The instability of the country on the verge of the Civil War may have contributed to the failure of the elder Menken's firm in 1861. Shortly after J. S. Menken opened his business in Memphis, he was joined by his brothers, Jules and Nathan. Once the store became well-established, the Menken brothers paid off all of the debt incurred by the bankruptcy of the Cincinnati business. Their creditors were so appreciative that they presented each brother with a "costly silver service" and gave a dinner for them at Delmonico's Restaurant in New York.[13]

---

[11]Daneel Buring, "Seessel's: The Development of Memphis Business, 1859-1964" master's thesis, Memphis State University, 1986; Henry Seessel, *Memoirs of a Mexican Veteran, 1822-1911* (Memphis: n.p., 1891).

[12]Bob Levy personal interview, September 1991.

[13]O. F. Vedders, *History of the City of Memphis and Shelby County* (Syracuse, New York: D. Mason and Co., 1888), vol. 2, 155.

Another store opened by Jewish merchants in 1862 was J. H. Lowenstein and Brothers, a department store sometimes called "The Southern Palace." Located at 197 Main Street, the store prospered from the beginning. In the year following its opening on 15 November 1863, it gained the distinction of placing the largest newspaper advertisement of any Memphis store.[14] It remained an important store throughout the Civil War years, but did not reopen after it was destroyed by fire shortly after the end of the war.

Immigrant Jews with ambition, energy, and little capital sought opportunities wherever they could find them, and many, guarding against ill fortune, had their fingers in multiple economic pies. As a result, few areas of commercial enterprise were without Jewish participation. There were Jewish cotton brokers and factors, real estate brokers, barbers, auctioneers, wholesalers, grocers, liquor and wine dealers, tobacco and candy merchants, dry goods and clothing merchants, both wholesale and retail, purveyors of leather goods, boots, and shoes, hatters, and dry-cleaners. Samuel Schloss, whose emigration from Bavaria in 1851 was followed shortly by that of his brother Daniel, was one of the first wholesale merchants in Memphis. He was with the Gerber dry goods store for a short time before joining the Pittsburgh Coal Company.[15]

D. Bloch's gentlemen's furnishings store was listed in the 1850 *Memphis Business Directory*. D. Levy and Company, 189 North Main, advertised in 1855 as "a purveyor of fashionable clothes." In 1857 city residents could shop for dry goods at Lehman and Company, Moses Levy and Company, the Samuel Levy Company, and S. Levy and J. Levy and Company. Peddlers could procure supplies at Charles Levy's. Hats were available at Jacob Bloch's, while boots and shoes could be bought at Strauss, Lehman, and Company, as well as at Zellner Shoe Company, the largest retail shoe business in the South.[16]

In the 1860s E. O. Goldsmith operated a men's clothing store bearing his name. M. Simon's store at 194 Main Street sold dry goods and clothing, both wholesale and retail. Lazard Kremer sold millinery, jewelry, and watches, in addition to dry goods. M. Friedlander of 231 Main Street

---

[14]James and Helen Wax, *Our First Century, 1854-1954* (Memphis: Temple Israel, 1954), 19; *Memphis Daily Bulletin*, 16 November, 1863.

[15]Twyman's *Business Directory and General Merchandise Advertiser for 1850.*

[16]Art Supplement to the Housewarming Edition of the *Memphis Press Scimitar*, 1903, 78.

"featured fancy goods at wholesale." L. D. Mayer, Fibelman and Elson, Goldberg, J. Alexander, L. Lieberman, and Loeb and Holland were all dry goods merchants.

Goldsmith's, a tiny store on Beale Street between Front and Main, was opened in 1870 by brothers Isaac and Jacob Goldsmith and later became Memphis's largest department store. The first customer of the day had a symbolic meaning for the Jewish peddler or shopkeeper; if he or she made a purchase, it was a signal that it would be a good day. When Isaac and Jacob Goldsmith opened the door of their store, a windowless room measuring fifteen by sixty feet, their first customer, a little girl named Loretta, bought two spools of thread her mother had sent her out to purchase. It was a favorable portent. So delighted were the young merchants that on the next Christmas they sent Loretta a present. The practice continued until Loretta died in 1921, with the presents increasing in grandeur—the last one was a fur coat.[17]

From the beginning Jacob Goldsmith ran his business according to the cliché, "the customer is always right." Customers could return anything at any time, even years after its original purchase. Goldsmith's optimism was famous and infectious, and he trained his sales force accordingly. In 1902 he moved the store to a large building and placed an expensive advertisement in the newspaper to announce the expansion and move. As opening time approached, a rainstorm drenched the area. One the sales clerks went to commiserate about the unfortunate weather with "Mr. Jacob." The response was "Don't worry, son. I have enough trouble competing with the man down the street (Elias Lowenstein) without competing with The Man upstairs. Besides, we'll sell a lot of raincoats and umbrellas."[18]

Goldsmith instigated many new ideas in building the largest department store business in the city. In the early 1900s he began going to the train depot to welcome Santa Claus to the city and to escort him to Goldsmith's. This Christmas tradition soon led to a parade that other merchants later joined. This parade preceded by more than a decade Macy's famous annual event in New York City. In the 1960s Goldsmith's also celebrated Christmas with the Enchanted Forest, modeled after the Disney Small World exhibit at the New York World's Fair. The Enchanted Forest became so

---

[17]D. Davidson, "A Biographical Sketch of Jacob Goldsmith, 1850-1933." Memphis. Unpublished pamphlet. n.d.

[18]Interview with Sylvia Goldsmith Marks, 1991.

popular that it kept three Santa Clauses busy dealing with the large numbers of children who attended.

While there may have been some uncomfortable feelings, there are no records of discussions by Jewish merchants regarding participating in the promotion of Christian holidays. In most instances, beginning with Jacob Peres in the 1850s, adherence to Jewish rituals and abstinence from those with Christian content yielded to the pragmatic urgency of making a living. Peres was an observant, orthodox Jew, but he was also a businessman, forced to accommodate himself to the world in which he was doing business. Stores serving the community as a whole, like Goldsmith's and Lowenstein's, operated on the Christian calendar, remaining open on Saturdays, the Jewish Sabbath, but also the most profitable business day of the week, and closing on Sundays. Exceptions to this were stores developed later in the area of the Pinch, where most of the Orthodox Jews from Eastern Europe resided. Living as they did in a largely Jewish neighborhood, they could more easily remain faithful to their own religious customs, closing their stores on Saturday instead of Sunday. When they closed their stores on Saturday and opened them on Sundays, however, they were found to be in violation of Sunday blue laws that prohibited such business practices. Thus their religious practices conflicted with the laws of the city.

In 1902 Goldsmith's was the first store in the south to arrange merchandise by departments, thus becoming a true "department store." It was the first store in Memphis to install air-conditioning, escalators, a bargain basement, and a mechanical credit system, called Charg-a-Plate. When Elias Lowenstein died in 1919, Jacob Goldsmith lost his last competitor for the title of the leading merchant in the city.[19]

Goldsmith was also a participant in the religious and civic life of the city. Among other activities, he was vice-president of the Memphis Chamber of Commerce; member of the boards of directors of several Memphis banks; a member of Odd Fellows for over forty years; and for many years he was a member of the Board of Trustees and an officer of Temple Israel. A few years before his death, while he was Warden of the Temple, the congregation created the office of Honorary President and elected Goldsmith to fill it.

Jacob Goldsmith died in 1933, followed a year later by his wife, Dora. Their home at 696 Vance was given by the family to St. Agnes Academy,

---

[19]Paul R. Coppock, "Mid-South Memoirs," *Commercial Appeal*, 28 November 1976, 7.

which was directly across the street, to be used as a library that was eventually named the Goldsmith Memorial Library. To honor his memory, his descendants created the Goldsmith Civic Garden Center in Audubon Park.

The business of Joseph Andrews, mentioned earlier as the virtual founder of the Memphis Jewish community, included banking, brokering, and cotton sales. Henry Frank and his brother Godfrey, also early residents of the city, were cotton factors. They came to Memphis after a flood in 1860 permanently inundated their little hometown of Napoleon, Arkansas. One measure of their prominence was the fact that the *Henry Frank* was the largest steamer on the Mississippi River at the time. Joseph Gronauer, who had moved to Memphis in 1862 with his brother Herman, was also in the cotton business.[20]

Many young Jewish businessmen began their careers as employees in established businesses and ventured out on their own after they gained experience, confidence, and capital. Sol Coleman was one. Arriving in Memphis in the 1860s, he worked as a traveling salesman for the Joseph Witkowsky Wholesale Cigar and Tobacco House until he opened his own business. Later, he became a director of both the Manhattan Bank and the German Bank and belonged to the Masons. Seymour Lee came from Prussia in about 1860 and teamed up with Dave Sternberg to establish a cigar and tobacco business. Lee eventually broke up the partnership to open his own S. L. Lee and Sons, a name the concern retained until 1932 when it, along with many other formerly solid businesses, was liquidated because of the Depression. Ike Samelson, who started out as a clerk in the firm of Sternberg and Lee, began his Samelson-Leon Tobacco Company in 1881.

Other German Jewish immigrant businessmen founded well-known and respected concerns in the middle of the nineteenth century: Julius Goodman brought fine jewelry and silver to Memphis in 1862; and Marx and Bensdorf established a real estate firm in 1868.[21]

Jewish businessmen who were engaged in more than one type of enterprise included Jacob Peres and Herman Gronauer, both of whom sold

---

[20]David Roller and Robert Twyman, eds., *The Encyclopedia of Southern History* (Baton Rouge: Louisiana State University Press), 484; Boshwit interview; Jack D. L. Holmes, editor, "Documents: Joseph A. Gronauer and the Civil War in Memphis," *West Tennessee Historical Society Papers*, vol. 22, No. 148, 1968): 75-76.

[21]*Press Scimitar* Art Supplement 78; Holmes, "Documents," 148; Wax, *Our First Century*, 31.

a diversity of products. Gronauer and his brother Joseph moved to Memphis in 1862 and went into the insurance business. Gronauer was a partner as well in the cigar, liquor, and wine business of Block, Gronauer, and Company. A. S. Levy, who was primarily in the auction and commission business, advertised "money on loan on all kinds of personal property." D. Hirsch, E. Mayer, H. and L. Morgenthau, and E. and L. Block were in the liquor business. A. S. Milius sold crockery and glassware; H. Koninsky sold tents; and M. L. Putzel opened a pattern business in 1864.[22]

Although the early Memphis Jews pursued many and varied commercial endeavors, a significant number were engaged in the clothing business, a natural outgrowth of a combination of circumstances. Many immigrants had gained knowledge and experience in Europe in the manufacture of clothing. Trained in the old country, they came to America at a time when ready-made clothing was becoming popular and their skills were timely assets in an industry boosted by the development of the sewing machine, invented by Elias Howe in 1845 and improved by Singer between 1851 and 1856. The early Jews participated in all aspects of the clothing trade. They were tailors; salesmen of dry goods, boots, shoes, clothes and millinery for all ages, shapes, and sizes; and dealers in second hand furnishings.[23]

In addition to their commercial activities, Memphis's Jewish citizens participated fully in the political and civic life of the city, a new experience for people who had been denied this opportunity in the lands of their birth. The public service of Joseph Andrews has been noted. Among others who served was William Goodman, alderman from 1845-1846. Tobias Wolf was wharfmaster in 1861, a position to which he was re-elected by a large plurality over five other candidates. Henry Marks was appointed to the police force in 1862. Paul Schuster was alderman of the Third Ward in 1863. As stated previously, In 1866 Jacob Peres was the president of the Board of Education on which A. E. Frankland and Henry Seessel Jr. both served.[24]

The prominence of the first Jewish settlers in Memphis, the German immigrants, may have had a positive influence on the future of Jewish-

---

[22]Holmes, "Documents," 148; *Memphis Daily Bulletin*, 11 August 1864, quoted in Wax, 25, 26.

[23]Fedora S. Frank, *Five Families and Eight young Men: Nashville and Her Jewry*, 1861-1901 (Nashville: n. p., 1976), 55.

[24]Eli N. Evans, *The Provincials* (Kingsport: Kingsport Press, Incorporated, 1973), 336; Carruth , "Israel's Children," 101.

Christian relationships in the city. Historian John Higham wrote that the degree to which Jews were involved in the early growth of a city, achieving a well-known and respected place in its public and private life before the era of mass immigration, was significant in cushioning the impact of that influx.

The Memphis Jewish community was well-established by the time of the Civil War. In other communities of the United States, especially in the North and East, new immigrants tended to recreate the community and culture they had left behind. This did not happen in Memphis. Most of the German immigrants of the first wave settled in the center of the city to be close to their businesses. They were never segregated in one living area either by their own choice or by pressure from others.[25]

Jews of the South have traditionally been the most assimilated segment of American Jewry. Generally, southern Jews have preferred to blend into the landscape, which their small numbers made possible. The southern Jewish experience has differed from that of the Jews in the North, particularly in the Northeast. In contrast to their co-religionists in the North, southern Jews have always been a tiny minority of the people among whom they lived. Thus, southern Jews did not affect the South as much as they were affected by it, imbibing its values and mores.[26]

At the same time, however, they retained a strong sense of Jewish identity, an association strengthened in part by their desire to conform to southern cultural norms, one of which is religious affiliation. The South leads the nation in number of congregations in proportion to number of Jews, with one for every six hundred, as compared to the national average of one for every 1,300. Paradoxically, by being more southern, and thus more involved in organized religious activities, southern Jews are at the same time more Jewish than many from other regions.[27]

Although Jews participated in the commercial and political activities of the city, they were less integrated into its social life, a condition that was probably mutually agreeable to both Jews and Christians. In response to the opportunity of religious freedom in their new homeland, immigrant Jews

---

[25]Richard F. Thomas, "The Residential Distribution of Immigrants in Memphis, Tennessee" (unpublished M.A. thesis, Memphis State University, 1970), 320.

[26]Stephen J. Whitfield, "Jews and Other Southerners," in Nathan Kaganoff and Melvin T. Urofsky, *Turn to the South: Essays on Southern Jewry* (Charlottesville: University of Virginia Press, 1979), xii, 103.

[27]Kaganoff and Urofsky, xii; Harry Golden, *Our Southern Landsmen* (New York: G. P. Putnam's Sons, 1974), 96.

often created their own communal and social institutions; Christians also developed their own separate social organizations. Nevertheless, except for General Grant's Order 11, (see Chapter 3), there is no record of prejudice as an on-going, serious problem despite the existence of some social barriers.

Social segregation has often been a device used by communities to try to ensure that their children marry within their own group. Some feel the group's very survival would be threatened by intermarriage. Because marriage records did not list religious preferences, it is difficult to obtain accurate information about the marriages of the early Jewish Memphians. All conclusions about these marriages are therefore speculative. But, judging by the familial names of those being married and by the name of the person officiating, many of the marriages listed appear to have been Jewish. Until 1864 in Tennessee, rabbis were not authorized to perform marriages. When Simon Tuska joined Julius Nathan and Hanna Ehrman in marriage on 21 May 1864, it may have been the first wedding performed by a rabbi. Intermarriage between Jews and Christians seems to have been rare in Memphis until the 1880s.[28]

The German Jews were great organizers, not only of businesses but also of institutions to support and provide structure for their lives in their new land. The development of Congregation B'nai Israel illustrates this ability. While not the oldest congregation organized in Tennessee (Bolivar had a short-lived one begun in 1851), it is the oldest extant congregation in the state. A charter granted by the state legislature on 21 March 1854, listed Joseph I. Andrews, Moses Simon, John Walker, D. Levy, Julius Dandac, T. Folz, M. Bamberger, N. Bloom, Joseph Strauss, and H. Reinach as organizers. Initially the congregation included thirty-six heads of families.[29]

After the departure of Rabbi Jacob Peres, Congregation B'nai Israel hired Rabbi Simon Tuska on the recommendation of Rabbi Isaac Mayer Wise. Born in Vesprin, Hungary in 1835, Tuska was the son of a rabbi in Rochester, New York. In 1858, upon completion of his education at the Rochester Theological Seminary, he became the first person to be sent (with financing) to Europe to study at the Jewish Theological Seminary at Breslau in preparation for the rabbinate in America. Two years later,

---

[28]Bettie B. Davis, compiler, *Shelby County, Tennessee Marriage Bonds and Licenses 1850-1865* (Memphis: Richard Harris), 23.

[29]Bernard Postal and Lionel Koppman, *American Jewish Landmarks: A Travel Guide and History,* (New York: Fleet Press Corporation, 1954) 241; Wax, *Our First Century,* 15.

although he had not yet completed his course of study in Europe, he returned to the United States to try for a position at Temple Emanu-El in New York City, but he was rejected because of his "small stature and thin voice." He then came to Memphis where he was warmly welcomed by the congregation. He served as rabbi of B'nai Israel for eleven years until he died of a heart attack in 1871 at the age of thirty-six. Among his papers when he died was a proposal for an American rabbinic seminary.[30]

Although most synagogues in the United States began by adhering to stricter, traditional practices, within a few years, influenced by American culture, many had shifted toward moderate Reform observance. Men and women were no longer seated separately, organ accompaniment was introduced, and prayers were delivered in the vernacular, at first in German, then later in English.

The dominant tide at mid-century favored the "moderate reformers," who were creating what they considered a "respectable" American Judaism that modified Jewish beliefs and customs that distinguished Jews from non-Jews. Judaism and the Jewish community were reshaped and used as instruments for, as well as symbols of, the success of Jews in American life. Synagogue ritual and religious practices were changed for several reasons: pragmatically, this change facilitated the Americanization of the Jews as rapidly as possible; intellectually it divested religion of what the reformers thought were superstitious rituals left over from the old country, which they determined had no place in an individual's relation to God; emotionally, it satisfied their desire to have a religious service at which non-Jews would feel comfortable and where the Jews themselves would not feel embarrassed.[31]

Reform Judaism began in Memphis with the arrival of Tuska in 1860. The first change in the service was the addition of a choir. Next came the confirmation service for young people. The prayer book was shortened and family pews where men and women could worship together soon replaced the traditional seating that separated the sexes.

More traditional Judaism was preserved in Memphis by Rabbi Peres and the forty former B'nai Israel members who left the congregation in 1861. Together, they became the nucleus of a new congregation called Beth El Emeth. The name, which means House of the True God, may have been

---

[30]Jacob Rader Marcus, *United States Jewry, 1776-1985*, Vol. 2 (Detroit: Wayne State University Press, 1989), 261; Kaganoff and Urofsky, *Turn to the South*, 23.

[31]Marcus, *United States Jewry*, 1, 622ff.

purposely chosen to imply that the congregation from which they departed was not the House of the True God because of its more liberal beliefs and rituals. Trustees of B'nai Israel seem to have deemed the new congregation unworthy of mention, since its formation is omitted from their records. The new congregation was dedicated to perpetuating intact the "minhag Polen," the Polish liturgy and practices of their forefathers. Beth El Emeth, chartered by the Tennessee legislature in 1862, listed the following among its founders: L. Alexander, F. Feldman, Jonas Levy, H. Blumenthal, M. Bren, H. Wright, and J. Barnett. The position of Peres in the congregation is unclear; one source says he was the "spiritual leader and served in all capacities"; another refers to him as secretary, later president of the synagogue." The first spiritual leader elected to the position was probably Rabbi Joel Alexander of Brooklyn, New York, who came in 1863. There is no reliable information about where the congregation met.[32]

In addition to the two synagogues, the early Jewish immigrants created other organizations in the pre-Civil War days. The Hebrew Benevolent Society was organized in 1855 to care for the needs of the community and to be responsible for the operation of the cemetery. It was strongly supported by Jewish merchants.[33] A female auxiliary, the Ladies Benevolent Society, was also founded in 1855, by women whose economic circumstances afforded the time necessary for charitable work.

The activities of men and women in the nineteenth century for the most part were divided into separate spheres: the women's sphere was the home, the men's was the business and civic life of the community. This division was consistent with Jewish teachings about women as "domestic caretakers, nurturers, child rearers, and moral instructors." It was also consistent with the role of middle class women in America as providers of charity. The entry of the Jewish women into organizational life as volunteers enlarged their traditional realm but was seen as an extension of their role as nurturers. For the first time they were expected to be involved in community affairs as well as to be guardians of religion and morality in the home. In their new activities, they joined other middle class American

---

[32]Wax, *Our First Century*, 12-14; Kaganoff and Urofsky, *Turn to the South*, 23; Sam Shankman, "History of the Jews of Memphis." Unpublished manuscript; *The American Israelite*, 12 December 1862.
[33]A. E. Frankland, *Fragments of History* (Cincinnati: American Jewish Archives: Hebrew Union College/Jewish Institute of Religion), 92ff.

women, which is evidence of the Jewish family's successful integration into the community and its adoption of values prevalent in the United States.

The Jewish men of Memphis were enthusiastic joiners of secret societies during the nineteenth century. Masons, Odd Fellows, Sons of Malta, and Druids were all organized during that period. Although some societies accepted Jewish members, many did not, and during the 1840s, Jewish men began to form their own fraternal orders. The most important of these organizations was B'nai B'rith, formally entitled the Independent Order of B'nai B'rith, in imitation of some of the non-Jewish orders of higher status. Its purpose was to unite the Jews of the United States, to provide sick benefits, and to help the members develop respect for themselves, and earn the respect of the community around them. It was established on 13 October 1843 by a group of twelve men who met at a cafe in New York City to organize "a secret society for the purposes of mutual aid and unification of American Jewry." Deliberately copied from other American fraternal orders, B'nai B'rith had strong religious overtones. In addition to providing benefit funds for the sick and for orphans and widows, it provided a sense of belonging to immigrant families searching for roots in a new, foreign environment. In this, as in many other activities, Jews were demonstrating that they were part of the general community. The Jews of Memphis organized the first B'nai B'rith lodge in the southern states, Euphrates Lodge No. 35 in January 1858, at the home of Mark Bloom on Market and Front Streets. Their stated purpose was "to relieve distress and perform good deeds." The lodge originally maintained a nurse fund, a weekly benefit fund, and a widow and orphan fund. Among the approximately thirty men who attended that first meeting were Samuel Schloss, Hart Judah, A. E. Frankland, Julius Nathan, and Rabbi Isaac Mayer Wise, who was in the city to dedicate the synagogue of Congregation B'nai Israel at Main and Exchange Streets.[34]

The first officers of the new B'nai B'rith lodge were Hart Judah, president; Theodore Foltz, vice-president; A. E. Frankland, treasurer; and Samuel Schloss, secretary. In addition to providing for the material needs of its members, the lodge planned lectures and entertainment. Like most other secret societies, the lodge had its own password, handshake, and

---

[34]Marcus, *United States Jewry*, Vol. 2, 239-40; Sam Shankman, "One Hundred Years of B'nai B'rith (Memphis: Sam Schloss Lodge #35, B'nai B'rith, 1958.); Arthur Hertzberg, *The Jews in America* (New York: Simon and Schuster, 1989), 115.

hailing signs. Applicants for membership were carefully scrutinized and some were rejected. During the early 1860s B'nai B'rith wives organized and collected five hundred dollars to buy a banner for the lodge. A second lodge, Simon Tuska Lodge No. 192 was formed in 1873, and a third, Tuska Lodge No. 301, whose membership was composed mostly of young men, was established in 1878. It did not survive the yellow fever epidemics and was consolidated with Simon Tuska Lodge in 1880. Six years later the two remaining lodges, Euphrates and Simon Tuska, merged to become Memphis Lodge No. 35.[35]

The first Memphis Jewish social club, one of the oldest in the South, was founded in 1860. Most of its all-male members were also members of B'nai B'rith, but the purposes of the two organizations were different. The new social club was organized purely for social reasons, while B'nai B'rith had religious and charitable as well as social aims. At first, the new club was called The Southern Club, but in 1865, the name was changed to The Memphis Club because the original name offended the federal military government then in control of the city. Solomon Hesse, N. Hoffheimer, Adolph Loeb, H. T. Tomlinson, J. Nathan, J. S. Menken, and Henry Seessel were charter members. The first president was Lazard Kremer, who was succeeded in office by Solomon Hesse. The club, which had one hundred members, sponsored regular evenings of entertainment during the winters at which were "assembled the elite of Jewish society.[36]

The United Hebrew Relief Association, begun in 1868, assumed responsibility for the relief of indigent Jews. It had one hundred twenty-five male members, each of whom contributed annually "according to his ability and benevolent feeling. Each year the association raised between fifteen and eighteen hundred dollars to be disbursed to the Jewish needy. The first officers were Angel S. Meyers, president; Sol Vendig, vice-president; Sol Harpman, secretary; Louis Goldsmith, treasurer; and Dr. R. L. Laski, physician[37]

While charitable contributions of Jews in the city were not directed only to Jewish institutions, Jews were always guided by their promise to Governor Stuyvesant that they would care for their own. The organization

---

[35]Samuel Schloss, "Memphis Lodge #35, I.O.B.B.: A Historical Sketch" 1-3.
[36]Shankman, "B'nai B'rith."
[37]Vedders, *History of the City of Memphis*, 286.

of benevolent societies specifically designed to accomplish this goal is evidence of the determination of the community to keep that promise.

3

THE CIVIL WAR YEARS

"Do not separate yourself from your community."

—Hillel

In the autumn of 1860 Memphis was enjoying great prosperity. It counted among its assets a flourishing cotton trade, railroad and river traffic, wholesale houses, professional offices, six newspapers, twenty-one churches, three female seminaries, two medical schools, twenty-one public schools, the Jenny Lind and Edwin Booth theaters, and a Philharmonic Society. It was the sixth largest city in the United State s. When the idea of secession first arose in the South, not wishing to endanger its advantageous position, Memphis was in favor of remaining in the Union. So too was the state of Tennessee, at least at first. In the special state convention called in February 1861, to consider secession, the majority of the delegates voted against it. But this sentiment changed in response to ensuing events: a peace conference called in February 1861 by the state of Virginia failed to bring any agreement on an acceptable compromise to save the Union; Abraham Lincoln was inaugurated in March 1861 as President of the United States and in April called for the mustering of troops; and Fort Sumter fell to southern troops in December 1861.[1]

In a dramatic reversal of opinion, by 2 April 1861 Memphis merchants unanimously resolved that, regardless of any action by the state, West Tennessee should join the Confederacy. Two weeks later, so overwhelming was the sentiment for secession that 3,000 citizens of the city supported it. In June 1861 the electorate ratified the ordinance for secession that had been approved by the state legislature in May with only five dissenting votes cast in Shelby County. The names of many Memphis Jews appeared on a

---

[1]Gerald Capers, *Biography*, 37; Charles W. Crawford, *Yesterday's Memphis* (Memphis: E. A. Seemann, 1976), 29; Richard Morris, *Encyclopedia of American History* (New York: Harper and Row, 1953), 229.

resolution calling for secession.[2]

Although Jews did not constitute a large presence at the time—the census of 1860 registered approximately four hundred Jewish men, women, and children in Memphis, out of a total population of 22,625—most of the Jewish citizenry concurred with the prevailing secessionist sentiment, a view from which in general they were not dissuaded by their rabbis. Thus, reflecting local attitudes, Rabbi Tuska denounced as "rabid" the abolitionist views of such men as Henry Ward Beecher, stating that "the Jews of Memphis are ready, in common with their Christian brethren, to sacrifice their property and their lives in defense of southern rights." Likewise, a Nashville rabbi defended slavery by quoting the Bible.[3]

Rabbis received little guidance on the issue. No national organization attempted to speak for American Jews, and national Jewish periodicals ignored the problem. Consequently, because they generally followed rather than led political opinion, American rabbis of the period seldom discussed slavery from their pulpits until a decision about it had already been made by the community. Most American rabbis, like most American Jews, with such notable exceptions as David Einhorn of Baltimore, had not yet adopted the view that Jews had a responsibility to promote social justice. Southern Jews before the Civil War accepted the Talmudic statement that "the law of the land is the law," and viewed slavery as a part of the law they were bound to uphold and follow. Very few believed that they should evaluate the institution in light of the teachings of the prophets.[4]

The relationship of Jews to the South is a subject of controversy. To W. J. Cash, the Jew was "everywhere the eternal alien, and in the South he was especially so." But Eli Evans wrote that Jews are "blood and bones part of the South itself, Jewish Southerners."[5] Bernard Postal and Lionel Koppman believe that the southern Jew became a super-southerner because his vulnerability made him reluctant to appear different, a point they illustrate

---

[2]Capers, *Biography*, 137-146; John Carruth, "Israel's Children: History of the South's Second Largest Reform Congregation," *Commercial Appeal*, 6 September 1953.

[3]Capers, *Biography*, 106; Lawrence Meyers, "Memphis Jews and Civil War Issues," unpublished paper, Memphis State University History Department, 1961, 2; *Memphis Daily Appeal* (Memphis: The Southern Association), 23 January 1861; Fedora Frank, *Five Families and Eight Young Men: Nashville and Her Jewry* (Nashville: n. p., 1976), 87.

[4]Bertram W. Korn, "Jews and Negro Slavery in the Old South, 1789-1865," in Leonard Dinnerstein and Mary Jane Pahlson, *Jews in the South* (Baton Rouge: University of Louisiana Press, 1973), 131.

[5]*Ibid.*

by citing how closely the stand of most southern Jews on the issue of slavery mirrored that of their fellow whites.[6] Most writers on the subject agree with Postal and Koppman: Jewish thinking on issues of the day, both in the South and the North, paralleled that of other white members of the community.

Rabbi Jacob Rader Marcus, considered the dean of Jewish American historians, has written that the southern Jew was a "regional type . . . frequently, although not always, he was a Southern particularist, and only secondly a citizen of the United States. . . . He could not escape his environment; the pattern he followed was the pattern of a host of Southerners."[7]

While Rabbi Marcus presented a convincing rationale for Jewish sentiment for secession, lingering questions remain. Many Jews came to America because they lacked the civil rights in Europe that they hoped to gain in the new world. How then could they in good conscience accept the principle of slavery, which so severely limited the rights of others? One factor that caused these early Jewish citizens of Memphis to acquiesce to the prevailing mood was an overwhelming need to demonstrate that they were an integral part of the community, as Rabbi Marcus suggests. They were too newly arrived, with the insecurity that implies, to be willing to be conspicuous by espousing opinions contrary to those of the majority.

One scholar has argued that Southern Jewish marginality has traditionally placed a high premium on conformity to the regional mores, and then even when there has not been a great deal of expressed bigotry, there has been enough latent anti-Semitism to make good southerners out of Jews.[8] Many southerners were free of anti-Semitism, their prejudices against blacks and Catholics leaving them little time or energy to hate Jews as well. In addition, they were well versed in the Old Testament, and much of their religious imagery was the same as that of the Jews. In the Bible Belt, the dominant community felt more tolerant of Jews than did non-Jews in other, less Bible-oriented sections of the United States. Economic rivalry was not a significant problem as Jews seldom engaged in direct economic competi-

---

[6]Bernard Postal and Lionel Koppman, *American Jewish Landmarks: A Travel Guide in History* (New York: Fleet Press Corps., 1954), 241.

[7]Leo E. and Evelyn Turitz, *Jews in Early Mississippi* (Jackson: University of Mississippi Press, n.d.) xvi.

[8]Lewis Killian, *White Southerners* (Amherst: University of Massachusetts Press, 1985), 80-81.

tion with non-Jews, largely establishing their own businesses. [9]

Slavery, in fact, boosted the status of Jews in the Old South. Jews gained in stature and security from the very presence of blacks who were objects of the prejudice that might otherwise have been focused on Jews. Because the overwhelming division was between the races, southern Jews, being white, attained higher social position than their counterparts in the North. In the South, many Jews held elective office; in the North, few did, despite constituting a larger percentage of the population. Many believe that Jews would not have achieved so high a level of social, political, economic, and intellectual acceptance and recognition without the presence of the lowly and degraded slave.[10] Thus, southern Jews supported secession *and* slavery.

A. E. Frankland, a fierce southern partisan who lived in Memphis during the Civil War, implied that a feeling of loyalty motivated the Jews' support of the South: "It was quite natural," he wrote, "they (the Jews) sided with the section that was their home." Jews, in sum, reflected little of their ethno-religious heritage, but were instead a mirror image of their city, region, and socio-economic position, all of which they desired to protect.[11]

Jews were guided by the practice of most other Memphians in regard to slave ownership as well; any Jew who had need for the services of slaves and could afford to own them would do so. Charles Levy, a merchant, is listed in the 1860 slave schedule as the owner of two slaves, one of each sex, for whom he paid $3,000. Henry Seessel owned four slaves when war broke out in 1861, and there were, no doubt, other Jewish slave owners as well. A poignant incident was recounted by the Reverend Blair Hunt, a black preacher, educator and civic leader. Before he died in the late 1970s Hunt told of his mother, Emma, the daughter of a slave and her Jewish white owner, who, realizing that slavery was doomed, decided to leave the South. Traveling north on the Mississippi River, he dumped Emma and her mother on a wharf on the river, promising to return to bring the child some jelly

---

[9]Thomas D. Clark, "The Post-Civil War Economy in the South," in Dinnerstein and Pahlson, *Jews in the South*, 164.

[10]Korn, "Jews and Negro Slavery," 132-34.

[11]A. E. Frankland, "Fragments of History" (Cincinnati: American Jewish Archives, n. d.), 93; Lawrence C. Meyers, "Evolution of the Jewish Service Agency in Memphis, Tennessee, 1847-1963," (Unpublished master's thesis, Memphis State University, 1965), 5.

beans. They never saw him again.[12]

Some Memphis Jews were slave traders. The following advertisement appeared in the local newspaper: "A. S. Levy, A. E. Frankland, and Company, Auctioneers and Commission Merchants, 1096 Main Street. Prompt attention paid to all sales of real estate, negroes, merchandise, furniture, groceries, in city and county." Slave trading as a Jewish occupation, however, was atypical. Primarily because most Jews were urban dwellers who had little need for the kind of agricultural labor supplied by slaves, very few became slave traders. In Memphis, only about one-twelfth of the slave traders were Jewish.[13]

Jews contributed broadly to the southern cause. They played an active role in Confederate military affairs, and supplied men and money to the war effort. Some served in the cavalry forces commanded by General Nathan Bedford Forrest. Isaac Strauss was elected third lieutenant by unanimous vote of the Washington Rifle Company. When asked by the mayor of Memphis to close their stores at four o'clock in the afternoon so that the men could train for the army, Jews complied, comprising one-half of the merchants who signed a petition acceding to the request. In the Shelby Grays Company listing of "gentlemen of Memphis who have kindly contributed to its comfort," the businesses of M. Simon and of Block-Gronauer and Company were specifically commended.[14]

Concerning Jewish men who served in the Confederate ranks, Frankland wrote: "Memphis . . . was not behind in her quota; nearly all her young men volunteered and went." He described an occasion during the war in which enlisted volunteers, all in Confederate gray uniforms, marched into Congregation B'nai Israel during a Sabbath service. Standing around the scrolls of the law, Major Abraham S. Levy, Captain Maurice A. Freeman, Lieutenant Isaac Strauss, Corporal M. A. Kuhn, Emil Gross, and "several others" recited the blessing in chorus. Following the service, the soldiers received a special benediction and returned to camp.[15]

Among other Jewish men who served in the Confederate army was

[12]Korn, "Jews and Negro Slavery," 96; Max Dimont, *The Jews of America: The Roots and Destiny* (New York: Simon and Schuster, 1978), 82; Interview with Blair Hunt, 1978.

[13]*Memphis Daily Appeal*, 17 February 1861; Korn, "Jews and Negro Slavery," 111.

[14]Chaim B. Seiger, "Immigration, Settlement, and Return: Jews of the Lower Mississippi Valley, 1865-1880," Memphis State University, unpublished paper, July, 1970, 2; *Memphis Daily Appeal*, 3 March 1860; 30 May 1860; 18 June 1860.

[15]Frankland, *Fragments*, 93-94.

Frederick Wolf, who joined the Washington Rifles, becoming second sergeant. Early in the war this company became a part of the Fifteenth Tennessee Infantry, and Wolf fought with it at the Battle of Shiloh. He was later promoted to the rank of captain, taking part in many other battles, including Chickamauga, Missionary Ridge, and Perryville. According to a family tale, Wolf was shot, but his life was saved because he wore a large pocket watch in a heavy metal case which deflected the bullet. Louis Hanauer, owner of a general store, enlisted in the Confederate army in 1861 and became an officer. It has been reported that Joseph Gronauer, a grocer and merchant, in a not uncommon practice, hired a substitute to serve for him in the Confederate army.[16]

Jewish contributions, both in the army and on the home front, received praise from the *Memphis Daily Appeal:* "The Israelites of this city have been behind none in showing their devotion to the South both by liberal contributions, and by taking arms in her defense." The New Orleans *Crescent,* in speaking of southern Jewish soldiers, said: "They can be found in considerable number . . . and they are well regarded by their officers, as well as cheerful and active soldiers." The Jewish women of Memphis also played an active role in the war by forming an association to collect donations for the benefit of the soldiers' hospital. Rabbi Tuska served by ministering to his own congregants and by working with other members of the clergy to provide counsel and aid for wounded soldiers.[17]

The deep sense of responsibility toward each other felt by the Memphis Jews continued during the Civil War. The by-laws of B'nai Israel stated that anyone who was sick could expect the assistance of two fellow-congregants for the duration of his illness. When a death occurred, two members of the congregation were also expected to attend to the corpse until the funeral and to observe the traditional seven days of mourning, if this was the custom or wish of the family.[18]

Congregation B'nai Israel in 1863 established a secular school, the

---

[16]Interview with Charles Goodman, 1990; Robert Rauchle, "Biographical Sketches of Prominent Germans in Memphis, Tennessee in the 19th Century," *West Tennessee Historical Society Papers* 22 (1968): 73-85; Jack D. L. Holmes, editor, "Documents: Joseph A. Gronauer and the Civil War in Memphis," *West Tennessee Historical Society Papers,* vol 22, 1968): 148-158.

[17]*Memphis Daily Appeal,* 27 September 1861; Keating, *History,* 504; *Memphis Daily Appeal,* 10 February 1861.

[18]Keating, *History,* 504.

Hebrew Educational Institute, which filled a pressing need because the war had forced the closure of many of the community's schools. The *Daily Appeal* reported that the school "opened with some of the best talent in our city. We look forward to a prosperous and flourishing career for this school where the children of the Hebrew and Christian will be educated side by side." It was supervised by Lazard Kremer, with Andrew J. Haile as principal. English, Hebrew, German, French, geography, and music were taught. One hundred students, both Jews and non-Jews, were given final examinations in the Assembly Hall of the Memphis Club; commencement was on June 23 at Greenlaw Opera House. Patrons and friends of the school and the general public were invited to attend.[19]

The faculty of the Hebrew Educational Institute included Principal Haile as professor of mathematics; the Reverend Simon Tuska, professor of languages; Annie Haile, instructor in the Female Department; Miss Annie Coolidge, teacher in the Primary Department; and Mr. Sigmund Schlesinger, professor of music and teacher of German and Hebrew.[20] The Hebrew Educational Institute operated for five years, closing for lack of funds in 1868, despite the community's continuing need for its services.

Schlesinger, of whose time in Memphis little else is known, was presented with a silver kiddush cup, traditionally used in a ceremony sanctifying the Sabbath, by Congregation B'nai Israel in 1864. This was probably the year he left Memphis, first for Somerville, Tennessee and later for Mobile, Alabama, where he spent the rest of his life pursuing his musical career. Schlesinger was among the first musicians to have a strong influence on the practices of the Reform movement in the United States. Recognizing the need for a musical component for the Union Prayer Book, he composed seven complete services, three for Sabbath evening and morning, one for the three festivals, and three for the High Holidays. His compositions, while widely accepted and used at the time they were written, have been supplanted in recent years by music that employs more of the Oriental characteristics of Jewish music.[21]

Meanwhile, as the Civil War continued, tensions grew in Memphis. The outbreak of the war had created an impasse. Supplies from the North were cut off and a Union blockade of southern ports prevented importation

---

[19]*Memphis Daily Bulletin*, 21 June 1864

[20]*Memphis Daily Bulletin*, 7 August 1874, 20.

[21]Irene Heskes, *Jews in Music* (New York: Bloch Publishing Co., n. d.), 26.

of products from Europe. Shortages of all manufactured goods resulted in rapid inflation and the beginning of illegal traffic between the North and South.[22] Because of its location on the Mississippi River, and because it was the nearest city to St. Louis, the source of badly-needed pharmaceuticals, Memphis became a major center of illegal trading after falling to Union forces on 6 June 1862. The newspapers were filled with reports of arrests: the Memphis *Daily Bulletin* of 25 February 1863, announced that two hundred ounces of quinine had been seized on the steamboat Rowena, "destined for the rebel army." All of those involved were imprisoned, including a St. Louis druggist. On 10 March 1863, General Grant issued stringent orders against contraband trade.

Although President Lincoln, Secretary of the Treasury Salmon P. Chase, and Generals Sherman and Grant had tried since 1861 to eliminate the flow of proscribed goods passing through the city, the traffic in contraband supplies exchanged for cotton remained undiminished.[23] Speculators, traders, and adventurers descended like vultures upon the area. They traded gold, silver, merchandise, arms, quinine to treat malaria, and surgical supplies, which the South wanted desperately, for the cotton and other southern raw agricultural products needed equally by the North. It has been estimated that between twenty thousand and thirty thousand dollars worth of supplies—the equivalent of between $7,408,000 and $11,112,000 in 1988 dollars—were funneled to the Confederacy through Memphis.[24]

General Grant feared that the black market in cotton would undermine the Union cause and was concerned about information leaked by the carpetbaggers. He and General Sherman considered all traders to be anathema and "rotten to the core."[25] Suspicion of traders is often commonly felt by soldiers who as a group find trade "disorderly." Added to this suspicion was the generals' deep distrust of Jews, a feeling he shared with

---

[22]Korn, "Jews and Negro Slavery," 145.

[23]Jeffrey N. Lash, "The Federal Tyrant at Memphis: General Stephen A. Hurlbut and the Union Occupation of West Tennessee, 1862-1864," *Tennessee Historical Quarterly*, Spring, 1959, S58, No. 1.

[24]Abraham J. Karp, ed., *The Jewish Experience in America: Selected Studies from the Publications of the American Jewish Historical Society*, (New York, KTAV Publishing House, Inc., 1969), 121.

[25]Berkley Kalin, "General Grant and the Memphis Jews," *Jewish Historical Society of Memphis and the Mid-South Newsletter* (Memphis: v.2, No. 4, October, 1989) 6.

many other Union officers.

General Grant's father, Jesse, who had long been critical of his son's lack of business success, had formed a partnership with three Jewish merchants in Cincinnati—brothers Henry, Harmon, and Simon Mack. The Macks came to north Mississippi to ask Grant for permits to buy and ship cotton, but they returned to Cincinnati without them. Grant was chagrined and angered by his father's attempt to use personal influence. It was true that, along with many others, some opportunistic Jewish merchants had entered the area as soon as it was conquered by the Union armies. It would have been unusual if Jewish businessmen, who had played a vital role in the expanding American capitalist economy, had not taken advantage of openings made available to the northern commercial world by Union successes. But Jewish merchants comprised a distinct minority of the traders who were engaged in the exchange of contraband goods. It was not in this instance what the Jews did, but *what they were* that was offensive to Generals Sherman and Grant.[26]

While the government authorized trading, even with the South, it wanted the generals to regulate it in a consistent and enforceable manner in order to eliminate smuggling. The generals in charge, on the other hand, deplored any trading with the South. They were thus placed in the awkward position of being responsible for implementing a commercial policy whose ambiguity was a constant temptation to exceed the limit of the law, and one with whose provisions they strongly disagreed. General Stephen A. Hurlbut, who had been put in charge of Memphis in November 1862, may have been placed in a difficult or even impossible situation when he was ordered to halt the smuggling that Sherman and Grant had been unable to control. But Hurlbut, instead of implementing the policy, participated in the smuggling himself, and then blamed Jewish merchants for the entire problem.[27]

Shortly after Hurlbut's appointment, General Grant sent him orders to "refuse all permits to come south of Jackson for the present. The Israelites especially should be kept out." The next day Grant instructed General Webster in Jackson to "give orders to all conductors on the road that no Jews are to be permitted to travel on the railroad southward from any point. They may go north, and be encouraged in it, but they are such an intolerable nuisance that the department [of Tennessee] must be purged of them."

---

[26]Ibid.
[27]Karp, *The Jewish Experience*, 134; Lash, "The Federal Tyrant," 19.

These instructions were the forerunners of Grant's notorious General Order No. 11, often called "the most sweeping anti-Jewish regulation in all American history."[28] Issued on 17 December 1862, the Order stated that:

> Jews as a class violating every regulation of trade established by the Treasury Department and also department orders are hereby expelled from the Department of Tennessee within twenty-four hours from receipt of this order.
>
> Post commanders will see that all of this class of people be furnished passes and required to leave, and anyone returning after such notification will be arrested and held in confinement until an opportunity occurs of sending them out as prisoners, unless furnished with permit from headquarters.
>
> No passes will be given these people to visit headquarters for the purpose of making personal application for trade permits.[29]

There is evidence that some of the staff officers who composed Order No. 11 signed by Grant were protecting large-scale smuggling engaged in by non-Jews. At that time, an order issued in Memphis indicted government trade with fifteen clothing firms said to have committed infractions of the laws. The order permitted two firms to continue furnishing uniforms to the troops. It is probably intentional that all of the prohibited firms were owned by Jews while the two deemed acceptable were not. Those who attempted to restrict the sources for military procurement stood to profit.[30]

Although illegal trading in contraband goods was widespread, the percentage of Jews engaged in these practices was a small, insignificant portion of the problem. In a report listing ninety-eight individuals accused of smuggling offenses, five names may possibly be Jewish. Those who were known to be trading illegally were denounced angrily and publicly by the leaders of the Jewish community, including Rabbis Tuska and Peres. Tuska vehemently criticized northern Jews who had come to Memphis as "greedy birds of prey." Peres, himself a businessman, expressed chagrin when he spoke of "Jewish law-breakers," describing their activities as "a profanation of the name of God." For his part, Rabbi Leeser, who wanted Jews to be

---

[28]Postal and Koppman, *American Jewish Landmarks*, 243; Evans, *The Provincials*, 66.
[29]Evans, *Provincials*, 42.
[30] Arthur Hertzberg, *The Jews in America* (New York: Simon and Schuster, 1987). 133.

farmers, not traders, wrote with shame of "the crowd of needy Jewish adventurers, who travel or glide . . . through the highways and byways of the land in quest of gain, often, we fear, unlawfully, who, in their material labors are perfectly indifferent to the duties of their religion." David Einhorn declared that Jews were no worse than others, but felt it was the duty of the Jews to uproot such crimes that brought disgrace to the whole Jewish community. The rabbis felt that while Jews were "over-represented" in smuggling, they were not the major figures in this trade.[31]

When Grant's infamous orders were issued, hundreds of Jews in both Union and Confederate forces were on active duty in the designated area from which Jews were to be expelled. Of the approximately two thousand Jews then living in Tennessee, forty were fighting with Tennessee regiments on both sides of the struggle. Of these, seven were killed in action, two died in prison, and three were wounded.[32]

Jews who for decades had considered Tennessee home were hurriedly forced to pack up their families and depart. When one perplexed man and his wife questioned a soldier as he was forcing them to leave, they were told, "It's because you are Jews, and neither a benefit to the Union nor to the Confederacy." Cesar Kaskel of Paducah, Kentucky, saw thirty men and their families deported without any sort of trial or hearing. He asked Rabbi Isaac Mayer Wise of Cincinnati for support. Together they gathered and forwarded to the White House petitions and letters of protest from Jewish leaders, objecting to "this inhuman order, the carrying out of which would place us . . . as outlaws before the whole world."[33]

With the assistance of Congressman John Addison Gurley of Ohio, a friend of Wise, and with affidavits from leading Republican party members and military authorities, Wise and Cesar Kaskel secured an appointment with President Lincoln. During the conversation, Lincoln reportedly asked, with biblical allusion, "And so the Children of Israel were driven from the happy land of Canaan?" Kaskel replied, "Yes, and that is why we have come unto Father Abraham's bosom asking protection." "And this protection," the president answered, "they shall have at once."

Lincoln immediately wrote a note to Henry W. Halleck, general-in-

---

[31]Evans, *Provincials*, 43; Kaganoff and Urofsky, *Turn to the South*, 29; Karp, *Jewish Experience*, 152; Hertzberg, *Jews in America*, 133.
[32]Ibid.
[33]Karp, *Jewish Experience*, 152, 158.

chief of the army, directing him to telegraph instructions canceling the order. Halleck dispatched the following message to General Grant: "A paper purporting to be General Order No. 11, issued by you December 17, has been presented here. By its terms, it expels all Jews from your department. If such an order has been issued, it will be immediately revoked." Three days later, Grant's office transmitted the order of recall, making sure that it was understood that he was not acting on his own volition, but was complying with orders from the general-in-chief of the army.

When some rabbis and other Jewish leaders thanked the president, he told them that he believed it wrong to "condemn . . . the good with the bad. I do not like to hear a class or nationality condemned on account of a few sinners." Lincoln's prompt action nullifying Grant's order reassured the Jewish citizens of Memphis and of the country as a whole that anti-Semitism had not become the policy of the United States government.[34]

At the same time that Lincoln was revoking Grant's order, a resolution to revoke the order was introduced in the United States Congress. The resolution's failure in both houses signaled that Congress was willing to believe that Jews were unusually prominent among the smugglers and speculators. Overt anti-Semitism of the economic kind, reminiscent of that in Stuyvesant's New Amsterdam, had now reappeared in America. A more general type of anti-Semitism surfaced in the Confederacy targeting two Jews who had abandoned their religion: Judah P. Benjamin and David Yulee, both former United States senators. Grant's Order No. 11, though rescinded almost immediately, was more a reflection of the growing anti-Semitism of the period than it was of Grant's own personal animus. It was an action he regretted later, and one that was not forgotten by the Jews of Memphis.[35]

When Lincoln was assassinated on 14 April 1865, the Jews of Memphis expressed their deeply felt grief. Both Jewish congregations joined with other religious institutions in a memorial service. The entire membership of Euphrates Lodge No. 35 of B'nai B'rith marched in the city's procession of mourning with Samuel Schloss acting as marshal. Later, when Grant ran for president of the United States in 1868, the Memphis Jewish community, led by its rabbis, held a mass meeting at which it adopted a resolution declaring him "a man unfit for the high position to which he aspires, and

[34]Evans, *The Provincials*, 2; Karp, Jewish Experience, 125.
[35]Hertzberg, *Jews in America*, 135.

incapable of administering the laws to all classes with impartiality and without prejudice." Memphis Jews urged all those attending to use "every honorable means" to defeat Grant, asking other Jewish communities throughout the nation to act in the same manner. Only the Nashville community joined them. This meeting was the only recorded time in American history that a Jewish community took such united action in an American presidential election.[36]

In June 1862 after Memphis was captured, political allegiance changed, in form if not in feeling, as people were expected to support the North. While most Jews continued to support the Confederate cause, others embraced the Union, indicated by the rolls of the Home Guards, a self-policing organization under Union auspices, which included many Jewish names, some of whom had been Confederate sympathizers. Some Memphis Jews also served in both the Emerald Guards and the Sherman Guards, Union organizations.[37]

The Department of the Treasury recognized the contributions of Second Lieutenant David Lowenstine to the Union in a ceremony on 22 July 1864, attended by "our most prominent and most influential citizens, and a number of the officers of the General government. . . ." He was presented with a ceremonial sword, designed and produced by Tiffany's, bearing the emblem of the United States and his initials in diamonds. Secretary of the Treasury, J. M. Tom Leavy, made the presentation with the following remarks:

> Your fellow citizens, desiring to give expression to their high opinion of you as an enterprising, successful merchant, and to show you their appreciation of your generosity and public-spirited liberality, your efforts to promote the public-spirited liberality, your efforts to promote the welfare of our city, and your devotion to the cause of the Union, here present you this sword, sash, and belt....

---

[36]Postal and Koppman, *Jewish Landmarks*, 243.

[37]Wax, *Our First Century*, 38-39. Names included Samuel Schloss, Harry S. DeYong, J. C. Cohen, David C. Lowenstine, Lazard Isaacs, Harry Newman, Charles Myers, Joe Wolf, Morris Stone, M. J. Levi, S. Loeb, A. Boshwetz, E. Messenger, Charles L. Brown, S. Meyer, George Abrahams, H. Berger, H. Cohen, P. Halle, J. Hecht, Joseph Freedman, Louis Cohen, Isaac Gross, H. Lazarus, Jacob Loeb, Joseph Leopold, N. Block, E. Lehmen, M. Cohen, M. Wolf, J. Frankland, John Stix, David Solomon, F. Feltman, and J. C. Lowenhaupt; Seiger, "Immigration," 2.

Responding with thanks, Lowenstine said,

> Reared, as I have been, under the glorious Star Spangled Banner, and having enjoyed the benefits of a republican government beneath its folds, my endeavors shall be to further in every way the cause of liberty and American union, and never shall I unsheathe the sword, except in their defense. . . .[38]

Lowenstine was not the only Memphis Jew to support the Union. Herman Gronauer was another active Union advocate during the Civil War. He joined the Enrolled Militia, which was organized in 1863 by the Union soldiers of Memphis. After the war he was rewarded for his loyalty to the Republican Party when he was appointed Inspector of Hulls for the city. Union partisan Dr. R. L. Laski was appointed a member of a three-man committee on arrangements for a demonstration by the Enrolled Militia.[39] At least four Memphis Jews, Edward Barinds among them, attended the Union-sponsored State Convention in 1864.

Federal control of Memphis brought with it many changes: prices rose, trade dwindled, a large number of families moved away, and newcomers arrived in droves. Not surprisingly, Memphians had problems with the Northern occupation of the city. Captured Confederate soldiers who had taken the amnesty oath before the war ended were forced to serve as military guards for their comrades who were still in arms. Taxes were levied and collected without authorization from either the president of the United States or the secretary of war. The propertied classes suffered along with all the rest of the inhabitants.[40]

The Civil War ended officially on 9 April 1865 with the surrender of General Robert E. Lee to General Grant at Appomattox, Virginia. Although this armistice took place three years after the cessation of hostilities in Memphis, it opened the way for additional changes in the city. One of the most important of these changes was the influx of newly freed slaves from the surrounding countryside. Blacks flocked into Memphis

---

[38]Wax, *Our First Century*, 87.
[39]Rauchle, "Biographical Sketches," 74; *Memphis Daily Bulletin*, 11 November 1862.
[40]*Memphis Daily Bulletin*, 7 December 1862; Robert Corlew, *Tennessee: A Short History* (Knoxville: University of Tennessee Press, 1981), 325.

leaving many rural areas short of labor. Officials of the Freedmen's Bureau, established in March 1866, attempted to keep them out of the cities, encouraging them to return to the farms and plantations where their labor was needed, but with no success. There was a widespread belief among the freedpersons that freedom connoted freedom from work, at least work for their former masters. Some who were willing to work would not work for white men; and many were advised falsely that they would be supported by the government if they refused to work for "rebels." The famous promise of "forty acres and a mule" kept many from signing work contracts until after 1 January 1866. Where blacks were willing to sign contracts, they often demanded money wages paid at frequent intervals, a demand that was completely beyond the capacity of most farmers after the war. As a result, the labor shortage on the farms continued throughout 1865 while towns and cities were swollen with black migrants.[41]

Most of the newly arrived blacks in Memphis were former farm laborers with few skills to equip them for life in the city. They settled in south Memphis in an area populated largely by recent immigrants from Italy, Ireland, and Germany. If the mere presence of blacks in a formerly white area were not exasperating enough to Memphians, the fact that many of these blacks had been Union soldiers was a painful reminder of the defeat of the Confederacy. "A black soldier in a blue Union uniform was a red flag for defeated southerners."[42] Racial tensions soon developed.

The stage was set for trouble in January 1865, when the Third United States Colored Heavy Artillery was ordered to patrol the city's streets. The police, largely Irish and all white, resented the black presence. Brawls between the police and the black soldiers were frequent. White citizens petitioned for the replacement of black troops with white ones. A near-riot occurred in December 1865, when a large crowd of blacks rescued a black soldier from police who had arrested him for stealing meat from a market. Police who had ransacked several homes in searching for the black soldier were chased from the scene.

After the last of the black troops was mustered out of military service on 1 May 1866, fighting broke out once again in the Memphis Riot of 1866, the worst racial conflict in Tennessee during Reconstruction. In several

---

[41]Thomas B. Alexander, *Political Reconstruction in Tennessee* (Nashville: Vanderbilt University Press, 1950), 53.

[42]Alexander, *Political Reconstruction*, 54.

hours of brawling, a white mob looted and raped and forty-six blacks were killed, with many more injured. There was widespread destruction of black property, including the burning of several churches and schools.

Most of the Memphis newspapers grossly misrepresented the whole affair, belittling and oversimplifying it. The *Daily Argus* blamed the "poor, ignorant, deluded blacks." The *Public Ledger* wrote: "While we cannot but condemn such conduct in every way, yet it will have a good effect, and may be the means of inculcating in the negroes that respect of the law which they seem to have been taught to disregard. . . . It will be a warning to the negroes not to attempt to riot again."[43]

A report by the Freedmen's Bureau summarized the causes of the Memphis Riot more truthfully: the feud between police and black troops; incendiary racist articles in Memphis papers; isolated outrages by black troops during occupation; economic competition between black and white laborers; lack of communication between blacks and whites; and the character of the all-white police, many of whom were unaware that the curfew for black slaves no longer existed.[44] Peace was restored on Friday, 4 May 1866, three days after the riot began, by the arrival of four companies of white Union troops from Nashville. According to official reports, forty-eight people had been killed and seventy-five wounded. A congressional committee investigating the violence uncovered ample evidence to lay the groundwork for prosecution of the rioters and their leaders, but only three Union soldiers were ever tried.

On the other hand, racial animosities elsewhere in West Tennessee seem to have quieted quickly after the Civil War. Unionists received the returning white Confederate supporters courteously and kindly, helping them to get back into business to resume their disturbed lives, and reclaim their fortunes.[45] But the lack of punishment for the white rioters in the aftermath of the Memphis Riot was a harsh and bloody signal to the community that blacks would be kept "in their place," regardless of the outcome of the Civil War. It was also a strong signal to the Jewish community that the primary role of scapegoat would not be theirs in Memphis. It reinforced the feeling of belonging that Jews in Memphis had

---

[43]Richard Banks, "In the Heat of the Night," *Memphis Magazine* 15 (June 1990): 72; Alexander, *Political Reconstruction*, 56, 181-182, 184.

[44]Alexander, *Political Reconstruction*, 56.

[45]Alexander, *Political Reconstruction*, 58.

enjoyed, in large measure, ever since their arrival in the city.

This feeling was enhanced by the fact that the South needed a working population to exploit its natural resources profitably. Because former slaves were viewed with deep enmity and distrust and because Yankee transplants were regarded with hostility, the South looked to immigrants to fill its labor needs. Between 1870 and 1900 it aggressively attempted to attract foreign immigrants by means of pamphlets, leaflets, handbooks, special reports, resource surveys, and land prospectuses. These were translated into several languages and distributed widely in countries from which large numbers of immigrants were coming to the United States.[46] These measures, friendly toward immigrants, encouraged Memphis Jews, not far removed from their own immigrant experience, to feel wanted and needed.

When the fighting stopped, Jewish Memphians reacted to the Union victory as did the rest of the population. Some were bitter at the South's loss and the resulting economic hardships; some made the necessary accommodation to the new order of things; and some made common cause with the victors. The records that remain were written by the first group. A. E. Frankland reported atrocities committed by the occupation forces. Henry Seessel wrote of the dishonesty of the Federal forces and of their rudeness toward his wife when he had to be absent from home.[47]

Nevertheless, the Jewish community of Memphis, except for the shocking events surrounding Grant's General Order No. 11, did not suffer greatly during the war. In Memphis, the war lasted for a relatively brief period, and was less disruptive than it was in many other southern cities. Resumption of regular activities occurred quickly.

The end of the war found Jewish Memphians engaged in many types of businesses; they were barbers, bankers, race track operators, retailers. Twenty clothing stores were owned by Jews. They were prominent in the cotton brokerage business. Solomon Levin operated a cotton gin. Jews were engaged in liquor, livestock, crockery, and glassware concerns; some were auctioneers and wholesalers. A. E. Frankland was in the real estate business. Jacob J. Peres, having been dismissed as rabbi by Congregation B'nai Israel for keeping his business open on the Sabbath, was engaged in foreign trade

---

[46]Thomas D. Clark, "The Post Civil War Economy in the South," in Leonard Dinnerstein and Mary Jane Pahlson, eds., *Jews in the South* (Baton Rouge: University of Louisiana Press, 1973),164.

[47]A. E. Frankland, "Kronikals of the Times" *American Jewish Archives*, vol 9, No. 2, Oct. 1957), 102; Henry Seessel, *Memoirs of a Mexican Veteran* (Memphis: n. p., 1891), 30.

and selling cotton to his native Holland. J. D. Blumenthal and Gensburger Brothers were involved in the manufacture of trunks. Arthur Seessel sold dry goods and was a jobber of shoes; his brother Henry was a butcher who also brokered livestock and kept a kosher meat counter. Menken Brothers and Lowenstein's had become major department stores. Joseph Goodman was in the jewelry business; H. Foltz operated a hotel, City House.[48]

While all businessmen in Memphis were bound by Sunday closing laws, Jewish businessmen encountered a particular problem because those who wished to observe religious practices could not do business on Saturday either. Sunday closing laws, called "Blue Laws," had been in force in Tennessee since 1803, only seven years after Tennessee became a state. When six people were arrested in 1862 for keeping their stores open on Sunday, only one was Jewish. Among those who had to pay a five-dollar fine for staying open on Sunday were Jewish businessmen Louis Just, Abe Brum, M. Levy, D. Asher, and D. Zweifel. M. R. Isaacs was fined ten dollars in 1863, for "not caring particularly for the Christian Sabbath."[49]

Newspapers often questioned the application of the Blue Laws to Jewish businessmen. On 28 May 1861, a report of the arrest of Moses Levy for Sunday trading concluded that "under our Constitution we have no right to compel a man to keep our sacred day as well as his own . . . . If so, he has the same right to make us keep his day as well as ours if he had the power." Of the same case, the Memphis *Daily Avalanche* opined, "Certainly such of our fellow-citizens of the Jewish persuasion as keep Saturday as a Holy Day should be permitted to sell on the Christian Sabbath. It is a matter of religious tolerance."[50] Despite sympathy for the civil and economic liberty of Jews, a case appealed to the Supreme Court of the Confederate States resulted in a decision that Sunday closing laws were in accord with the State Law, "and therefore . . . constitutional in a state point of view." The Blue Laws were retained.

In 1865 Jews were officers of several banks and held important positions in Memphis life insurance companies. In contrast, among the few Jews in the professions in Memphis at the end of the Civil War were Dr. R. L. Laski, a physician, and Leopold Lehman who, upon opening a law practice

---

[48]Seessel, *Memoirs*, 30.

[49]*Commercial Appeal*, 13 January 1966, "100 Years Ago"; *Memphis Daily Bulletin* 12 August 1862, quoted in Wax 32.

[50]*Memphis Daily Appeal* 28 May 1861, and Memphis *Daily Avalanche*, quoted in Wax, 32.

in 1869, became the first Jewish lawyer listed in the City Directory. Lehman practiced law in partnership with his brother Irving. Born of wealthy parents from Alsace, Leopold Lehman was an authority on the law and on the French philosopher and writer Montesquieu. When Justice Peter Turney of the Supreme Court of Tennessee became ill in 1892, Lehman served for six months as a judge in his stead. Elias Gates associated with the Lehman firm for many years.[51]

Once the hostilities were over, Memphis's Jewish community resumed its active role in civic affairs. In the realm of education, D. C. and H. W. Lowenstine and the Herzog brothers helped to establish Christian Brothers College in 1871. Louis Hanauer was a member of the Board of Trustees of Memphis Medical College in 1878. In the realm of politics, Paul Schuster was elected alderman from the Third Ward; Dr. Laski also became an alderman, filling a vacancy that occurred. In the election of 1864, L. Hanover was chosen clerk and J. Hanover, returning officer. Jacob Peres was elected president of the School Board. Dr. R. Loewenthal, who in 1861 had been appointed Memphis city hospital physician, was appointed to the same position for the county in 1866. He had been named to fill a vacancy as alderman in 1863. He became director of the County Pest House in 1874. In 1872 Joseph Gronauer was elected as a delegate to the Republican National Convention from the Ninth District of Tennessee.[52]

Articles in *Commercial* indicated the way non-Jews of Memphis regarded the Jewish community. On 7 March 1867 the newspaper wrote:

------

[51]Seiger, "Immigration," 9, 12. Mechanics Savings Bank employed M. H. Katzenberger as president; I. Katzenberger as teller; A. Cohen, Jacob Marcus, A. S. Meyers, H. Henochsberg, and Merrill Kremer as directors. Memphis National Bank named Joseph Fader, Hardwig Peres, and Benedict Lowenstein as directors. Germania Bank's letterhead listed Louis Hanauer, Edward Goldsmith, Sol Coleman, and Jacob Weller. Manhattan Savings Bank's directors included S. Goldbaum, Lazarus Levy, Sol Coleman, Hardwig Peres, Louis Hanauer, and Edward Goldsmith. Arthur Seessel was a director of Carolina Life Insurance. He was also a director of Mississippi Valley Fire and Marine Company, as were S. Menken and Benedict Lowenstein. Herman Gronauer was the secretary, and G. H. Judah, Benjamin Eiseman and Jacob Peres were directors of Tennessee State Mutual Fire Insurance Company; *Bench and Bar of Memphis* 196, and Judge Irving Strauch lecture, Memphis, TN, Memphis Jewish Community Center, 12 January 1992.

[52]Seiger, "Immigration," 12; *Memphis Daily Bulletin*, 2 July 1864, quoted in Lawrence Meyers, "Memphis Jews and the Civil War Issues," unpublished term paper, Memphis State University, 1961; E. B. Washburne, "Memphis Riots and Massacres" (Washington, D.C., United States House of Representatives Select Committee on Memphis Riots of May, 1866.); *Memphis Daily Bulletin*, 3 March 1863; Shankman 4-5..

The Hebrews of Memphis rank among the most enlightened and enterprising citizens of the United States. In all the relations of life they are eminently prosperous. As a business people, none are more strictly just; as neighbors they are sociable and kind-hearted, and as donators of assistance to the wretched and needy they are among the most liberal, giving with unsparing hand and with a willingness of disposition that sheds a luster about their bountiful generosity.[53]

Another article in the same month said:

A lecture for the benefit of widows and orphans of Confederate soldiers was delivered at the Tabernacle by Rabbi Simon Tuska, whose subject was "The reformed Israelite of the nineteenth century . . . ." Those who attend will have a rare treat. The discussion by so learned a divine of such an interesting subject cannot fail to fill the Tabernacle to its utmost capacity.[54]

A further sign of Jews' acceptance in the city was their membership in several non-Jewish social and fraternal organizations. Louis Hanover was vice-president of the Order of Masons. The Masonic Directory included both the Hebrew and the Masonic calendars. Samuel Rosenheim, Jacob Goldsmith, and L. Rosenheim were members of the Ancient Order of United Workmen. S. Dreyfus and Daniel Schloss were charter members of Unity Lodge, organized in 1875. Nathan Bach and L. Goldsmith were officers of Diamond Lodge No. 583; Gus Haase was a member of Esperanza Lodge No. 3105. Louis Ottenheimer was treasurer of Knights and Ladies of Honor.

Jewish organizations continued to grow. B'nai B'rith created a separate branch in Memphis in 1875. The Memphis Club expanded its membership and elected new officers on 30 October 1869.[55] The Memphis Mennerchor, a German Jewish social society, was organized in 1871 by Otto Zimmer-

---

[53]*Commercial Appeal* ,7 March 1867.

[54]*Commercial Appeal*, 24 March 1867.

[55]O. F. Vedders, *History of the City of Memphis and Shelby County* (Syracuse: D. Mason and Co., 1888), vol. 2, 274; *Commercial Appeal*, 20 January 1973; Isidor Rosenbach, president; Lazard Kremer, vice-president; L. Wertzfelder, financial secretary; E. Lehman, D. Langsdorf, L. Iglauer, trustees; L. Feucht, J. Marrhentz; S. Hirsch, librarian. *Memphis Daily Appeal*, 16 June 1869.

mann, A. Goldsmith, P. Kohler, S. Darmstadt, A. D. Schimmels, and M. Gottleib.

The Young Men's Hebrew Association (YMHA), a social and educational organization, was founded in 1881. YMHAs were indigenous to the United States, patterned after the Young Men's Christian Association (YMCA), which appeared in the country in 1851 and by 1874, numbered almost 1,000 branches. While the YMCA was religious in orientation, the primary goal of the YMHA was social. It sought to promote intra-Jewish fellowship and catered generally to young, middle-class Jews aged eighteen through thirty. Thus, it was a Jewish organization, but its emphasis was secular. The Memphis YMHA originally met in rented rooms at the corner of Second and Union. The facility was open evenings and Sundays and provided a reading room stocked with a library of 1,500 volumes. Members produced semi-monthly literary and musical entertainments and presented other programs of interest.[56] The *Commercial Appeal* wrote on 23 October 1890:

> The hall of the Young Men's Hebrew Association would not contain the crowd gathered there last evening to hear the speeches of the Honorables John P. Buchanan and William C. P. Breckenridge. The audience was composed of representative businessmen of the city and a large number of farmers from the country adjacent to the city. . . .[57]

The Jewish community, in creating such an organization, was conforming to the practice of establishing its own separate institutions comparable to the non-Jewish ones in which Jews were denied membership.

When the Hebrew Orphans Asylum was established in Cleveland, Ohio, in 1869, the B'nai B'rith lodges of Memphis hosted a picnic for its benefit in June of the same year. The committee for the affair included a

---

[56]Jacob Marcus, *United States Jewry, 1776-1985* (Detroit: Wayne State University Press, 1989), vol. 3, 412.Its first officers were Dave Gensburger, Emil G. Rawitser, Harry Rosenthal, and Dr. Harry S. Wolff., E. E. Becker, Charles J. Haase, Simon Levi, Otto Metzger, and Hardwig Peres were members of the Finance Board. Emanuel Klein was chairman of social affairs; Dr. A. L. Blecker, debates; Gilbert P card, entertainments; Sidney Seligstein, athletics, and Dr. Alphonse Meyer, Sr., educational affairs. All were Reform Jews.; Vedders, *History*, 289.

[57]J. P. Young, *History of Memphis, Tn.* (Knoxville: N.W. Crew and Co., 1912), 557.

large percentage of the Jewish community. Extensive publicity appeared in the *Daily Appeal,* both before and after the event. The picnic was held at James Park, a site used frequently for civic events, and was attended by an estimated 6,000 persons, both Jewish and non-Jewish. An orchestra played for dancing from eleven a.m. until midnight, and arrangements were made for streetcars to extend their normal hours of operation. In July, the *Daily Appeal* published a letter from the secretary of the Orphans Asylum, acknowledging receipt of proceeds from the picnic, and of a contribution from the Ladies Hebrew Benevolent Society. The newspaper congratulated "our Jewish friends upon their success and hope that they will often be able to contribute to their noble institution."[58]

Another fund-raising event of 1869 was a fair held by members of Congregation B'nai Israel. Again the newspaper supported the efforts of the Jewish community by announcing the project and urging attendance by the community at large:

> It is to be hoped that the good work of the ladies and gentlemen of the Temple will prove, in the highest sense, remunerative, and that the result will be such as to meet their expectations and the necessities of their organization. Our Hebrew fellow-citizens seldom make an appeal and seldom resort to expedients other than that of direct subscription, in aid of their charities and synagogues, while they are accounted among the most liberal "givers" for all purposes that we have in our community.

The congregation presented a "handsome gold-headed cane" to Lewis Wexler in appreciation for his services to the fair.[59]

In 1871, at age thirty-six, Rabbi Simon Tuska died suddenly of a heart attack.[60] Tuska had led his congregation, B'nai Israel, in the direction of moderate Reform Judaism. His activities also involved him in the community as a whole. He had participated in interfaith services during and after the war, and had introduced patriotic services for Thanksgiving and National Fast Day.

---

[58]"100 Years Ago," *Commercial Appeal,* 27 January, 1990; *Memphis Daily Appeal,* 16 June 1869.

[59]*Sunday Morning Appeal* ,4 July 1869.

[60]*Memphis Daily Appeal,* 27 November 1869.

Tuska was succeeded in 1871 by Rabbi Max Samfield, whose long and fruitful ministry furthered the ideals of Reform Judaism and advanced the commitment to public service demonstrated by his predecessors, Peres and Tuska. Samfield served as rabbi for more than four decades. He joined the B'nai B'rith when he arrived in Memphis, and became the president of the Memphis lodge where he was committed to the support of widows, orphans, and delinquent and handicapped individuals. For many years he was a director of the Cleveland Orphans Asylum, one of the institutions supported by the organization.

He had joined the Masons in Shreveport, where he had been before coming to Memphis. In 1872 he joined the Lelia Scott Lodge, attaining the rank of Thirty-Second Degree and remaining a member until his death. He had been a member of the Elks for ten years before he died, serving as President of the Tennessee Elks Association.

During his forty-four years in Memphis, Samfield helped the Jewish communities in the towns surrounding the city, organizing many congregations and Sabbath schools. He was a founder of the United Charities of Memphis, the YMHA, the Hebrew Relief Association formed during the yellow fever epidemics, and was the first vice-president of the Federation of Jewish Charities of Memphis. He was a governor of the Hebrew Union College, and a trustee of the New Orleans Orphan Asylum Home. He helped found the Tennessee Society for Prevention of Cruelty to Animals and Children. His broad activities included work on improvements to the Memphis school system, and assistance in the building of St. Joseph's Hospital, which honored him posthumously at its one hundredth anniversary for his role in its founding.

Samfield established a weekly journal in 1885, the *Jewish Spectator*, devoted to Judaism, science, and literature. It enjoyed a large readership, especially in the South and Southwest. The respect Samfield won throughout the city was reflected in the large number of pallbearers from all faiths who served at his funeral in 1915. For ten minutes during the services, every business house in the city shut off its power, and every streetcar came to a halt for a minute.[61]

---

[61]Dr. Norman Shapiro, "Our Rabbis and Their Times." Unpublished paper.

4

THE YELLOW FEVER EPIDEMICS

"Gloom hung over the city, which was silent by day, desolate by night."

—J. M. Keating

Memphis was affected by three important events in the second half of the nineteenth century—the Civil War, Reconstruction, and the yellow fever epidemics. Most scholars who have studied the history of the city at this period conclude that it was least damaged by the Civil War. "Few towns suffered as little from the four years of war as did Memphis," wrote Gerald Capers. "Reconstruction, however," according to Capers, "was a different story, bringing Memphis to a new low as local Radicals gained control of the city government, robbing the treasury, resulting in the deterioration of city services, while crime, vice, filth, and disease flourished."[1] The yellow fever epidemics were even more significant in the history of the city.

Memphis in the 1870s was a prime candidate for a medical disaster. Although in that era little was understood of modern methods of sanitation, it was known that cities with sewers, indoor plumbing, and paved streets were safer than cities without them. In Memphis, sewage was dumped into open rivers or bayous that often became infested with rats and other animals. The streets were surfaced with Nicholson pavement, a substance composed of cypress logs that became poisonous as it decayed, and there was no organized system of garbage disposal.[2]

As early as the 1850s Memphis newspapers issued warnings about unsanitary conditions and sponsored a health campaign. Doctors urged the city to install a sewage system and a water works, and to adopt hygienic practices. But the Board of Health was only an advisory body; and the

---

[1]Gerald Capers, quoted in William D. Miller, *Memphis During the Progressive Era, 1900-1917* (Memphis: Memphis State University Press, 1957), 6.

[2]J. M. Keating, *A History of the Yellow Fever Epidemic of 1878 in Memphis, Tennessee* (Memphis: The Howard Association, 1879), 13.

aldermen, who were authorized to initiate such measures, did not imple-ment the progressive recommendations. When a quarantine was proposed in 1858 to avoid an epidemic of yellow fever, an alderman expressed the fatalistic attitude of many citizens: "[I] never knew any good to come from quarantine," adding, "if Providence intended the fever to come here, it will come in spite of all we can do."[3]

The Civil War, with its military occupation, had brought better standards of sanitation to Memphis, but the benefits of the wartime cleansing were only temporary. In 1866 the Memphis Board of Health advocated a quarantine and strict sanitation measures to fight the threat of cholera, but authorities again declined to provide funding. In fact, no health board was appointed in 1867. City officials also fired the street cleaners and sanitation officers and sold the city's slop carts and mule teams. The Memphis charter of 1878, completely ignoring the dangers of epidemic and recent discoveries about hygiene, made little provision for sanitation and none for cases of emergency.[4]

In part, the city's failure to adopt preventive sanitary measures can be attributed to its financial position. Before the Civil War, Memphis's taxable wealth amounted to $28 million; after the war that total was reduced by almost one-half. The city was unable to fund the necessary sanitation projects. But failure to adopt hygienic practices can also be attributed to its citizens' complacency. Memphis was wounded by the yellow fever epidemic of 1873, but not mortally, in part because the fever that year arrived only six weeks before the first frost. Even so, there were eight thousand cases with twenty-five hundred fatalities. Four summers free of the fever followed, encouraging the city fathers to overlook the still-present danger and setting the stage for the catastrophe of 1878.[5]

As it had done in the 1850s, the Memphis Board of Health again pleaded with the city administration after the 1873 epidemic to clean up the streets and to improve sanitation. The *Daily Appeal* supported those efforts, but instead city leaders and merchants invested in public relations schemes to make Memphis a manufacturing center. Private investors financed the

---

[3]Capers, *Biography*, 130.

[4]John Duffy, *The Sanitarians: A History of American Public Health* (Urbana and Chicago: University of Illinois Press, 1990) 114.

[5]Keating, *Yellow Fever* 13; Mimi White, "Yellow Fever," a special section of the *Centennial Edition of The Commercial Appeal* (Memphis, October 31, 1978) 13; White, "Yellow Fever," A6.

largest fireworks display ever seen in the South for the 1878 Fourth of July celebration.

Early in May 1878 an outbreak of yellow fever in the West Indies came to public attention. By 5 July 1878 New Orleans had reported thirty-six cases of "virulent yellow fever." Nevertheless, four days later the Memphis City Council ignored a petition by the Board of Health to impose a quarantine on the city. Most of the business community viewed the quarantine as an unnecessary and costly impediment to the trade it was promoting, an attitude that coincided with the opinion held by most urban southerners who believed the proper functions of government were to protect property and to preserve the existing social order. Business leaders were supported by the majority of the city's physicians who said emphatically, "There is absolutely no danger from yellow fever, and no need for a quarantine."[6]

By August the dreaded fever had killed several Memphians. People began to flee the city by every available means, often leaving businesses and property unattended. Most of those who fled were white and affluent, including many Jews, some of whom, like other Memphians, never returned. In that exodus Memphis lost a large percentage of its cultured, wealthy citizens, who relocated both themselves and their businesses farther north.

Twenty-five thousand Memphians had left by August 24; two weeks later, five thousand others had taken refuge in temporary camps outside the city. Jacob Kohlberg, acting president of the newly organized Memphis Hebrew Hospital and Relief Association, noted that the effects of the epidemic were evident not only in Memphis, but also in the areas surrounding the city: "To our utter dismay, we found every avenue leading to the city densely packed . . . with Jewish families, and, with few exceptions, did any escape the force of the fever."[7]

Of the forty thousand people who had lived in Memphis before the fever, only twenty thousand remained. Of those, most were poor whites and blacks who were at first popularly, but incorrectly, believed to be immune to the disease. By the end of August, three thousand cases were reported in the city. Hot, dry weather exacerbated an already desperate situation. There was no trade or traffic; those who could do so isolated themselves in their

---

[6]Keating, *Yellow Fever*, 24ff; Duffy, *The Sanitarians*, 114; White, "Yellow Fever," A6.

[7]"Memphis Jewish Community, 1840-Present," Center for Southern Folklore pamphlet (Memphis: Center for Southern Folklore, 1987.)

homes. During the worst months of the epidemic, both church and synagogue services were discontinued. The streets were strewn with bodies awaiting disposal.[8]

Individuals and organizations made heroic efforts to help. Many of those who were free of the disease worked to bring relief to the afflicted. Among the societies set up to deal with the crisis was the above-mentioned Memphis Hebrew Hospital and Relief Association, established probably as a branch of the United Hebrew Relief Association. Its members, according to J. F. Keating, editor of the *Memphis Appeal*, "were especially notable for ardor, for steadiness, for single-heartedness, and for unstinted charity. They were no respecter of persons. They went from house to house, asking but one question, 'Is aid needed?' They made no distinction." The Jewish population of the South, mobilizing once again to deal with the crisis at hand, established a Yellow Fever Fund. The fraternal, social, and charitable organizations throughout the region collected monies, food, and clothing, while their individual members helped to care for the sick, the widows, and the orphans.[9]

The B'nai B'rith called upon the resources of its member lodges outside the South to help. Jewish assistance was widespread, as it had been in previous epidemics. In 1873 a Des Moines congregation sent a gift for the relief of Memphis yellow fever victims. Members of the Indianapolis Tree of Life Mutual Benefit Association, a typical Jewish self-help organization of the period, sent one hundred dollars to "their suffering co-religionists" in Memphis and Shreveport to relieve the victims of yellow fever. The Philadelphia *Times* reported: "There has been a regular flow of money from Jewish circles in aid of the sufferers. . . American Jews, who number 250,000, have sent sixty thousand dollars to the infected region."[10]

One of the Jews who remained was City Alderman David Gensburger, who in 1873 signed a pact with fellow Memphian, the non-Jewish A. Compton, to remain in the city "until the epidemic reaches three hundred deaths a day." They did so. E. M. Levy, A. E. Frankland, Rabbi Max Samfield of B'nai Israel, and Rabbi Ferdinand I. Sarner of Beth El Emeth also remained. Sarner, who came to Beth El Emeth in 1872, had been the

[8]Keating, *Yellow Fever*, 126.
[9]Lawrence Meyers, "Memphis Jews and Civil War Issues." (Unpublished paper, University of Memphis, 1961), 15; Keating, *Yellow Fever*, 126; Louis Schmier, ed., *Reflections of Southern Jewry: The Letters of Charles Wessolowsky* (Mercer Univesity Press, 1962), 61.
[10]Rader, *United States Jewry*, vol 2, 99; Schmier, *Reflections*, 61.

first rabbi to serve as a regimental chaplain in the United States Army. He enlisted in 1863 with the 54th New York Volunteer Infantry and was wounded at Gettysburg. During the epidemic Sarner reportedly attended Friday night services at B'nai Israel. In times of trouble, Jews buried their liturgical and organizational differences in favor of their communal identity. Sarner became a victim of yellow fever.[11]

Despite the efforts of individuals and of the hospitals and nursing facilities that normally ministered to the sick, the epidemics overwhelmed the capacities of regular caregivers. New Orleans already had encountered this problem. During its 1853 yellow fever epidemic, volunteers in that city created an organization known as The Howard Association, named for an English philanthropist and geared specifically to deal with the devastation of the disease. "The Howards," as members of the organization were called, gathered medicines, nurses, doctors, and provided for other kinds of needs.[12] In Memphis, which had formed its own chapter, they supplied much-needed assistance.

During the yellow fever epidemic of 1873, A. E. Frankland was a member of The Howards. Frankland and his non-Jewish partner, S. W. Rhodes, were assigned to Ward Three, charged with visiting all the sick in the area, morning and evening. When the association solicited funds in 1873, Frankland was one of four who signed the appeal. In its final report, the association praised Frankland

> who labored so assiduously to relieve the suffering and distressed, and who lost his son in the fever. The boy frequently assisted his father, one of the most indefatigable of The Howard Association visitors, and in the path of duty was attacked with the disease. . . .[13]

Frankland was a director of The Howard Association in 1876 and 1877. Frankland did not remain in Memphis during the epidemic of 1878. Wishing to avoid a repeat of his terrible loss of 1873, he joined the general exodus from the city and went to St. Louis. For this move he was dropped

---

[11]Postal and Koppman, vol. 2, 245; Schmier, *Reflections*, 69; Postal and Koppman, *Landmarks*, 245.

[12]Keating, *Yellow Fever*, 126.

[13]*Memphis Daily Appeal*, 29 October 1873.

from The Howard Association.[14] But other Jewish members of the group chose to stay. Among those who made significant contributions, perhaps none is more notable that Nathan D. Menken.

Menken had been preceded in Memphis by his brother, Jacob, who established a dry goods business in 1862. Nathan and another brother, Jules, joined Jacob in the growing business. The store became one of the most prosperous retail and wholesale businesses in town, and according to a newspaper article, "did much to make Memphis a commercial city." Even before the yellow fever epidemic reached its height, Menken was persistent in pointing out the need for good pavements and a thorough system of sewerage. He personally made a generous donation to a general sanitation fund.

When the fever struck, and the ranks of The Howard Association were depleted by defection and death, they issued an urgent call for volunteers. Menken was among those who responded. Sending his family away to safety, he remained behind as a member of The Howards to nurse the sick, eventually succumbing to the disease. One of the women who remained to answer the call for nurses during the 1878 epidemic was Henrietta Pump. She survived the fever, dying in 1916.[15]

One unfortunate result of the yellow fever epidemics was the large number of children orphaned by the disease. The Memphis Jewish community hosted a picnic on 21 May 1875 to benefit the Hebrew orphan asylums in Cleveland and New Orleans. A newspaper explained the connection: "Many Memphis children who were orphaned by the yellow fever epidemic were taken by these institutions," it reported, adding that "the Memphis public should feel an obligation to make this picnic a success."[16]

The scourges of the decade that had destroyed so many lives threatened the existence of the city itself. Some five thousand of those who fled the city, many of whom were affluent, productive citizens, never returned. The Jewish population, which had numbered twenty-one hundred before the Civil War, was reduced to three hundred.[17] City coffers were virtually empty. By 1878 the amount of money due to the city in taxes had dimin-

[14]Anne Marie McMahon Falsone, "The Memphis Howard Institute: A Study in the Growth of Social Awareness" (unpublished M. A. thesis, Memphis State University, 1968).
[15]Keating, *Yellow Fever*, 140-41; "Bygone Days," *Commercial Appeal*, 17 January 1991.
[16]"100 Years Ago," *Commercial Appeal*, 21 May 1975.
[17]"Memphis Jewish Community, 1840-Present." Center for Southern Folklore Pamphlet.

ished from $28 million to $18 million. But even this amount, one-third of which was expected to be generated by a sales tax, was uncollected, primarily because the population was unable to pay.

Despite the ravages of yellow fever, the city's population had doubled since 1860, whereas trade had increased only slightly. One third of the new black immigrants to the city were very poor. With severely curtailed income and a continuing need to provide services, the city could not meet its financial obligations. As a last resort, the city government went into the banking business, broadcasting promises to pay its expenses and issuing scrip.

Among the expenses it could not pay was money owed to the State of Tennessee for taxes on the city charter. When the city's debt reached $5.5 million in 1878, the state took possession of one-third of Memphis real estate in exchange for the delinquent taxes. In response, a mass meeting was held on 31 December at the Greenlaw Opera House, where officials adopted a plan to relinquish the charter, believing this to be the only course of action that would allow Memphis to survive. Louis Hanauer was active in the campaign for the charter's repeal. Accordingly, the Tennessee legislature abolished the corporate charter of Memphis on 31 January 1879, appointing Dr. D. T. Porter as mayor of the newly created Taxing District of Memphis.[18] Under this arrangement, which lasted for fourteen years, Memphis yielded to the state the authority for selection of city officials and control of finances.

Yellow fever struck the city again in June 1879, but this time the epidemic, while serious, did not approach the severity of 1878. City authorities finally accepted the fact that sanitation was a necessity for which funds had to be found. Among those appointed to committees to secure sewers were Ben Eiseman and Elias Lowenstein. Lowenstein also served on the Executive Committee of the Board of Health of the Taxing District and was one of a committee of ten men appointed to find a way to restore the city's charter. Major sanitary reforms were in place by 1880, and the population had increased to sixty-five thousand as rural people poured in.[19]

---

[18]Keating, *Yellow Fever*, 101-102; White, "Yellow Fever," A7; Lynette B. Wrenn, "The Impact of Yellow Fever in Memphis: A Reappraisal," *West Tennessee Historical Society Papers* 12 (1987): 14; Rubin Bruesch, *Yellow Fever in Tennessee, 1878* (Nashville: Tennessee Medical Association, 1979), 305.

[19]Bruesch, *Yellow Fever in Tennessee*, 305; Interview with Ira Samelson, 1995; Keating, *Yellow Fever* 189.

Jews were active in civic endeavors throughout the period. Henry Eschman had become an alderman in 1876. Joseph Gronauer was appointed United States Inspector of Hulls in 1879. The first Tennessee Society for Prevention of Cruelty to Animals and Children, organized on 15 March 1880, chose Rabbi Max Samfield as its vice-president. J. S. Menken, a member of the Memphis School Board, advocated a general kindergarten system in 1895. Israel Peres, son of Rabbi Jacob Peres, was elected president of the Memphis School Board in 1900.[20]

Despite the severity of the epidemics, business activity continued. A. Schwab opened a dry goods business on Beale Street in 1876 in the location which still houses the store, operated by descendants of the founder. A. Simon and Brother also opened a dry goods store in the same year.[21]

As the city of Memphis and its environs recovered from the war and its aftermath, and from the more devastating epidemics of yellow fever, the citizenry exhibited a growing sense of confidence in the future. Congregation Children of Israel, as B'nai Israel was now usually called, voted in 1882 to purchase property on Poplar Avenue between Second and Third Streets. Less than two years later, a new building was erected at a cost of $39,130, and was dedicated on 18 January 1884. Within a year, forty-five new members had joined and the congregation was free of debt. There were so many young Jewish men in the small towns surrounding Memphis, as well as in the city itself, that the young ladies of Memphis held open house for them during religious holidays when they came into the city to attend services. Hattie Schwarzenberg, Birdie Hesse, and Mattie Goldsmith advertised in the Memphis *Avalanche* that "they will tomorrow receive at their home."[22]

The relationship of Jews to the rest of the Memphis population seems to have been strengthened by the tragedy they had undergone together. The performance of Jews as members of the caring community gave evidence of their feeling of oneness with the city in its time of great trouble.

[20]James D. Davis, *History of Memphis* (Memphis: Hite, Compon, and Kelly, 1873) 42; Keating, *Yellow Fever*, 271; *Commercial Appeal*, 31 March 1970; Sterling Tracy, "The Immigrant Population of Memphis," *West Tennessee Historical Society Papers* 4 (1950): 17.
[21]Postal and Koppman, *Landmarks*, 245.
[22]James A. and Helen G. Wax, *Our First Century, 1854-1954*, 41; Postal and Koppman, *Landmarks*, 245.

5

EASTERN EUROPEAN IMMIGRATION

How came they here? What burst of Christian hate?
What persecution, merciless and blind
Drove o'er the sea—that desert desolate
Those Ishmaels and Hagars of mankind?

They lived in narrow streets and lanes obscure
Ghetto and Judenstrass, in mirk and mire;
Taught in the school of patience to endure
The life of anguish and the death of fire.

— Henry Wadsworth Longfellow

By 1880 there were three hundred thousand Jews in America. Most were well-established and integrated into their communities. Historian John Higham wrote that "the degree to which Jews were involved in the early growth of a city and had achieved a notable and respected place in public and private life before the era of mass immigration directly influenced how later generations of Jews were received." Higham's thesis is borne out by the experience of Jews in Memphis. The prominence of the German Jews in the city's early history has had a positive effect on the later relations between Jews and non-Jews. Most Jews by 1880 had adopted Reform Judaism, finding in this method of observance a way to accommodate old traditions to American reality. They saw themselves as part of the American culture, their religion one of the many religions in the New World.[1]

This adjustment was to change with the arrival of the Eastern Europeans. Czar Alexander II of Russia was assassinated on 1 March 1881.

---

[1]Higham is cited in Wax, *Our First Century*, 41; Oscar Handlin, *A Pictorial History of Immigration: A Dramatic Story of the Builders of America from Prehistoric Times to the Present* (New York: Crown Publishers, Inc., 1972), 240-41.

Under his successor Alexander III, official Russian policy, never friendly to the Jews, became virulently anti-Semitic. Seeking a scapegoat to divert attention from the government in a time when economic conditions were bad and growing worse, Alexander encouraged peasants to blame Jews for their problems. The resulting animosity prompted a devastating series of pogroms in hundreds of towns between 1881 and 1884. The government produced and distributed anti-Semitic tracts, including the infamous *The Protocols of the Elders of Zion*, rumored to have been written by an official of the Russian secret police. According to this document, Jews were part of an international conspiracy directed by a central body of influential Jews whose purpose was to dominate the world.[2]

For centuries Jews had lived in Eastern Europe, Russia, Romania, and Austria-Hungary, subject to the tyranny of the czars and the violence of Christian peasants. Since the Middle Ages, in these countries as well as in the countries of Western Europe, their occupations had been restricted to those of traders and artisans. But in Russia, which then included much of modern Poland, Jews were also confined to living in a prescribed area of approximately 380,000 square miles in the eastern part of the country between the Baltic and the Black Seas. This vast ghetto was called the Pale of Settlement.[3]

Although his regime discriminated against Jews and severely limited almost every area of their lives, Alexander III left them free to worship as they pleased. This freedom allowed the Jews, living in shtetls, little villages within the Pale, to develop a rich and meaningful religious and cultural life. Although poor and parochial, Jews of the Pale centered their attention on the family, the celebration of traditional rituals, and the study of Talmud and Torah.[4]

Restrictions even more severe, limiting further where they could live, were imposed on the Jews of Russia in 1882. Shtetl life became so intolerable that one-third of the Jewish population, often entire families, came to America. These new immigrants were poor, hungry, and ill-clothed. Many were illiterate and carried their meager belongings in old suitcases held

---

[2] Arthur Herzberg, *The Jews in America: Four Centuries of an Uneasy Encounter* (New York: Simon and Schuster, 1989), 240-41.
[3] Steven Lowenstein, *The Jews of Oregon, 1850-1950* (Portland: Jewish Historical Society of Oregon, 1987), 72.
[4] Joshua Rothenberg, *The Jewish Religion in the Soviet Union* (New York: KRAV Publishing House, Inc., 1971.); Lowenstein, *Jews of Oregon*, 72.

together by ropes. The men were usually bearded, the women dressed in peasant fashion with babushkas on their heads. Yiddish was their own language, and Orthodox religious observance was the core of their lives. The Eastern European Jews were not only foreign to America in general, but seemed especially so to the Jews already established here and who wished to blend unnoticed into the general populace. Americanized German Jews cringed at the "backwardness" and orthodoxy of the newcomers, fearful of being overwhelmed by their numbers. They questioned whether the newcomers would ever be assimilated and worried that their own recently achieved acceptance would be threatened by the influx of these different, clannish immigrants with whom they shared the designation of Jew.[5] They were embarrassed by the newcomers, the "greeners" or "greenhorns," who brought with them not only strange customs and manners, but also strange political and social ideas and a language that sounded to them like jargon.

The Eastern Europeans, denied so many rights in the countries from which they came, often adopted Socialism and Zionism, philosophies that offered hope for escape from their miserable lives. Historian Arthur Hertzberg theorizes that the identification of the Eastern Europeans with Zionism reflected their sense of powerlessness. In America they were told that they were inferior both by German Jews, who tolerated but did not accept them, and by non-Jews. By joining the Zionist movement, the new immigrants declared their independence from their German predecessors. By not allowing the German Jews to speak for them in the non-Jewish community, the immigrants took an important step toward feeling that they belonged in America.[6]

The German Jews, who had learned to accommodate themselves politically to the American mold, rejected both Socialism and Zionism. German Jews, having attained a measure of wealth and prestige in the United States, feared that the pro-Zionist Easterners would undermine them, bringing into question their loyalty to America. They felt strong pressure to meld with the dominant culture, and did not wish to espouse anything that differentiated them from their non-Jewish neighbors. As a result, the German Jews of Memphis, like those in the rest of the South, were thus reluctant to identify with Zionism. Their position was validated

---

[5]Lowenstein, *Jews of Oregon*, 75.
[6]Hertzberg, *Jews in America*, 229.

by the fact that the Hebrew Union College, the institution that trained Reform rabbis, was the citadel of the fight against Zionism. Its president, Kaufmann Kohler, elected in 1903, was an outspoken anti-Zionist, as was his predecessor, Isaac M. Wise.[7] Locally, Rabbi Max Samfield of Temple Israel wrote that "Zionism is an abnormal eruption of perverted sentiment."

The Eastern Europeans, on the other hand, felt that the German Jews were so thoroughly assimilated as to be barely Jewish. When they arrived in Memphis, the new immigrants were shocked at the Reform measures adopted by Temple Israel. Use of the word "temple" by the Reform Jews was an insult to the Orthodox Jews, who felt that designation belonged only to the Temple in Jerusalem. They were horrified by this imputed infraction as they were by other Reform rituals they viewed as betrayals of Judaism, changing and even eliminating much of the old tradition.

What brought the first Eastern European Jews to Memphis, a city whose Jewish population was composed almost entirely of Western European Jews? Some came in response to advertisements in European periodicals of the time placed by southern interests who touted the advantages of the South in the hope of attracting a population of skilled workers. Others were drawn by letters sent back to Europe by successful immigrants who wrote that the streets in America were paved with gold. And, as with the German Jews, when one family member came to America, he sent for the rest of the family as soon as he could afford the tickets. Immigrants were also sent to the South by the Hebrew Immigrant Aid Society (HIAS), which worked to disperse Jewish immigrants throughout the United States rather than their congregating in the large cities of the eastern seaboard. The philosophy of HIAS was totally compatible with that of the German Jews of Memphis, who did not wish to see the embarrassing new immigrants arrive in large numbers with high visibility. The German Jews agreed with the policy of scattering them to create less impact. Some, of course, found their way to Memphis. Five immigrant families were sent to the city by HIAS in 1895.[8] Most of the newcomers originally stayed with a relative, or even a *landsman*, a fellow countryman, who would give them a room or a floor, and help them

---

[7]Lowenstein, *Jews of Oregon*, 75; Alfred O. Hero Jr., "Southern Jews," in *Jews in the South*, ed. Leonard Dinnerstein and Mary Jane Pahlson (Baton Rouge: LSU Press, 1973) 19; Marcus, vol. 3, 110; Herman Landau, *Adath Louisville: The Story of a Jewish Community* (Louisville: Herman Landau and Associates, 1981) 198.

[8]Lawrence Meyers, "Evolution of the Jewish Service Agency in Memphis, Tennessee 1847-1963," (unpublished M. A. thesis, Memphis State University, 1965), 17.

get started in an occupation.

Some of the Eastern Europeans settled in north or south Memphis in neighborhoods that included both non-Jewish and Jewish residents. Most lived behind or over their businesses. But Laizer Shendelman operated a hat business downtown on Adams Street, and bought a two-story home on Polk Avenue for his family. The Levys lived on one corner of the same street where they operated a grocery store; the Fleishman family, whose father had a horse and wagon to peddle fruit, lived nearby; on another corner were the Katzes, also in the grocery business; and there were the Alexanders and the Lewises. The block was all-white, but mixed religiously; there was an all-black street a block away.[9]

Not only did the Eastern European and German Jews differ in language, background, and religious practices, but economic difference also created barriers between them. Before the new immigrants arrived, Memphis had had almost no Jewish poor, and, unlike New York City, no true Jewish working class. Nearly all the children of the Jewish tailors, carpenters, and peddlers had graduated from high school; many were able to attend college. The Eastern European Jews, however, had little in their segregated, Old World existence to equip them for the lifestyle of the southern urban environment of Memphis. Very few had any secular education.[10]

With the arrival of immigrants from eastern Europe, Memphis gained its first Jewish neighborhood, sometimes called "the Memphis version of the Lower East Side." Most of the newcomers were impoverished and needed affordable housing and most preferred to live near others who shared their language, customs, and religious practices. They satisfied these requirements by settling in the district called the Pinch, a twelve-block area just north of downtown, extending from Front Street to Third, east to west, and Auction to Poplar, north to south.Evelyn Weiss says that her father came to the Pinch because "he could only speak Yiddish, so he had to go where there were Jewish people who could understand."[11]

The Pinch historically housed the poorest immigrants who came to Memphis in ethnic waves, sometimes overlapping so as to create in the

---

[9]Interview with George Shendelman, 1990.

[10]Judith Endelman, *The Jewish Community of Indianapolis, 1849 to the Present* (Bloomington: Indiana University Press, 1992) 5ff.

[11]R Steve Stern, "Echoes of the Pinch" *Memphis Magazine,* 8 (March, 1984): 66-73; Rachel Saltzman, "Shalom, Y'All" *Southern Exposure* (Durham: Institute for Southern Studies, September-October, 1983): 28-36.

district a mixture of races, religions, and nationalities. They were attracted to the area because it was close to the bayou that provided an abundance of fish and a source of wood. Its reputation from pre-Civil War days was legendary; then, its streets were filled with bordellos, gambling houses, river rats, and drunken Indians. Among the many stories of how the Pinch acquired its name is the more commonly accepted explanation that the Irish refugees from the potato famine who settled there in the 1840s and 1850s had pinch-gutted faces of poverty. However the name began, it persisted; later residents so completely accepted it that they painted the word "Pinch" in large block letters on a sign on an octagon-shaped box that stood at the corner of Market and Main Streets.[12]

By the 1890s Italian immigrants joined the Irish in the Pinch, followed by eastern European Jews by 1900. Ten years later some 947 Russian immigrants lived in Memphis. Most were Jewish and sought Jewish neighborhoods that could provide moral and material support. Sixty-one percent of the Russian immigrants lived in the four downtown wards. Between 1910 and 1920, 290 Poles arrived, thirty percent of whom joined the Russians in the Pinch. Nearly all these were Jewish as well. Pinch newcomers found rooms above and behind shops, often boarding with another family. Most began to earn a living by peddling, financed by established merchants like Jacob Goldsmith and Moses Lewis.[13]

The family of Rosalee Abraham exemplified life in the Pinch. Her mother came to America from Odessa, Russia. Her father arrived in New York from Kounas, Lithuania, when he was fourteen years old. He spent a month with a sister and brother, then came to Memphis and lived with relatives who later moved on to Australia. He opened a confectionery store, then a delicatessen and a fruit stand. The family lived upstairs over the stores.[14]

Max Gerber arrived in Memphis in 1904 and lived at 228 Exchange

[12]James Roper, *The Founding of Memphis, 1818-1820* (Memphis: Memphis Sesquicentennial, Inc., 1970); J. M Keating, v.1, 183; Stern," Echoes," 68; Interview with Fagie Schaffer, 1990.

[13]Stern, "Echoes," 68; Richard K. Thomas, "The Residential Distribution of Immigrants in Memphis, Tennessee," (unpublished M. A. Thesis, Memphis State University, 1970), 20; Interview with Jack Lewis, 1992. When Moses Lewis arrived from Russia at Ellis Island, he told the officials his name was Moses Tarshish. H was asked to spell it, which he could not do in English, so an official, in a not uncommon practice, told him that his new name was Moses Lewis.

[14]Interview with Rosalee Abraham, 7 July 1995.

with his wife, Rebecca, and his children, Morris, William, Israel, and Esther, all born in Russia, and Joseph and Sol, who were born in the United States. He was vouched for by earlier Jewish immigrants and residents of the Pinch —Louis Springer, a hardware merchant, and Isidore Sarsar, a grocer. [15] Gerber's second son, William, became an influential citizen of the city. William was six years old in 1904 when his family emigrated from Russia, following extremely harsh pogroms of 1901 and 1902.

After attending Market Street School, Will Gerber went to Tech High. For eight years, he delivered the *Commercial Appeal* in the mornings and sold afternoon papers in the streets in the evenings. After service in the army in the first World War, he married Fannie Kabakoff of Memphis and attended law school in the evenings. He passed the Tennessee State Bar Exam in 1923 and joined the law firm of William Tyler McLain and Lois Bejach, men in high positions in the Crump organization. When Bejach became District Attorney, he took Gerber with him as his assistant. This experience turned Gerber into a first-rate trial lawyer.

Thus began a career that was to make Gerber politically important. He became Assistant City Attorney under Mayor Walter Chandler in 1934, and the following year, when Chandler went to Congress, Gerber succeeded him as City Attorney, a post he retained for seven years. He was appointed Shelby County Attorney General by Governor Prentice Cooper in 1940. Young Gerber was recommended to Crump as "a man who had come up in the world," a type Crump particularly liked. This was an unusual appointment because at that time in Memphis there were no other Jews in public office, either as commissioners or judges. Gerber traveled to Nashville regularly with the Shelby County delegation to the state legislature, and he met with Crump at least weekly.[16]

All members of the Crump organization did not share the Boss's opposition to anti-Semitism. But Gerber fought for the organization with a fierceness equalled only by Crump himself. When Turner Catledge of the *New York Times* came to Memphis to investigate local voting practices, Gerber attacked him at the voting precincts, destroying his camera. When Catledge protested to Crump, Crump advised him that, since Crump

---

[15]Records of Bureau of Immigration and Naturalization of the United States of America, Department of Commerce and Labor.
[16]Interview with Hal Gerber, 1995.

certainly did not want "to see any of his friends get hurt," Catledge should stay away from dangerous places in the future.

Politically, Gerber served Crump well. He brought the "Main Street Jews with their financial support" into the system. He also served as a visible reminder to the community at large that anti-Semitism was discouraged by the Crump administration. William Miller, the official biographer of Mr. Crump, wrote:

> Although Gerber left the bruised sensibilities of those scalded by his invective, he also left a city completely clear of racketeering, loan sharks, medical quacks, and soothsayers. His objective was a clean city, and he worked indefatigably to get it. The gamblers and confidence men who fixed an eye of Memphis had always found Gerber way ahead of them.

Life in the Pinch was devoted to the necessity of making a living. When the father of a family had accumulated enough capital to start a small store, the family helped to make ends meet by using part of the space for living quarters. Usually the wife worked in the store along with her husband, sometimes keeping the account books. The children also worked, but this did not excuse them from attending school. Because secular training had been difficult to achieve in Eastern Europe, education was a high priority. The immigrants knew that it was through education that their children would attain a "better life."

The public school just off Market Square, called Market Street School in 1872 when it was originally named, served the Pinch. The name was changed to Smith School in 1882 to honor Thomas R. Smith, a member of the Board of Education. Most people continued to refer to it as Market Street School, however, until 1920, when its name was changed to the Christine School in memory of its popular principal, Miss Christine Reudelheuber. The latter name remained until the school was closed.[17]

Reudelheuber was dedicated to teaching the immigrant children to become Americans. The school's celebratory Anniversary Souvenir Edition notes: "Many influential citizens of Memphis are children of the 'new' school." The school offered more than formal education to these immigrant children, it was the center of activities as well. Sports, organized by the

---

[17]Interview with Dr. Abe Bass, 1992.

Memphis Park Commission, helped create close bonds of friendship between neighborhood children, both Jewish and non-Jewish."[18]

In addition to secular school, the immigrant parents insisted that their children attend cheders, or Hebrew schools, in the hope such education would preserve traditions which seemed in danger of being lost in the new world.[19] Classes were held in the Menorah Institute, an educational and cultural center created by Baron Hirsch Synagogue on Washington Street, in the Arbeiter Ring at Jefferson and Orleans, or in the homes of the teachers.

Meanwhile, The German Jews, despite keeping their religious and social lives separate from those of the newcomers, felt it essential to Americanize the embarrassing greenhorns as soon as possible. Charity, traditionally a Jewish virtue, now became an imperative. Sick benefits, free loans, money for fuel, food and clothing, and goods to peddle were often available to the newcomers. By 1899 the Hebrew Relief Association had 115 members and assets of fifteen hundred dollars. To facilitate the integration of the Eastern Europeans into American life, the German Jews, paralleling a national trend, established the Jewish Neighborhood House on Market Square in 1901. They created it, supported it, and volunteered their services.[20] Despite its name, Jewish Neighborhood House did not restrict its services to Jewish immigrants, but served all who lived in the Pinch.

English, the facts required for naturalization, hygiene, the social graces, and the arts were all taught at Jewish Neighborhood House.[21] It has been described as

> a place where the Yancey, the Goldstein, and the Jones kids play together, when Russian meets Greek and they sit down with an Italian and a Frenchman to learn to read English. . . where people who fled the tyranny of native lands and religious persecution study the functions of democracy and prepare to become United States citizens . . . where ill babies receive doctors' care and cod liver oil . . . .[22]

---

[18]Bass interview.
[19]Stern, "Echoes," 72.
[20]Saltzman, "Shalom," 22.
[21]Stern, "Echoes," 72.
[22]*Press Scimitar* 6 January 1938.

Neighborhood House also became the immigrants' community center. There was a nursery for infants and kiddie bands for those a little older.[23] Fagie Schaffer remembers it vividly:

> We had a house called the Jewish Neighborhood House. And there was a very lovely lady, Miss Miriam Goldbaum, a spinster with a sweet smile, most helpful and very understanding toward children. She taught us the niceties of daily living, like brushing our teeth, and "this is the way we comb our hair." We used to sing a little ditty, and she would show us the proper techniques . . . the fundamental bits of hygiene that were necessary. Taught us to embroider and crochet and read. The main purpose was to teach us how to be Americans so we could help our parents with English. You didn't need to speak too much English; everyone spoke Yiddish.[24]

Schaffer also reme mbered a shy, polite young man who lived with his mother and father in the downstairs half of a duplex at 462 Alabama owned by her parents, Molly and Aaron Dubrovner. Her mother called him Elvis'll, but his name, later to become the internationally best known name ever to originate in Memphis, was Elvis Aaron Presley. When Aaron DuBrovner died, Molly lived with Fagie and her husband, Dr. Ben Schaffer and Jeannette and Rabbi Alfred Fruchter occupied the upstairs apratment. In order to obvserve the Sabbath in a proper orthodox manner, the Fruchters could not turn on theirr gas or electricity, but needed a non-Jew called a *Shabbos goy* to perform these functions. "The King" became their *Shabbas goy*, and they reciprocated by lending him their phonograph and telephone, which the Presleys didn't have. A close relationship developed between Elvis and the Jewish community he grew up around. When he had the means to do so, he shopped for clothes at Lansky's, for jewelry at Levitch's, and had close companions like Geroge Klein. Later, when the Jewish Community Center was built in Memphis, Elvis donated the money for an entire room. He had a six-point star engraved on his mother's footstone and often wore a *Chai*, the Jewish symbol for life, around his neck.

---

[23]Lakee Brooks interview, conducted by Steve Stern, 27 June 1983, Center for Southern Folklore Archives, Holocaust Interviews.

[24]Saltzman, "Shalom," 32.

In the early 1900s the Pinch housed four Jewish grocery stores, three delicatessens, numerous butcher shops, and a kosher fish market. At the kosher butcher store, the customer could select a live chicken; a *schochet*, the ritual slaughterer, would kill it there.[25] Sam Cooper describes in detail the businesses of the Pinch, both Jewish and non-Jewish:

> Beginning on the north, there was a grocery at Overton and Main run by Moskovitz. Just west of that, one block on Front, was Blockman's Junk Store, which is still there. On the north side of Auction, Davidson had an indoor pool with massages and hot baths. Next door to them was the Herbert Rosenberg family. Just south of the grocery store was Ridblatt's Bakery, which baked most of the kosher bread served in the Jewish community. The son of the owners, nicknamed "Rye," was a well-known prizefighter. Across the street was Walter the tinner, because roofs in those days were made of tin.
>
> Just south toward Jackson was the Memphis Pie Company. On the northeast corner of Jackson and Main Street, Mr. Schneider had a fruit stand. Turning south at Commerce and Main, on the northeast corner, was a big store run by Mr. Walsh. Across the street at Commerce and Main, on the southeast corner, was a grocery store run by the Minor family. South on that block, from Commerce to Winchester, was a soda fountain. Next door, the Sebraning family sold and repaired shoes. Next door was a salvage store of Sam Crowe; next door to that was Hanover's. Across the street from Winchester on the southeast corner was Levy's Drug Store.
>
> Coming down Commerce and Main, on the west side was Aaron Dubrovner's kosher butcher shop where Mr. Turetsky koshered the chickens in the back; next door was Hanover's Shoe Store. On the corner of Winchester and Main was Bower's Grocery. Across the street on Winchester was a fish market run by Bennie Sacharin's father. Going south on Main was Goldstein's Delicatessen on the west side. Next to the delicatessen was a fire station with engines pulled by horses. When the fire bell rang, all the kids would quit playing ball and go to the fire. Across the alley was Suzore's Theater.

---

[25] Alan Singer, "A Self Guided Tour of Jewish Memphis, Past and Present," Memphis Jewish Federation, June 1980, 15.

On the east side of Main from Winchester was a dry goods store. Across the alley was Taubenblatt's delicatessen, with Bluestein's Dry Goods Store next door. Zito's Restaurant, with Schlesinger's Dry Goods store, was at the northeast corner of Market and Main. Nathan Loskovitz's pool room stood on the southeast corner of Market and Main. Siskin, the tailor, was next door. Then there was a wholesale fruit stand, Blen's dry good store was next, followed by Zimmerman's big dry goods store, and a non-Jewish barbershop.

On the west side of Main, between Market and Exchange, was Samuels's Furniture Store. A pool hall for blacks was located on the west side of Main, between the alley and Exchange. On the southeast corner of Exchange and Main was a drug store, also a yeast store and a bakery. Second Street from Auction to Poplar was mostly residential, but on Jackson, between Main and Second, was the Jackson Avenue Synagogue. Also called Anshei Mischne, and across the avenue was Anshei Galicia.

The Phoenix Boxing Arena was at Winchester and Auction; Jack Dempsey fought a demonstration match with Bennie Leonard there. At Overton and Third, a saloon was run by Mr. Weiss. Nat Buring's father had a tailor shop above it. The Loskove family lived in the alley before Overton, between Third and Second streets. (Sam Cooper's father had a tailor shop at Main and Exchange, the site of a building erected and occupied later by the Eighth District of the Federal Reserve, on whose board Cooper later served.)[26]

T. E. Hanover has also left a description in his own colorful style of daily life in the Pinch when he was growing up there. He believes that it was "ninety percent Jews, five percent Irish and Italian." He remembers the non-Jewish Walshes, whose wagon yard in back of their place of business, facing on Commerce between the alley and Second Street, was where all the country farmers brought their chickens, eggs, and butter; they would unhook their horses and line up their wagons. The Jewish women would go down there and buy eggs, butter and live chickens. According to Hanover:

> About nine o'clock at night, when the farmers had not sold all
> their . . . wares . . . , they would have about a dozen live chickens
> on one arm, a basket of eggs and butter on the other arm, and start

---

[26]Sam Cooper interview, conducted by Steve Stern, 8 July 1983, Center for Southern Folklore.

up Main Street from the wagon yard. They would come up Main Street and in them days all the Jewish merchants would sit out on Main Street in chairs. Every store on Main street had chairs there, and that's the way they'd pass their evenings, and the customers came anyway, they waited on customers until eleven or twelve at night . . . These farmers would go up the street and they would stop at everybody sitting in chairs, asking if they wanted to buy a chicken or eggs or anything . . . . So I remember my mother would get a chicken, start tapping on the back of them to see whether they were fat or not . . . . The guy who wanted fifty cents for a chicken, they would start arguing with him and get him down to forty cents. Same thing with butter and eggs. They would buy two or three chickens . . . and there was Aaron the butcher . . . and Dubrovner was there, and Makowsky was there . . . and they would take them down there and the shochet would kill the chicken and cut their throats and put them over a stick in a barrel . . . and then, when they were clean, they had to pay five cents for flicking (removing the feathers of) the chicken . . . . We had kosher groceries. Rosen's had a kosher grocery delicatessen on the west side of Main Street . . . . They used to go in there if someone wanted a schmaltz herring. They had a big barrel . . . and they would go and pick out themselves a herring with a piece of newspaper and wrap it in the newspaper. . . . We would come home (from school) for lunch every day, and we would get two cents apiece . . . and after we got through with lunch, we would run down to the grocery store at Winchester and Third and buy a pickle in a wine bowl . . . and we would eat that every day.

When Hanover was older, a young man about town, he reports going to a house of assignation, run by a Jewish women, "in a cottage at 321 Monroe . . . and so we would go there and she would have fried chicken, spaghetti dinner for us every Saturday night at twelve o'clock."[27] Hanover's reminiscences reveal the closeness of community life where neighbors lived largely outdoors sitting in front of little stores in the summertime. There seems to have been a great spirit of interdependence with neighbors and friends only a chair away.

---

[27]I. T. Hanover interview, Memphis, 1982 and 1987.

As had been true in Europe, the central institution of life in the Pinch was the synagogue. Religious practices and traditions were the focal point of the lives of the Eastern Europeans in the old country. They suffered for their religion and were identified by it. There was scholarship within its province, beauty in its rituals, and social life in its celebrations. Several Orthodox synagogues were located in the vicinity of the Pinch. Each had its own variation of ritual, usually reflecting the specific area of the world from which its members had emigrated; thus, Anshei Galicia —already mentioned—was the religious home for Jews from Galicia.

The largest of these synagogues, now the largest Orthodox synagogue in the United States, is Baron Hirsch. The history of its early days is clouded by a lack of adequate records. It was named in honor of its benefactor, a wealthy Belgian Jew, the Baron Maurice de Hirsch, who, working with HIAS, devoted much of his fortune to helping Russian and Polish Jews flee pogroms in their native lands and find new homes in places of safety and freedom. At the same time, the Industrial Removal Office of New York City was created to encourage immigrants to leave the East Coast where they might overwhelm available resources and jobs.[28] Both HIAS and the Industrial Removal Office worked to establish Galveston as an alternate landing point for Jewish immigrants.

One shipload of Eastern European immigrants that landed in Galveston in the early 1860s was sent to Memphis. According to one source, the newcomers joined a minyan formed in 1862 by people who were dissatisfied with the rituals practiced at Beth El Emeth. That congregation was virtually destroyed by yellow fever. The epidemic killed Jacob Peres, the congregation's leader in 1879, and caused an already small membership to decline further. Those who did not at that time join B'nai Israel as well as those in the minyan became the nucleus of Baron Hirsch.[29]

Another source reports that the Baron Hirsch group had been worshiping together in homes and vacant buildings since 1884, with no established meeting place. Between 1886 and 1890, the members met on

---

[28]Oscar Handlin, A Pictorial History of Immigration: A Dramatic Story of the Building of America from Prehistoric Times to the Present (New York: Crown Press, 1972), 200; Joseph P. Schultz, Mid-America's Promise; A Profile of Kansas City Jewry (Joint publications of the Jewish Community Foundation of Greater Kansas City and the American Jewish Historical Society, 1982), 10.

[29]Sam Shankman, History of the Jews of Memphis. Unpublished Manuscript; Perre Magness, "Jews Come to Memphis in the 1840's," Commercial Appeal (7 April, 1988): 2.

the second floor of the Cochran Hotel on North Main Street near Poplar. A permanent place of worship was acquired either by 1892. At that time, the congregation, through financing provided by the sale of fifty-dollar bonds to members and the Jewish and to non-Jewish communities, purchased a Negro church at Fourth and Washington for five thousand dollars and converted it into a synagogue. S. Isaacs, J. Croner, H. A. Cohen, N. Hanoch, and W. Brodowsky applied for a charter for Baron Hirsch Benevolent Society on 3 June 1892. Four days later the Secretary of State of Tennessee issued the charter that served the congregation until it changed its name in 1941 to Baron Hirsch Congregation. Several rabbis occupied the Baron Hirsch pulpit in its early years: Benjamin Meyerowitz, an otherwise unknown Bressler, Lieber Cohen, and one M. Franklin served in 1890 and 1891. M. Springer was cantor. The first known officers, serving in 1890 and 1891, were Jake Croner, president; H. Glickman, vice-president; and Ferdinand Loewenberg, secretary. David Goldberger, Leopold Goldberger, J. Croner, A. Weiss, A. Lipman, Sam Rosenheim, S. L. Benowitz, F. Franklin, Max Brode, Dave Hammer, and A. Isaacs were members of the Board of Directors.[30]

Baron Hirsch also acquired a cemetery, buying property it had leased for several years from B'nai Israel. The cemetery originally had belonged to Beth El Emeth congregation and had been acquired by B'nai Israel in 1890 for one thousand dollars.[31]

Shortly after Baron Hirsch bought its new home, a committee consisting of S. D. Benovitz, Moses Lewis, David Goldberger, Leopold Goldberger, and Hyman Kovinsky organized a Talmud Torah for the children of the congregation. It lasted only a few years, following which, in 1897 a Sunday school for the children of Baron Hirsch members was organized and staffed by women of the Reform synagogue who felt the children needed religious school training. The women included Mrs. Meyer Gattman, Mrs. George Hexter, Miss Beatrice Hildreth, Mrs. B. Friedman, and Mrs. Ike Ochs. They were assisted by their rabbi, Max Samfield.[32]

In 1898, a few years after Baron Hirsch was organized, twenty Polish Jews, in order to be able to observe the Sephardic Orthodox tradition,

---

[30]Shankman, *History of Jews*, and *Jewish Spectator*, Thirtieth Anniversary Issue 119; Singer, "A Self-Guided Tour," *Baron Hirsch Family Album*.
[31]Wax, *Our First Century*, 31.
[32]Shankman, *History of Jews*.

founded their own synagogue, Anshei Sphard.[33] Meetings were held initially in the home of Samuel Baruchman. In 1904, Israel Peres, the son of Jacob Peres, drew up a charter and constitution for the new congregation, which then had a membership of twenty-five families. Between 1898 and 1904 the congregation rented a brick and stone building at Main and Beale and in 1906 purchased a home on Maiden Lane, later called Market Square, and remodeled it into a synagogue that served for twenty-one years. Residents of the Pinch sometimes called the synagogue "the Market Street Shul."[34] In 1907, just three years after it was incorporated, Anshei Sphard purchased land on Airways Boulevard for use as a cemetery.

Anshei Sphard was organized by S. Dlugach, S. Baruchman, H. I. Schaffer, and S. Weinberg. Important roles were played by S. H. Epstein, M. Hyman, H. Goldman, N. Tannenbaum, I. Sebraning, Jake Felt, Sam O'Mell, I. Geldman, and M. Padawer. Zalke Kanarek was the first president. In 1925, when Nathan Kapell was president, the congregation replaced the old wooden structure with a brick synagogue. Its main sanctuary seated 250 and its balconies held seventy-five women.[35]

Two other synagogues existed in the early part of the twentieth century in the vicinity of the Pinch. Congregation Anshei Mischne was organized in 1900 by Polish immigrant Judah Friedman, who originally rented a frame building at 108 Jackson Avenue, where he conducted services for two years. Led by Rabbi Ignatz Isaacs, along with Morris Blockman, William Blockman, H. Blockman, and M. Loskove, the congregation in 1907 built a Greek-style brick building containing an auditorium that seated 350. It also built and maintained the only mikveh, or ritual bath, in the city.[36] When the new synagogue was erected, the Blockman family and M. Loskove guaranteed the mortgage. M. D. Blockman became president, an office he held for thirty years until his death. Because by that time most of its congregants had moved to the eastern part of the city, Anshei Mischne also ceased to exist.

Congregation Anshei Galicia, formed in 1912, was also located near the Pinch, at Second and Jackson. Its founders came from southern Poland, or

---

[33]"Fifty Years of Faith," Anshei Sphard's Golden Anniversary, 1906-1956.

[34]Sam Alabaster interview, conducted by Steve Stern, July 25, 1983, Center for Southern Folklore archives.

[35]"Fifty Years of Faith"; Eli Evans, *The Provincials* (Kingsport: Kingsport Press, 1973), 336.

[36]Shankman, *History of Jews.*

Galicia, a region, not a nation, that before 1918 belonged partly to Russian Poland and partly to Austria-Hungary. The people called themselves "Galitzianers."[37]

Anshei Galicia's first officers were Sol Kanarek, president; Sol Belz, vice-president; and S. Zwechenbaum, secretary. Sol Kanarek and Sol Belz were also charter members along with L. Binstock, D. Weiss, M. Belz, M. Padawer, B. Hurwitz, M. Wolf, S. Zwechenbaum, Louis Weinman, and Israel Peres. Peres was not a "Galitzianer," but he helped the congregation apply for a charter and joined the synagogue, as he did every other synagogue in the city, regardless of its orientation. Asher Blockman, whose father was for many years the leader of Anshei Mischne, recalls that he and his friends used to call members of Anshei Galicia "the G. Men."[38]

While the first Jewish immigrants had in some other areas of the United States tried to reproduce in the new land the community and culture they had left behind, this had not happened in the early years of Memphis: the German immigrants were never segregated, either by themselves or by others, in one living area. In the 1880s a little group of well-to-do German Jews lived in one of the newest residential sections of the city. Typical of them was Seymour L. Lee and his wife, Fannie, whose home was on Adams Street, where they lived with their four sons, Louis, Julian, Ernest, and Clarence. The Harry Schloss family was next door with their children, Irene, Gilbert, and Lucille. Bensdorfs, Sondheims, and Isenbergs lived on the next block.[39]

Seymour Lee had come from Prussia in about 1860. In Memphis, he went into the cigar and tobacco business with Dave Sternberg, and the business prospered. The social mores observed by the Lees reflect the high standards and attention to appearances that were characteristic of the non-Jewish milieu in which they lived. The porch of their house extended across the front and around one-half of the east side of the dwelling. Although summers in Memphis were hot and humid, Fannie Lee required that men who wished to sit on the porch, regardless of the heat, wear one of the jackets that were always hanging on hooks just inside the front door. Social life at the Lee's included a Sunday night poker game with six other people,

---

[37]Singer, "A Self-Guided Tour," 16; Neil M. Cowan and Ruth Schwartz, *Our Parents' Lives: The Americanization of East European Jews* (New York: Basic Books, 1989), xviii.

[38]Shankman, *History of Jews.*

[39]*Commercial Appeal,* 23 October 1990; Shankman, *History of Jews.*

which ended at midnight, followed by "almost a complete meal" offered to the guests by the family's servants. The home itself was large; one of its more notable features was a detached laundry room for which water was collected in a cistern in the side yard. The houseman and his wife, the cook, lived above the stable.

Joseph Newburger was another German Jew who lived in an elegant, more suburban neighborhood settled by Jews and non-Jews alike. In 1912, he built a home at East Parkway South and Union Avenue. In 1963 the home was purchased by the Memphis Theological Seminary of the Cumberland Presbyterian Church; and in 1982, the seminary building, formerly Newburger's home, was placed on the National Register of Historic Places.[40] Newburger was the owner of a twenty-three-year-old firm, the Newburger Cotton Company, which he moved in 1896 from Coffeeville, Mississippi, to Memphis. The firm had established connections with mills in New England, selling cotton to them directly. Once situated in Memphis, the company, "a pioneer in the cotton industry and in the development of the Mississippi Valley," grew to become one of the largest spot-cotton operations in the world. At one time the firm had offices in Germany, Italy, Switzerland, Sweden, and Greece, and representatives in England, France, Holland, and Russia. Newburger had many other business interests: he was the principal owner of the Federal Compress and Warehouse Company; he was also president of the Memphis Packing Corporation. His broad business concerns included farming, the Arkansas rice industry, and their related agribusinesses.

Newburger was one of Memphis's leading philanthropists; he helped lead the committee that raised money to build St. Mary's Cathedral of the Episcopal Diocese of Memphis and served on the boards of several organizations, including Methodist Hospital.[41] It was during his presidency of Temple Israel that the Poplar Street Temple was built.

The German Jewish women of Memphis shared with their husbands a sense of obligation to their less fortunate fellow Jews and to the community as a whole, and in the 1880s and 1890s often served as volunteers outside the home. The Willing Hands Sewing Circle came into existence in December 1895, at the home of Belle Herrmann. The name was later

---

[40]Interview with Ernest Lee, Sr.
[41]Ann Leach Stovely, "The Newburger Mansion of Memphis, Tn.: Founders' Hall of Memphis Theological Seminars," *Memphis*, June 1992.

changed to The Pauline Levy Sewing Circle to honor leader Pauline Levy who died in 1908, and who, along with her four daughters, was among the original members of the club.[42] The purpose of the club was to "give to any needy person we could hear of . . . regardless of creed and color: Jewish Federation, Goodfellows, Christine School, Jewish Children's Home in New Orleans, Colored Juvenile Court, Red Cross."

By the end of the century, the German Jews were solidly integrated into the life of Memphis. Their Eastern European counterparts, more parochial and poorer at first than the Germans, already had made great progress in adjusting to their new environment and, as they became more secure economically and culturally, would make significant contributions to the community.

---

[42]Hattie Brooks, "History of Pauline Levy Sewing Circle." Unpublished paper. 14 March 1948; Other charter members were Harriette Wexler, Belle Harris, Lelia Sternberger, Stella Dreyfus, Belle Herrmann, Fannie Lee, Marie Halle, Bertha Kern, Hattie Brooks, Julia Brooks, Eva Halle, Rosie Gabay, Sally Ashner, Lily Ashner, and Serette Hirsch. They were joined later by Yetta Levy, Caroline Gronauer, Fannie Marcus, Fannie Buxbaum, Malinda Kaufman, Bessie Summerfield, Jennie Cohen, and Pauline Samfield. Several years later new members were installed: Nannine Gellher, Mary Hirsch, Sophie Gensburger, Lula Loeb, Jennie Jonap, Bobette Goodman, Estelle Hattendorf, Minnie Mook, Bertha Bluthenthal, Mollie Rosenfield, Connie Isenberg, Edna Jarecki, and Celia Felsenthal.

6

THE EARLY TWENTIETH CENTURY

"The prominent Jews of Memphis are more than owners of most of the city's department stores and movie houses; they are on the first string in civic affairs."

— Shields McIlwaine

By 1890 the population of Memphis had reached 103,320, more than three times the 33,000 it numbered in 1879 at the end of the yellow fever epidemics. Only two southern cities, New Orleans and St. Louis, were larger at the turn of the century. Most of the new inhabitants of the city were rural people, both black and white, who came from the depressed areas of north Mississippi and west Tennessee. While the majority of white Memphians had always believed blacks to be inferior to whites, the rural whites brought with them a plantation mentality whose primary goal was the preservation of white supremacy. This attitude was one important cause of the reputation for violence associated with twentieth-century Memphis. In an article entitled "Explaining our Homicide Record" which appeared on 19 October 1912, Memphis was named "the murder capital of the country." In 1910 the national homicide average for cities was 7.2 per one hundred thousand population; for Memphis, the average was a shocking 47.1, a number that climbed to 63.4 by 1911, and to 89.9 by 1916.[1]

The Jewish population of the city, which had been reduced by the yellow fever epidemics from twenty-one hundred in 1877 to three hundred by the end of the seventies, began to rebound, reaching four hundred by 1882. Internal southern migration as well as immigration from abroad boosted Memphis's Jewish population to twenty-five hundred by 1907, and

---

[1]William D. Miller, *Mr. Crump of Memphis* (Baton Rouge: Louisiana State University Press, 1964), 29; *Quoted* in Capers, *Biography*, 29; Andrew A. Bruce and Thomas S. Fitzgerald, "A Study of Crime in the City of Memphis, Tennessee, *Journal of American Institute of Criminal Law and Criminology* 19 (August 1928): 14.

to six thousand by 1912. As the population grew, so did commercial enterprise, leading by the turn of the century to the establishment of many Jewish businesses, some of which continued to operate for many years. Among them were Julius Goodman and Son, jewelers; Godfrey Frank, cotton; Sternberg and Sons, merchants; Ike Samelson, cigars and tobacco; I. Oppenheim and S. Bejach, clothiers; and Harpmann Brothers, tobacco. B. H. and I. W. Ashner, who came to Memphis in about 1867, established with the Seessel Family the firm of Seessel and Ashner in 1886, a wholesale produce business.[2]

On his twenty-seventh birthday in 1887, Henry Loeb Sr. borrowed money to build an all-steam laundry, a service for which he had discerned a need in the community ever since he had assisted his mother with the Monday morning family wash. By 1905, Loeb's business had achieved sufficient success to prompt him to build a new, revolutionary plant, "the biggest power laundry plant in America." Dubbed "Loeb's Folly," by skeptical Memphians, it was located four blocks from the center of town at 282 Madison Avenue. Time was to prove the skeptics wrong. Loeb pioneered door-to-door deliveries with a fleet of horse-drawn wagons and advertised his services by hiring a lady to wear a white suit and ride in a white carriage pulled by a white horse. White trucks eventually replaced the horse-drawn wagons. Cleaned clothes were packed in distinctive purple boxes with purple tissue paper. In 1939 Loeb's acquired Memphis Steam Laundry Cleaner with its twelve branches, ending fifty-two years of competition between the two businesses.[3] In the late 1990s Loeb's was still a widely-diversified business owned and operated by descendants of its founder.

Samuel Steinberg had a successful mercantile business in Clarksville, Tennessee, before he moved to Memphis in 1909. He opened a fur and hide business that became a significant factor in restoring Memphis to its former position as a leader in that market and in enhancing the city's commercial strength. During World War II, Steinberg helped the federal government obtain the hides it needed to make shoes for servicemen.[4]

---

[2]J. P. Young, *History of Memphis, Tn.* (Knoxville: H. W. Crew and Co., 1912), 570.

[3]John E. Harkins, *Metropolis of the American Nile: Memphis and Shelby County*, ed. by Charles W. Crawford (Woodland Hills, Cal.: Windsor Publications, Inc., 1982), 147; Margaret Hirsch personal interview; "25 Years Ago," *Commercial Appeal*, 19 January 1964.

[4]Lester Sewel Lecture for Jewish Historical Society of Memphis and Shelby County, Winter. 1991.

Because Memphis was viewed as a gateway to the West for the retail and wholesale pane and glass installation business, Milton Binswanger Sr. moved to Memphis in 1906 to start a Tennessee branch of Binswanger and Company, which had been begun by his father in Virginia in 1872. In addition to heading an expanding business, Binswanger played an important role in the community. He was a founding member of the Memphis Rotary Club in 1914 and the Memphis Community Chest. Convinced that natural gas would be of great benefit to the city, providing both economic gains and cleanliness, he was a prime mover in securing it for Memphis.[5]

Abe Simon arrived in Memphis from Poland in 1897 and started a wholesale dry goods business "on a shoestring." Within twenty-five years, he had built one of the largest dry goods establishments in the city. Located at first at Main and Jefferson, the A. Simon and Brother Company later moved into larger quarters on Second between Monroe and Union. Simon was prominently identified with many charities, especially with drives to aid German Jews settling in Palestine.[6]

Nathan and Louis Bry, along with Ike Block, founded Bry's Department Store in 1902. The business opened on the southeast corner of Main and Adams streets, then relocated in 1905 to Main and Jefferson. In the same year the Black and White Store was opened by Daniel Lewis "with a knapsack full of dry goods taken from his earlier days as a peddler." Lewis's daughter married Sam Shainberg who took over the store's management. By 1914 Shainberg had constructed a new building on a lot across from the original store. That establishment was the first of a large chain originally called Black and White Stores after the paint color scheme on the front of the stores, then renamed Shainberg's in the mid-1950s to upgrade the image of the business and to recognize its owner. Daniel Lewis's brother Moses opened a small dry goods store in 1890in a building he rented for fifteen dollars a month. Moses's enterprise also grew into a prominent business, later named Julius Lewis when Moses's son took over its management.[7]

Two businesses established in 1908 have become major companies in

---

[5]Interview with Milton S. Binswanger Jr., 1990.

[6]*Commercial Appeal* ,10 February 1937.

[7]Robert A. Sigafoos, *Cotton Row to Beale Street: A Business History of Memphis* (Memphis: Memphis State University Press, 1979) 114; Fred Hutchins, *What Happened in Memphis* (Kingsport: Kingsport Press, Inc., 1965) 90; Mel Grinspan personal interview; Hutchins, *What Happened*, 90.

the city: Wurzburg Brothers, begun by brothers Abe and Reggie Wurzburg to distribute office equipment and supplies and Plough, Incorporated, organized by Abe Plough. The Wurzburg brothers built on a foundation established when their father, Seymour, bought the Rosemore Company, a brokerage firm. After Seymour died in 1917, Abe Wurzburg assumed the leadership role. Making several moves to accomodate growth, the business finally moved to South Front Street, where it has grown and acquired adjoining property. By the late twentieth century Wurzburg Brothers became one of the top twenty-five industrial employers in Memphis.[8]

Born in Tupelo, Mississippi in 1892, Abe Plough moved to Memphis with his parents Julia and Moses Plough and seven siblings in 1903. Moses operated a clothing and furnishings store. The family lived in the Pinch where Abe attended the Market Street School and encountered teacher Lorene Banks, who taught him to calculate figures without pencil or paper. He called it "mental arithmetic." This ability was to serve him well in his business career. He said, "I happened to acquire thirty companies for over one billion dollars for Schering-Plough Corporation, and at no time did I ever use a pencil. I figured it in my head."

Plough received his only other formal education at St. Paul Street Grammar School, from which he was graduated. After school and on weekends he worked at George V. Francis's drug store without pay, because he wanted to learn the business. He was determined his future would be in the drug business. In March 1908 Plough's father lent him $125 to start his own business, the Plough Chemical Company, in one small room above his father's store. Using dishpans for mixing the chemicals, Plough initially developed a formula for "Plough's Antiseptic Healing Oil, a "sure cure for any ill of man or beast." Using his father's horse-drawn buggy, he set out to sell his product to drug stores and country merchants.

Success came almost immediately for the new enterprise. In 1915 Plough again borrowed money from his father to enter the patent drug business. Within a short time he branched out into the cosmetics business. He added aspirin to his line of products in 1920, buying the St. Joseph company. This was his "first step on the road to the big time." Plough was known by 1929 as the "multimillionaire drug store clerk" because he continued to spend Saturday nights working at his three Memphis drug stores.

---

[8]Interview with Warren Wurzburg Sr., 1992.

Although his business accomplishments were well known, Plough was equally renowned for his generosity. After the devastating stock market crash of 1929, the American Savings Bank of Memphis closed, leaving 6,000 Christmas savings customers facing a bleak holiday. Plough "came on like Santa Claus." He personally advanced $175,000 and raised $60,000 more among his friends to cash the Christmas savings checks of the bank's customers. Even as the Depression spread throughout the world, Plough was able to raise the salaries of his employees and add 100 additional ones to his labor force. He drew no salary for himself, however, saying that the company needed it "more than he did." (The company's rapid expansion required financing.) Plough bought two radio stations in 1944: WMPS in Memphis, and WJJD in Chicago. In 1951 Plough Incorporated moved to a $2,000,000 plant on Jackson Avenue encompassing 250,000 square feet on six acres of land. Jack Benny, the prominent star of radio, screen, and television, entertained at the opening of the plant. The company reported net sales of $24,500,000 by 1954, a figure that doubled by 1962.

In 1971 Plough Incorporated merged with the Schering Corporation of Bloomfield, New Jersey, primarily a manufacturer of prescription pharmaceuticals. Plough was Chairman of the boards of both Plough, Incorporated, and Schering-Plough. He retired in 1976 to devote his talents and energy to his other chief interest, philanthropy.

The business ability of Plough prompted *Forbes Magazine* to call him "as shrewd a horse trader as Tennessee ever turned out." Among the honors and awards accorded him are the Memphis Newspaper Guild's Citizenship Award in 1960 and the National Conference of Christians and Jews annual Human Relations Award in 1964. Memphis State University recognized him as its first Master of Free Enterprise. The University of South Carolina gave him an honorary Doctor of Science Degree, and the University of Tennessee College of Pharmacy gave him the Dean's Award for "extraordinary contributions to the profession of pharmacy." Plough received the first award ever given to an individual by the United States Consumer Product Safety Commission in 1983 for his pioneering efforts to ensure the safety of products for children. The Tennessee State House of Representatives recognized his outstanding contributions to the state in both 1976 and 1979.

Plough's gift of $1,000,000 in 1973 to the Memphis Community Foundation prompted its directors to change its name to the Memphis Plough Community Fund. Another fund, the Plough Foundation, was created by money he left to advance the public good.

The most significant contribution Abe Plough made to the city of Memphis was not, however, his largest monetary gift. Memphis was the site of the April 1968 assassination of Martin Luther King Jr., who had come to lead the sanitation workers in their strike against the city. Settlement of the long-running strike proceeded rapidly after King's death. The last remaining obstacle was the workers' demand for a pay raise. Negotiators recommended a raise of ten cents an hour effective on 1 May 1968, with an additional five-cent raise on 1 September. Estimates were that the raises would total about $558,000 for the coming fiscal year, which could then be made a part of the new budget. The problem was the city had no money in the current budget to provide for raises. Plough's assistance broke the impasse. He proposed to contribute to the city the money to pay the raises before the beginning of the new fiscal year on 1 July 1968, on the condition that his name not be made public. Although those most intimately involved with the final deal respected his wish for anonymity, before long his identity became public knowledge.

"It [the pay raise] could have presented an almost insurmountable problem had he not come forth," said Frank Miles, negotiator for the city. James Reynolds, negotiator for the United States, commented: "I had never heard of such a thing. I think it was one of the most remarkable and noble gestures that I have ever heard of." Plough's generosity benefitted, among others, the Goodfellows, the United Way, the Memphis Area Chamber of Commerce, Memphis Boys Town, the Salvation Army, St. Jude's Children's Research Center, the Memphis Arts Council, the Memphis Zoo, Memphis Memorial Stadium, several colleges and universities, and Temple Israel.

In addition to his generosity in material terms, Plough was extremely generous in giving his time, expertise, and efforts to organizations. He was a member of the Board of Trustees of Boys Town, The William R. Moore School of Technology, the Crippled Children's Hospital, the Memphis Street Railway Company, and the Toledo Museum of Art. He was honorary Chairman of the Board for Life of the United Way of Greater Memphis; he was also a Shriner, a 33rd Degree Mason, and honorary president of Temple Israel.

On the occasion of his ninetieth birthday, the *Commercial Appeal* paid tribute to Plough as "a man whose generosity and vision have enriched this city and its citizens." His legacy lives on in his deeds of generosity and leadership, and through the continuing contributions of the Plough

Foundation that is administered in his name by his heirs.[9]

Jewish Memphians continued to embark on new business enterprises. Jake Haas opened United Bedding Company in 1919. Within eighteen years the company had gained a national reputation, with warehouses throughout the country and advertising on the radio and in national magazines the *Saturday Evening Post* and *Liberty*. The Belz Corporation, a real estate development company, was launched in 1912. The circumstances of Philip Belz's early life were typical of the lives of many Eastern European immigrants. His father left the little town of Lancut in Galicia, a province of Austria-Hungary, in 1904 to avoid serving in the army where he would have had to violate, among other practices, the prayer requirements and dietary laws of Judaism . Belz was ten months old when his father came to Memphis to join a brother already living in the city. The two brothers lived together over the Grand Leader, a store on Beale Street.

Belz's father was a peddler for five years until in 1910 he had earned enough money to send for his wife and six-and-a-half year old son. At first the family lived at 310 Hill Street, in an area where other Jewish immigrants had settled. The living room was rented to a peddler who played the flute. In exchange for a reduction in rent, the peddler taught Philip to play the flute. At the age of twelve, he played in the Tennessee Regimental Band; at fourteen he played second or third flute with the first Memphis Symphony Orchestra. Belz became a soloist with the Baron Hirsh Choir; later he studied voice with Madame Valentina Tumanskaya, formerly a prima donna of the Moscow Imperial Opera. In 1932 Belz won a scholarship to study in New York with Amelia Roxas, the coach of opera singers Giovani Martinelli and Jan Pierce.

Business interests soon superseded musical ones. In 1935, when the federal government was interested in inexpensive housing for the poor, Belz and his father-in-law built apartments that rented for fifteen dollars a month. This venture was the beginning of what has become Tennessee's largest commercial and industrial property company.

One of Belz's primary concerns always was the practice of his religion. He was active in the organization and development of the Baron Hirsh congregation and served on its Board of Directors, of which he was vice-president and president for eight years. He made a significant donation to

---

[9]William Thomas, *Commercial Appeal*, 15 September, 1984; *Commercial Appeal*, 17 June 1951; 15 September 1989.

the building of the synagogue on Vollentine and to the new one in the eastern part of the city. He donated the money to build the Belz Synagogue in the B'nai B'rith Home for the Aged. He has contributed to many other Jewish organizations, as well as to the state of Israel. Belz was awarded the title "Man of the Decade" by Israel in 1958.

The fast-growing Belz Enterprises Company grew even faster after Belz's son Jack was graduated from the Massachusetts Institute of Technology in 1948 and joined the firm. (Two other sons, Leslie and Paul, who were also in the business, were tragically killed in a plane crash while on a business trip in a small plane.) The company has remained family-owned; today many of the grandchildren participate. Among other large acquisitions of property is the Peabody Hotel, now a landmark restoration involving creative financing by the community with loans from the federal and city governments. As developers, Belz Enterprises has changed the face of Memphis, and altered the aspects of many other cities.[10]

The early history of Jews in Memphis includes many who participated in the insurance and banking businesses.[11] The involvement of Jewish Memphians in these occupations is especially noteworthy because Jews in the United States were generally excluded from ownership of banks and insurance companies, despite statements by their enemies that they controlled banking and finance. Jewish participation in the banking business was limited by the requirement that banks could be established

---

[10]Harkins, *Metropolis of the American Nile*, 175; Interview with Philip and Jack Belz.

[11]Among them were Nathan Annotate, director of the First National Bank; Edward Goldsmith, cashier, and Sol Coleman, Director of The German Bank; Benedict Lowenstein, officer of State National Bank; Joseph Sugarman and Elias Lowenstein, directors of Bank of Common Savings; A. S. Myers, A. Cohn, Jacob Marks, H. Henochsburg, and Merrill Kremer, directors of Mechanics Savings Bank; M. Friedman, director of the Mercantile Bank; Edward Goldsmith, vice-president, James Nathan, cashier, E. L. Goldbaum, I. Samelson, I. Hirsch Morris, Samuel Mook, Godfrey Frank, L. Hanauer, Sol Coleman, L. Levy, and Hardwig Peres, directors of the Manhattan Savings Bank and Trust Company; Samuel Hirsch, secretary, Edward Goldsmith, treasurer of Memphis Building and Savings Association; Samuel Hirsch and Edward Goldsmith, directors of Bluff City Building and Loan Association; Herman Bensdorf, secretary, General American Association; Samuel Hirsch, secretary, Equitable Building and Loan Association; Abe Goodman, I. Mendel, J. Scharff, and David Sternberg, directors, the American Savings Bank. L. Hanauer was a director of the Hernando Fire Insurance Company; Sam Slager and Jacob Marks, directors of the Germania Insurance Company; Hardwig Peres, director of Planters Fire and Marine Insurance Company; H. Furstenheim, director of Memphis City Fire and General Insurance Company; Elias Lowenstein and Joseph Sugarman.

only through state or national charters. Only one such charter, to the New York concern called the Bank of the United States, had ever been issued to Jewish owners. Similarly, there were almost no Jews in the central management of insurance firms.

Although Jewish participation in the professions was similarly limited at the beginning of the twentieth century, the work of a number of Jewish professionals was noteworthy. Judge Israel Peres, appointed in 1917 to fill an unexpired term in the Tenth Chancery Division was elected to the office in 1918 by a large majority. Only ten of his decisions were reversed, a record on the bench. Elias Gates was another outstanding lawyer who made important contributions to his field. He was born in the small southern town of Des Arc, Arkansas in 1873 to wealthy landowner Ferdinand, and Sally Mayer Gates. His parents sent him to preparatory school in Philadelphia, then to the University of Pennsylvania for undergraduate school, followed by Harvard Law School. Upon graduation he joined the Memphis law firm of Irving and Leopold Lehman, which in 1904 became Lehman, Gates, and Lehman. When Leopold Lehman retired in 1911, the firm became Lehman, Gates, and Martin; by 1915 it was Gates and Martin. In 1920, Gates joined the law firm of Walter P. Armstrong and Judge Julian Wilson to form the firm of Wilson, Gates and Armstrong.

Gates was widely recognized by his legal colleagues for his ability to interpret the law. He was considered to be a "master of chancery practice and commercial law." Gates gained wide fame for writing the complicated, intricate legal document, a Creditors' Agreement, later accepted as a model by bankers and attorneys all over the United States, and which has become the standard instrument of its kind. He served at many levels in legal organizations: he was the president of the Lawyers' Club in 1918; president of the Tennessee Bar Association in 1921; and he was elected vice-president of the American Bar Association for Tennessee in 1919-1920. He was chairman of the legal advisory board, Division Two of the Chancery Court during World War I. He was vice-president and director of the Memphis and Shelby County Bar and Law Library Association, a leader in the movement to bring the annual meeting of the American Bar Association to Memphis, and chairman of the committee to plan the event.

In addition to his contributions to the legal profession, Gates was a prominent civic and religious leader. He became a trustee of Temple Israel in 1913, a position he held until his death in 1929. Temple Israel annually presents the Elias Gates Award to the outstanding senior Sunday School student. For many years, Gates was president of the Federation of Jewish Charities. He was president of the YMHA from 1902 to 1904, of the Rex Club from 1912 to 1914, and the non-sectarian literary club, The Egyptians, in 1917. Gates was a director of the Memphis Chamber of Commerce, and of the Union Planters National Bank.

Dr. Max Goltman became prominent in the medical profession in Memphis. He was Professor of Surgery in the Medical College of the University of Tennessee and Chief Surgeon at Memphis General and Baptist Memorial Hospitals; from 1910 to 1914 he was superintendent of the Health Department of the City of Memphis.[12] Born in Glasgow, Scotland, and moving to Canada as a young man, he was graduated from Bishop's University, and received his medical degree from McGill University in Montreal. He did postgraduate work in Montreal, London, Edinburgh, Glasgow, Boston, Baltimore, and New York, often paying his way by working on cattle boats during vacations. He began his practice in Pennsylvania in 1894, but the following year he married Mollie Sternberg from Memphis, moved to Memphis in 1897 and opened his practice in medicine and surgery.

Shortly after his arrival in Memphis he was named Assistant in Microscopy at the Memphis Hospital Medical College. He was promoted to Professor of Clinical Surgery at the College of Physicians and Surgeons in 1908. Goltman was intimately involved when the University of Tennessee Medical School moved to Memphis from Nashville in 1911 and merged with the College of Physicians and Surgeons, which resulted in the current University of Tennessee Medical School. He was made a Fellow of the American College of Surgeons in 1914. He acted as Chief of the Division of Surgery at the University from 1917-1919; he was Professor of Surgery from 1920-1933, when he was named Professor Emeritus. He served as head of the Memphis Board of Health from 1911-1914.

While he was in charge of the Board of Health, Goltman performed what is regarded as the most unusual operation ever performed in Memphis up to that time, when he put five stitches in the heart of a patient. A few hours after the surgery the patient was recovering satisfactorily. Goltman's interest in the control of tuberculosis led to his serving on a state commission dedicated to that purpose. Goltman was the first Memphis physician

---

[12]Patricia LaPointe, *From Saddlebags to Science: A Century of Health Care in Memphis, 1830-1930* (Memphis: University of Tennessee Center for Health Sciences, 1984), 45.

to use X-ray as a diagnostic tool, only a few months after it was developed in Germany.[13]

When his two younger sons were graduated from medical school in 1929, Goltman realized his dream of having his three sons join him in the medical profession. (His oldest son, Alfred, had already joined his father over six years earlier.) In gratitude, Goltman established a scholarship fund for medical students at the University of Tennessee Medical School. The "Thanksgiving Memorial Fund," as it was named, was inspired by the near-tragedy of a pharmaceutical student's attempted suicide because of fear of failing his examinations. The eighteen-year-old student was forced to keep an after-school job to sustain himself, and found he was unable to adequately perform his duties as both student and worker. Local medical men knew of no similar circumstance of a father and three sons all in the practice of medicine. Goltman's pleasure at this realization of his fondest hope reflects his love of family, love of his profession, and great respect for the value of education.[14]

The services of Dr. Henry Rudner Sr. were so sought after that an entire floor of Baptist Memorial Hospital was occupied by his patients. He was "regarded as a god" by residents of the Pinch, whom he often treated without charging a fee. He was considered to be an expert, intuitive diagnostician.[15]

Dr. Max Herrman and his nephew, Dr. Alphonse Meyer Sr., were called upon as expert witnesses to testify about "A Miracle in Memphis," the medically unexplained healing of Mary Magdalen Hodges, on 1 August 1913, at the Convent of the Good Shepherd. Catholic sisters at the convent devoted their lives to the re-education and rehabilitation of young girls with problems too serious for their parents to handle. Hodges had been ill since 1900. Surgery performed by Herrman and Meyer in 1912 revealed inoperable cancer. The Mother Superior had ordered a novena for the afflicted woman and the nuns prayed for the intercession of the deceased Mother Mary Euphrasia, founder of the Generalate of the Sisters of the Good Shepherd. Hodges' cure was instantaneous. After the testimony of the two doctors at two separate trials, it was recognized by the church as a true miracle, the third performed by Sister Mary Euphrasia. The process of

---

[13]From *Saddlebags to Science*, 45.

[14]Interview with Joanne Brod, 1991.

[15]Interview with Dr. Charles Olim, 1991; Schaeffer interview.

beatification requires that the person so elevated perform three miracles; the ceremony of the nun's beatification took place on 30 April 1933 at St. Peter's Basilica in Rome.[16]

In the 1920s the Jewish community raised money to build a Jewish hospital. The project was halted, however, when Jewish doctors felt that their relationships with the city's non-Jewish doctors and hospitals were so good that "we hesitated . . . taking a step in the direction of cutting ourselves off to disturb this very friendly and cordial relationship among the medical profession." Dr. Neuton Stern said that seventy-five percent of his patients were non-Jewish and that he felt there was no stigma attached to his being Jewish. The money collected was either returned to the donors or contributed toward the building of the B'nai B'rith Home, a residence and nursing-care facility for the Jewish aged unable to care for themselves.[17]

Stern, the first cardiologist in the Mid-South, received his undergraduate and medical school training at Harvard University. He enlisted in the army during World War I, during which the French government awarded him a medal for his work in the prevention of epidemics. Following the war, Stern remained in England to study for a year with the foremost cardiologist of his time. Returning to Memphis, he brought with him the first electrocardiagraph machine in the South, only eleven years after the first commercial one was developed. He embarked on the practice of internal medicine and cardiology, sharing office space with Drs. Jake Alperin and Gilbert Levy.

Stern was involved in numerous civic endeavors, often connected to medical and public health matters. He was a founder of the American Heart Association, of the local Heart Association, and of the Memphis Academy of Medicine, an organization of internists. He was the editor of the Memphis *Medical Journal* and the author of several books, among them: *Physical and Clinical Diagnosis: Rare Diseases Bases of Treatment*, co-authored by his son, Dr. Thomas Neuton Stern; and *Understanding Sexual Behavior*. He also wrote two unpublished books on philosophy and one on art, indicative of the breadth of his intellectual curiosity and interests. Stern's hobby was painting, which he began after a heart attack. To honor him on

---

[16]Paul R. Coppock, *Mid-South Memoirs*, "St. Mary Euphrasia's Miracle at Good Shepherd," *Commercial Appeal*, 13 July 1975, Section 6, 7.

[17]Dr. Neuton Stern interview by Dr. Berkley Kalin, 1968, Memphis State University, Mississippi Valley Collection.

his seventy-fifth birthday, his students, friends, and patients endowed a visiting professorship at the University of Tennessee Medical School, where he was a clinical professor. The endowment provides for an annual lecture by an outstanding cardiologist. Stern's son and daughter-in-law, Harriet Wise Stern, in 1992 endowed the Dr. Neuton Stern Chair in Cardiology at the University of Tennessee Medical School. A requirement of the endowment is that the person selected to occupy the chair must be "a teacher, researcher, and clinician"—as was the man in whose name the chair was established.[18]

In this regard, Memphis differed from the many American cities that did build Jewish hospitals. In Louisville, for example, a Jewish hospital was established in 1905 to serve 107 patients. By 1978 the hospital had served 17,874 patients of whom only four percent were Jewish. When it was organized, its sponsors were committed to fulfilling the need of Jewish patients for a facility in which they could receive proper attention and to fulfilling the need of Jewish doctors and nurses for a facility in which they could practice and further their medical education. At that time, Jewish doctors, although a tiny minority, were denied staff privileges in most Louisville hospitals. The founding of the Jewish hospital was also a response by German Jews to the demand of the Eastern Europeans for food that was prepared according to dietary laws and for a place where they would be free from Christian missionaries. The Jewish hospital satisfied those desires.[19] Like Memphis, other Southern cities chose not to build Jewish hospitals. Notably among them are Birmingham, Nashville, Knoxville and Chattanooga. Evidently, southern doctors were not discriminated against as were those in the North.

The Memphis Jewish community produced an important American actress in 1900 when Richard Mansfield, considered the foremost actor in the United States at the time, chose Florence Kahn as his new leading lady. Performing for a few years on the London stage, she married the well-known author, critic, and artist, Max Beerbohm in 1910 and later became Lady Florence when her husband was knighted by the King of England. Kahn's father had come to Memphis from Germany in the 1860s and established a dry goods business, Kahn and Freiburg, on the west side of Main at Poplar.

---

[18]Interview with Dr. Thomas M. Stern, 1992.

[19]Herman Landau, *Adath Louisville: The Story of a Jewish Congregation* (Louisville, KY: Herman Landau and Associates, 1981), 113.

One of her brothers, Samuel, became city editor, then Sunday editor, of the *Commercial Appeal*.[20]

As in years past, the Jewish community remained active in Memphis's civic and political life during this period. Abe Goodman was treasurer of the City Club, organized in 1907 "to facilitate government."[21] In the same year, Dr. Marcus Haase was one of the incorporators of the Public Education Association, created to boost public support for city schools.

The elder of two brothers, Marcus Haase was born in Natchez, Mississippi on 31 September 1870 and moved to Memphis in 1882. Most of his higher education was obtained in the city, including the degree of Doctor of Medicine awarded him by the Memphis Hospital Medical College in 1896. This institution later merged with the University of Tennessee and retained the name of the university, where Haase occupied the chair of Professor of Dermatology at the time of his death in 1924. Haase received post-graduate training in dermatology in England, France, and Germany, following which he returned to Memphis to practice his specialty. He made numerous contributions to medical literature of a variety of dermatological problems.

Dr. Marcus Haase was appointed secretary of the Memphis Board of Health in 1897. He was Chief of the Medical Advisory Board of the Memphis General Hospital for twelve years. During a crucial time when the hospital was without a superintendent, Haase served voluntarily, at considerable personal sacrifice, until a new superintendent could be hired. Perhaps his most important contribution to the hospital, however, was his organization of the medical records, greatly facilitating medical treatment. The efficient Outpatient Department of the hospital was largely his creation. Haase also coordinated the activities of the hospital with those of the University of Tennessee Medical School. Nationally, he was chairman of the Dermatology Section of the American Medical Association in 1923. Always concerned about the welfare of children, Haase was among the organizers of the Memphis Council of Social Agencies, established in 1920, and served as its president until his death. One of its projects was the Child Guidance Clinic. He spent much time and effort working for the Associated

---

[20]Paul Coppock, *Memphis Sketches* (Memphis: Friends of Memphis and Shelby County, 1976) 251.

[21]J. P. Young, *History of Memphis, Tennessee* (Knoxville: H. W. Crew and Co., 1912), 574.

Charities of Memphis.

In 1915 when Dr. Joseph Goldberger was working to find the cause of pellagra, a disease that took a terrible toll on the poor, he went to Parchman Prison in Mississippi to experiment on prisoners in exchange for pardons. Goldberger theorized that inadequate nutrition was the culprit, since he had found a high incidence of pellagra in individuals whose diets differed from those of persons around them, living in the same environment. Goldberger consulted with Haase because skin problems were a factor. Of his colleague, Goldberger wrote, "Professor Haase . . . is in the front rank of American dermatologists with a large experience in pellagra . . . There are few, if any, larger pellagra clinics in the United States than that of Professor Haase in the Memphis City Hospital."[22]

Charles J. Haase, the second Haase brother to have a distinguished career in Memphis, was mainly active in the fields of real estate, insurance, and loan businesses. He was also deeply involved in many of the charitable institutions of the city. Born in 1873, he began to work at the real estate company Marx and Bensdorf at the age of fourteen as a "runner." In 1930 he became its president when the firm was incorporated. Haase was president of the Building and Loan Association. When this federal program was established as part of the New Deal in the 1930s, Haase was called to Washington to be an advisor. He was named a director of the Fifth District Home Loan Bank in Cincinatti in 1932.

Haase was a director of the Bank of Commerce and Trust Company, and vice-president and a director of the Manhattan Savings Bank and Trust Company. He was chairman of the Committee on Farm Development for the Rotary Club, which he helped found, and which was the first organization in the Memphis area to advocate diversification. He was president of the Tennessee Building and Loan League, a member of the Board of the Memphis Power and Light Company, and a director of Lowenstein's at the time of his death in 1950.

Like his brother Marcus, Charles Haase was associated with many philanthropic endeavors. He was one of the oldest active members in the seven southern states of District Seven of B'nai B'rith and served as its president. He was the first president of the Leo N. Levi Hospital at Hot Springs, Arkansas, a national hospital mainained by B'nai B'rith. When the

---

[22]Joseph Goldberger, *Goldberger on Pellagra*, ed. Milton Ternes (Baton Rouge: Louisiana State University Press, 1964), 64-65, 74-75.

B'nai B'rith Home for the Aged was established in 1927, Haase became the first chairman of its Board of Governors, a position he held for over forty-five years, when Leo Bearman Sr. succeeded him.

In 1925 Charles Haase began a twenty-year term as president of the Memphis Eye, Ear, and Throat Association, which built a hospital at 1060 Madison. He was a charter member of the Memphis Rotary Club, and served as president of the Rex Club and of Ridgeway Country Club, when it adopted the latter name. During World War I, Haase was Food Administrator for Shelby County.[23]

The first playground director for the city was Irene Schloss Cohen, who operated three social centers providing classes in physical training, and offering various entertainments, including square dancing. In 1909, Schloss became the first woman in Shelby County to be granted a driver's license.[24]

The Egyptians, "a club for discussion of scientific, religious, and economic questions, was organized by Rabbi William Fineshriber of Temple Israel. Elias Gates, Charles Haase, Dr. Marcus Haase, and Herman Katz were among its fifteen Jewish and non-Jewish charter members. The club was to have "no more than thirty-three members of recognized standings, ability, and influence in Memphis and Shelby County, Tennessee." The name was suggested by Fineshriber.[25]

In business, philanthropic and civic affairs, Jews cooperated easily with non-Jewish Memphians, but in religious matters they were sharply divided among themselves. There was a deep division between Reform and Orthodox Jews in their social lives, as well as in their religious practices. Both were highly organized into separate institutions. An important group created by the Orthodox community was the Arbeiter Ring, or Workmen's Circle, a secularly oriented organization. One of its primary functions was the preservation of Yiddish culture and language. While nationally it was associated with the labor movement, in Memphis its focus was more philanthropic, cultural, and social than political. It was organized in 1909 by Nathan Cherry, Charles Farber, Julius Rosenblum, Sam Sharpe, L. Miller, Isaac Brenner, Max Silberberg, Frank Perlman, Jacob Scheinberg, Sam Rothstein, Raphael Rosenblum, and Saul Rosenblum. Four of their

---

[23]Neuton Stern interview.

[24]Polly Cooper personal interview; Wilma Dykeman with Carol Lynn Yellin, *Tennessee Women, Past and Present* (Nashville: Tennessee Committee for the Humanities, 1977) 60.

[25]Young, *History*, 570.

wives were involved: Mmes. Cherry, Farber, Rosenblum, and Silberberg. The Arbeiter Ring maintained a relief fund for its members, which later became a loan association; it sponsored a Yiddish concert every year and a school to teach the language. It supported strikers with funds and collected money for many Jewish institutions. The organization dedicated its own house on 11 January 1925, in a building on the corner of Jefferson and Orleans.[26]

Lewis Kramer, an active member and Yiddish performer, said of the Workmen's Circle that it "projected a better and more just and righteous world. . . . After all, the Torah and Yiddish law is all about justice and righteousness and brotherhood, and that's what the Workmen's Circle stood for."[27] Rosa Lee Abraham remembers the social aspects of the group:

> Everybody would go, and several mothers would cook one Sunday and several mothers some other Sunday . . . and they'd take the children and spend the whole day there . . . they'd show movies and play in the yard and have a wonderful time. We'd have more fun on Sundays than doing anything else in the world.[28]

Another Orthodox fraternal order, the Sons of Israel, was founded in 1900. A branch of a national organization, the lodge aspired "to take care of its own, to relieve distress caused by sickness or death, or to alleviate financial stress of its members."[29]

Memphis was also home to Zionist organizations, but unlike the YMHA and the later Federation, these were the creations of Eastern European Jews. Zionism had become an organized international movement by 1897 when Theodore Herzl convened the First International Zionist Conference in Basel, Switzerland. Although it was rejected at this time by many Memphians, Rabbis Samfield and Fineshriber of Temple Israel and Rabbi Bacarat of Baron Hirsch Synagogue among them, in 1896 a group of mostly Orthodox men established a local Zionist organization, the Lovers of Zion

---

[26]Interview with Ethel Kramer, 1989; Milton Goldberger and Joseph L. Malamut, eds., "Southern Jewry: An Account of Jewish Progress and Achievement in the Southland" (Memphis: *The Hebrew Watchman*, 1933): 33.

[27]Steve Stern, "The Pinch: Portrait of a Jewish Neighborhood, 1880-1950," *Memphis Magazine*, v.8, E12, March 1984.

[28]Stern, "The Pinch."

[29]Stern, "The Pinch," 98.

society. It was led by Samuel Baruchman, T. Miller, Herman Moskovitz, Sam M. Franklin, Israel Peres, and Dr. I. Stadper, who wrote a series of articles on Zionism for the *Commercial Appeal*. In that same year the society conducted a membership drive, visiting most of the Jewish homes in the city and securing eighty-one new members. Among them were Robert Cohen, S. L. Benowitz, Jack Moskowitz, Hardwig Peres, and Eli Davidson.

Theodore Herzl, the founder of Zionism, sent out a call in 1898 for members of the organization to provide financial aid for the movement by buying shares in the newly established Jewish Colonial Bank. Memphis Zionists sold 1,235 shares, amounting to an investment of $6,175. Herzl died in 1904 and the Memphis Zionist movement seems to have died along with him. However, in 1912, S. Shebs, a young Polish Jew, came to Memphis. He reorganized the group and became its president, with Sam Shankman as secretary, later president. Under their leadership Memphis again became a locale of Zionist activities. Hardwig Peres, who rejoined at that time, remained a staunch supporter of the cause.

In the beginning, men and women belonged to the same Zionist organization. Dues were two dollars a year. Meetings were held on Sundays and were usually family picnics. These functions continued until the establishment of Hadassah as the women's Zionist group. One of the causes Memphis Zionists supported was the Jewish National Fund, which planted trees for the revitalization of Israel. Early workers for the Jewish National Fund included Pearl Baruchman, Mary Weiss, Regina Goldberger, Mary Blockson, the Davidson sisters, and Rose and Ray Jaffe. Dora Weiss, Mr. and Mrs. H. Rosen, I. Istrov, Mr. and Mrs. H. G. Schaffer, Harry Dlugach, H. Blumenfeld, Elias Kabakoff, and Aaron Meltzer were also early Zionists in Memphis. In 1914 Sam Shankman became president of the Memphis Zionists.[30]

Between 1905 and 1912, the heavy influx of Eastern European immigrants to Memphis doubled the Jewish population of the city and strained the community's charitable resources. Most of the newcomers, who were poor, unskilled, and unable to speak English, settled in the Pinch, often living without adequate sanitation facilities. The established Memphis Jewish community held out a helping hand: Jewish doctors offered their services without charge; a free kindergarten was established; and a Mother's Circle presented regular lectures on child welfare. The Salon Circle, a

---

[30]Sam Shankman, "A History of Zionism in America." Unpublished manuscript, 3.

women's club of mostly German Jews, supplied clothes, conducted English classes, and gave parties for the immigrant children. The aforementioned Jewish Neighborhood House was organized in 1913. A Free Loan Society created in 1914 was functioning well by 1916.[31]

The Hebrew Benevolent Society, originally established in 1850 in connection with the care of the cemetery, had been reorganized in 1864 to alleviate conditions left in the wake of the Civil War. The influx of newcomers sparked the establishment of a successor, the Federation of Jewish Charities, in March 1906, as a family agency

> to initiate and carry out a unified program of social work among Jews of Memphis and Shelby County; to aid and assist Jewish families, children, young men and women who may be in need of material or other assistance or advice with a view of promoting . . . individual and family life and improving standards of living.

The agency offered help for the aged; financial assistance; service to the foreign-born; immigrant resettlement; aid to transients, and an information and referral service. All of the original organizers were from the Reform community: Emil Nathan, Rabbi Max Samfield, H. Warhaftig, David Sternberg, and Mitchell Rosenthal. They were committed to the vital work of the agency. But it was noted that although they wished to help the immigrants, often their attitude toward them was condescending. This situation persisted until 1916 when, of the new organizations that joined the Federation, thirty-seven percent were Orthodox.[32]

The benevolent societies that arose to take care of the needs of the immigrants were soon competing with each other for funds and often duplicating services. Some central organization was indicated as it was in communities all over the country. The concept of federation was encouraged by businessmen annoyed by constant solicitations and multiple appeals. They insisted on one annual drive. By 1920 about fifty cities in the United States had established federations differing in size, scope, and

---

[31]Lawrence Meyers, "Evolution of the Jewish Service Agency in Memphis, Tn., 1847-1963." Memphis State University, unpublished paper, 19-22.

[32]Shankman, "History of Zionism"; Jewish Service Agency Minute book.; Meyers, "Evolution," 18-22.

effectiveness. Memphis was one of those cities.[33]

In 1920 the Federation of Jewish Charities in Memphis changed its name to the Federation of Jewish Welfare Agencies, and was incorporated to allow direct collections of donations through one agency. Concurrently, the Hebrew Relief Association ceased operation as a separate entity, joining the Federation as its Social Service Committee. Health and Legal Committees were also added.

The Memphis Federation, organized originally in 1854 to provide relief to indigent Jews, has continued to respond to the changing needs of the Jewish community. While the Federation remains a source of financial aid and probably always will, it has adjusted its programs to address its constituents' other needs as they have arisen.[34]

Other organizations were also in flux. Some young members of the Reform group, not satisfied with the management of the Memphis Club, organized the Rex Club. They rejoined the Memphis Club in 1909, then merged the two organizations into what became known as the Rex Club. It occupied quarters over the Lyric Theater on Madison Avenue.[35]

The YMHA bought a lot on Dunlap and Madison in 1906 and, with the Rex Club, constructed a building. The Rex Club later bought 178 acres at 5854 Poplar Avenue and in 1921, began to build a golf course, tennis courts, and a clubhouse. The Rex Club became the Rex Ridgeway Club and in 1941, the Ridgeway Country Club. Its first five presidents were Sol Hesse, Charles Haase, Sam Friedlander, David Sternberg, and Milton S. Binswanger Sr. The YMHA established a junior group in 1910. Its first officers were Abe Waldauer, president; Joseph Goldstein, vice-president; Earl Heyman, secretary-treasurer; Sig Harpmann, Harry Bernstein, M. Bronstein, I. Cohen, Ike Alperin, and Herman Bacharach, directors. The group ceased to exist in 1920.[36]

Another organization that arose at about the same time was Pi Tau Pi fraternity, a national social club whose local branch was established in 1912. Officers were H. B. Cohn, president; Ben Sachs, vice-president; Albert

---

[33]Jacob Marcus, *United States Jewry: 1776-1885* (Detroit: Wayne State University Press, 1989), vol 3, 481-84.

[34]Jewish Service Agency Minute book.

[35]Ridgeway Country Club Rules and Membership Roster.

[36]Ridgeway Country Club Rules and Membership Roster; Shankman, "History of Zionism"; *Universal Jewish Encyclopedia* (New York: Universal Jewish Encyclopedia, Inc., 1948) 464.

Rosenfield, secretary; and Leo Wurtzburger, treasurer.[37] Because members were required to belong to Temple Israel, the organization served to further widen the breach between Orthodox and Reform Jews. While the Jewish community of Memphis was organizing itself in business, social, and philanthropic areas, the city was entering a new era in its political life when Edward Hull Crump was elected mayor in 1909. The city's middle class was expanding and, with the expansion, progressive ideas developed. Crump was elected as a "reform" mayor, his candidacy profiting from the increasing interest in municipal reform.[38] A basic change, strongly advocated by Crump and adopted by the city, was the shift from a council to a commission form of government.

Thus began a career that was to change every aspect of Memphis for years to come. Crump was twice re-elected as mayor by large majorities and later held the post of county trustee for eight years. He retired from local public office in 1924 to give his full time to the firm of Crump and Trezevant, a real-estate, mortgage, and insurance business, in which he had previously been a less active partner. In the 1930s he won election to Congress, serving two terms and in 1940 was elected Mayor by prearrangement. In a ruse designed to enable him to retain control of city government, he resigned one minute later in favor of his chosen candidate. Although he never held public office again, these years saw the consolidation of his control of the city as political boss and the increase of his influence throughout the state. Crump's influence lasted until the 1948 election when Estes Kefauver defeated the Crump candidate, John Mitchell, for the United States Senate.[39]

Crump's domination of the political life of Memphis was accomplished in large part by clever manipulation of the forty percent black population of the city. Blacks for years had been allowed to vote in Memphis, even as other sections of the South restricted their voting rights. The Negro community of Memphis, however, had little political power because their vote, when it was needed in an election, was cast by one white political group or another. Crump's control of the votes of the forty percent black population of the city was achieved in part by his domination of black

---

[37]Ibid.

[38]William D. Miller, *Memphis During the Progressive Era, 1900-1917* (Memphis, Memphis State University Press, 1957) 115.

[39]Capers, *Biography*, 194; David Tucker, *Memphis Since Crump: Bossism, Blacks, and Civic Reformers, 1848-1968* (Knoxville: University of Tennessee Press, 1980), xii.

leaders whose loyalty he commanded because his leadership had given blacks the nominal right to vote in Memphis, a privilege that was unusual in a southern city of that period. He further exploited this situation to his advantage, combining fear and intimidation with patronage, services, and less brutality than other southern cities, in order to tighten his hold on black voters. He entered each election campaign backed by a solid bloc.[40]

The large black presence in the city existed alongside a plantation mentality that emphasized the ideal of white supremacy. Although this sentiment always had characterized the city to some degree, it became more pronounced after Reconstruction, after the yellow fever epidemics, and after the flight of the more affluent foreign-born. Before 1860, thirty-seven percent of Memphis's population was foreign in origin; by 1900, both the foreign-born and those whose parents were foreign-born comprised only fifteen percent of the city's population. As foreign-born Memphians departed, their broader perspective and cultural interests were replaced by the narrow and provincial outlook of migrants from the southern countryside. The values of these migrants now became the ones adopted by the majority of the whites in the city. In particular, they exalted the Old South's ideal of white dominance, seeing espousal of this ideal as a way to preserve their social and economic status. Earlier, the institution of slavery had helped to boost the status of whites. But with the demise of slavery, many Southerners turned to vigilante activity as a means of maintaining their own position in society. The idea of white supremacy was held above religion, morality, or love by adherents in all classes, and the fanaticism with which it was defended explains much of the violence in the city during the early years of the twentieth century.[41]

Lynchings, in which the victims were almost always black, were popular entertainment, attracting fascinated audiences. A Beale Street character, Wild Bill Latura, was well-known for killing blacks. For no apparent reason in 1908, he entered a black saloon and, after proclaiming loudly that he was going to "turn the place into a funeral parlor," shot and killed six customers. Latura was acquitted of this crime, but not without protest from the *Commercial Appeal*. The newspaper said that the killing of blacks without cause was "being overdone," and ought to be stopped "because it was wrong

---

[40]Robert A. Lanier, *Memphis in the Twenties: The Second Term of Mayor Rowlett Payne, 1924-1928* (Memphis: Zenda Press, 1979), 96; Tucker, *Memphis Since Crump*, 17.
[41]Miller, *Progressive Era*, 6-7, 19.

in itself," and because "those men who kill Negroes as a pastime . . . usually end up by killing white men." The newspaper said in 1909 that no white men had been hanged in Shelby County since 1890, but added: "Since then we have had a hanging of Negroes pretty much regularly every year."[42]

The presence of anti-black feeling in Memphis probably deflected some discrimination that would have been directed toward the city's southern newcomers. It almost certainly deflected much overt discrimination that would have been directed toward the city's Jews and Catholics, groups who were often the targets of prejudice in Protestant America. But some credit for the city's tolerance toward religious minorities belongs to Crump himself whose benign attitude toward these groups was sometimes criticized, but not publicly. Like most early twentieth century city bosses who, in the interest of harmony, tended to include members of every constituency in their circle, Crump played ethnic politics well. Both Catholics and Jews held high places in his organization. Frank Rice, a Catholic, and William Gerber, a Jew, were among his top lieutenants. Abe Goodman Sr. was treasurer of Crump's first campaign for public office.[43] Judge Lois Bejach and attorneys David Ballon and Abe Waldauer were other Jews who played important roles in his organization.

Abe Waldauer was admitted to the bar in Memphis in 1916. He was a dedicated Boy Scout, the leader of Troop No. 25 at Temple Israel for many years. That troop sold more war bonds than any other troop in World War I. One of Waldauer's political connections had its roots in World War I, when he served in the 114th Artillery under Captain Gordon Browning. Browning's campaign for Congress was "planned in the dugouts of the Argonne Forest." When the war was over, Waldauer allied himself with Browning's political fortunes as Browning rose to become governor of Tennessee. Waldauer then became the liason between Memphis and the governor's office in Nashville. Browning named him a member of the State Election Board.

Browning's break with Boss Crump, to whom Waldauer was also loyally devoted, placed him in an awkward position. Waldauer was Assistant City Attorney until 1936, when he resigned rather than vote against his old friend Browning, who was a candidate for the United State Senate running

---

[42]Miller, *Progressive Era*, 96.

[43]Schaeffer interview; William Goodman interview by Berkley Kalin, 1968, Memphis State University, Mississippi Valley Collection.

against Crump-supported Nathan Bachman. Later, however, when Browning wanted to enlarge the State Board of Elections, Waldauer viewed it as an expression of no confidence in the board's members. Therefore, he severed his long-held friendship with Browning. Waldauer, progressive and astute, then became a welcome and close Crump ally.

Waldauer demonstrated his strong support for Jewish refugees even before World War II, when the United States quota system made it virtually impossible for an immigrant to gain entry to the country unless he had a job waiting for him. (The labor movement was a strong legacy of World War I; the Immigration Law acted as a protective tariff for American labor.) When a Rabbi Wise, in Germany, wanted to immigrate before World War II, Waldauer found a small congregation in Clarksdale, Mississippi which needed a rabbi. Rabbi Julius Mark of the Vine Street Temple in Nashville agreed to pay Rabbi Wise's salary; Waldauer, his father-in-law, leading citizen Lee Loventhal of Nashville, and others joined the small Clarksdale congregation to make it sufficiently large to secure the rabbi's employment. Waldauer asked Senator Kenneth McKellar to arrange an appointment for him with Secretary of State Cordell Hull, a Tennessean whose wife was Jewish. Even Hull could not expedite the visa, so Waldauer called President Franklin Delano Roosevelt, and the visa was issued.

Later, in the late 1930s and early 1940s, when the need to save European Jewry was urgent, Waldauer used his political influence to rescue as many as he could. He became a member of the Society for the Aid of Refugees, Scholars, Rabbis and Doctors. When a bill was introduced in the Tennessee legislature to prohibit the practice of medicine by immigrants, Dr. Justin Adler, then on the staff at Western State Hospital in Bolivar, called on Waldauer for help. Disturbed at the potential consequences of the bill, Waldauer told Governor Browning: "If that bill passes, you had better close up every mental institution operated by this state, because you do not have an adequate number of American doctors."[44] The bill was withdrawn.

President Roosevelt appointed Waldauer the Collector of Customs of the Port of Memphis; he was a trustee of the Henry George Foundation of America; a member of The Egyptians literary society, and a committed vegetarian. He was an active member of the American Legion. His wife

[44]Miller, *Progressive Era*, 247.

Dorothy shared his interests in scouting and in Zionism.[45]

Sometimes Crump would place a late-night call to a Jewish member of his circle to inquire about the basic beliefs of Judaism. He was curious about the place of the Jews in "the plan of Providence," and he admired their historic struggle to prevail in spite of suffering and deprivation. He apparently was determined that Jewish citizens in "his" city would receive equal treatment and respect. Because his control was effective for many years, this climate of acceptance predominated. Crump was the first non-Jew in Memphis to contribute to the Jewish Welfare Fund.[46]

Memphis, however, was not representative of the entire South. Atlanta Jews, for example, endured the lynching of Leo Frank. As a Jew and a Yankee, Frank was falsely convicted of the murder of Mary Phagan, a female worker in the Atlanta factory he managed, and was sentenced to death. When, two years later, Georgia's governor John Slaton commuted his sentence to life in prison, Frank was kidnapped from the prison in Atlanta by a mob of vigilantes and lynched on 16 August 1915. The lynching stirred up the subdued but ever-present fear of anti-Semitism that had been quiescent since Grant's Order No. 11 during the Civil War and inspired the B'nai B'rith to create the Anti-Defamation League "to work for equality of opportunity for all Americans in our time."[47] Some Atlanta Jews moved to Memphis to live in a friendlier atmosphere. Among them was Lewis "Red" Kramer, who became a leader in Zionist and charitable organizations in the city. Kramer recalled incidents in which the Jews of Atlanta were terrorized and their businesses boycotted:

My folks had a store in the neighborhood where Mary Phagan lived, the girl that was killed, and they were boycotted because they were accused of giving $500 to Leo Frank's defense fund. It was the only lynching of a Jew in the United States. . . . The governor

---

[45]Interview with Mr. and Mrs. Abe Waldauer. Memphis State University Oral History Project.

[46]Miller, *Progressive Era* 198; Hal Gerber, Anna Gruber and David Ballon personal interviews.

[47]Rachel Saltzman, "Shalom Y'all," in *Southern Exposure* (Durham: Institute for Southern Studies, Sept.-Oct. 1983): 35; Nathan Kaganoff and Melvin Urofsky, *Turn to the South: Essays on Southern Jewry* (Charlottesville: University of Virginia Press, 1979), 29; Lucy S. Davidowicz, *On Equal Terms: Jews in America, 1881-1981* (New York: Holt, Rhinehart, and Winston, 1982), 76.

was almost lynched himself because he commuted Frank's sentence from death to life so he could gather more evidence, because he was not satisfied with the evidence that was presented at the trial. When I first got married and we were going to a place called Stone Mountain to a wiener roast, there was a Ku Klux Klan demonstration with all the white hoods, sitting on the fenders of their cars. And it scared my wife and she hid under the dashboard. And I told her, "If you're going to live in Atlanta, you might as well get used to this, because it's an everyday occurrence. . . ."[48]

The Leo Frank case became a cause célèbre for Jews. The *Commercial Appeal* reported the case widely, stressing the illegality of the mob's action, expressing horror at it and condemning anti-Semitism. At the same time, the newspaper also carried reports almost daily of the lynchings of blacks, but did not express opposition to anti-black sentiment. Anti-Semitic incidents did occur in Memphis, but they were isolated events, unsupported by local government and opinion makers. Anne Phillips, born in 1911, lived on Azalea Street amidst a small group of Jewish families that included the Nathan Epsteins, the Morris Kaplans, the Ettingoffs, Levitzes, Katzmans, Schiffmans, Rosenblums, Starks, Greens, Katzes, and Margolins. She recalls the group as "pious Jews with a small synagogue in the Kaplan home where they held holiday services," and remembers that at Cummings Elementary School, neighborhood boys often called the Jewish children "Christ Killers." She feels that in general, however, there has been little anti-Semitism in Memphis, attributing this lack of prejudice to the civic contributions of the Jewish community.[49]

While the attitudes that led to the Leo Frank lynching were not typical of Memphis, they reflected the anti-Semitism that had begun to pervade the United States in the last quarter of the nineteenth century. New, open social discrimination was evident. In 1877 the Grand Union Hotel in Saratoga Springs, New York refused to admit a wealthy Jewish banker, Joseph Seligman,[50] despite the fact that Seligman had reserved accommodations there and with his family had been a guest of the hotel on many

[48]Ethel Kramer interview.
[49]Saltzman, "Shalom," 36; personal interview with Anne Phillips, 1990.
[50]Frank Coppa and Thomas Curran, *The Immigrant Experience in America* (Boston: Twayne Publishers, 1976), 160.

previous occasions. In 1878 the New York City Bar Association blackballed a Jewish applicant, the first in a long series of actions to restrict entrance of Jews into the lower rungs of the legal profession.

The same year, the Greek letter fraternities at New York City College excluded Jewish members. In 1879 the president of the Manhattan Beach Company barred Jews from his Coney Island hotel. The social anti-Semitism of the late 1800s was given a boost by the nouveau riche captains of industry who thought they would elevate their own social standing by excluding Jews from the hotels and clubs they frequented. It did not take long, however, for the old elite to rival the newcomers in hatred of Jews. Feeling displaced by America's increasing emphasis on material wealth rather than ancestry as a determinant of social status, members of the elite directed their frustrations against Jews rather than against the industrial moguls who were replacing them as leaders of society. The increase in discriminatory attitudes was coincidental with, and exacerbated by, the great mass immigration of Eastern European Jews at the turn of the century. In the now more polyglot nation, racist ideologies and rampant nativism began to develop.[51] There were night riders in Mississippi, and the Ku Klux Klan grew and prospered. Some southern Jews, many of them foreign-born merchants, were subjected to xenophobia, class hatred, militant Christian fundamentalism, and political demagoguery. In Memphis, however, these sentiments never became dominant.

Boss Crump openly opposed the Ku Klux Klan, as did the editor of the *Commercial Appeal*, C. P. J. Mooney, and it did not gain a stronghold in Memphis. Lynching of Negroes, however, remained accepted as normal procedure, judging by a newspaper report of 1917:

> The recent lynching in the vicinity of Memphis was in a spot ten miles from the city. As lynchings go, it was orderly. There was no drunkenness, no shooting, and no yelling. No stores were closed in Memphis, and no papers went to press early in order that the reporters might attend.[52]

Rabbi William Fineshriber, who served Temple Israel from 1911 to 1924,

---

[51]Charles E. Silberman, *A Certain People: American Jews and Their Lives Today* (New York: Summit Books, 1985) 47; Coppa and Curran, *Immigrant Experience*, 160.

[52]*Commercial Appeal*, 25 May 1917.

was a vigorous and outspoken foe of lynching. One of his sermons in which he denounced a lynching received widespread public attention, both favorable and unfavorable.[53]

The most explosive event of the early twentieth century was the world war that began in 1914. In addition to the larger hardships it caused, the war posed a problem for all German-born Memphians, including Jews, who saw their heritage, previously an advantage, become a source of concern. As America inched closer toward joining the Allies in the war, all things German fell into disfavor and were scorned. Thus, when the United States declared war on Germany on 6 April 1917, German Jewish Memphians were eager to demonstrate their patriotism. They joined the armed forces in great numbers, as did the rest of the community. Temple Israel's four hundred fifty families alone supplied one hundred thirty-one servicemen. Among them were Dr. Alphonse Meyer who was in France when his first child, Alphonse Meyer Jr., was born. Dr. Gilbert Levy served in the Medical Corps, and Dr. Marcus Haase in hospital management. Henry Frank volunteered and went to war when he was only seventeen years old. Memphis Jews killed in action included Albert Cohen Jr.; James Nathan Jr.; Elias Kiersky; Harry Kemker; Avrome N. Hexter; William Epstein; Edwin W. Halle; Samuel A. Lovenson; Herbert Seigel; and Harry Weiss.[54]

The nationalism and xenophobia fanned by war created a clamor for the restriction of immigration. After many earlier attempts and two vetoes by President Woodrow Wilson, Congress passed a literacy test for immigrants in 1917. Mass immigration, which had ceased naturally when the war began, was halted legislatively after the war, first in 1921 and then, even more stringently in 1924. In reaction to the Russian Revolution, the nation was swept by a Red Scare. Fear and hatred of foreigners, directed against German-Americans during the war, was transferred to alien radicals and revolutionaries. Many were seized in raids by Attorney General Mitchell Palmer and hundreds were deported in the prevailing hysteria.

An emergency immigration law passed in 1921 introduced a quota system favoring northern and western, as opposed to southern and eastern, Europeans. Immigration declined immediately. In 1923 the virulently

---

[53]Bernard Postal and Lionel Koppman, *American Jewish Landmarks: A Travel Guide and History* (New York: Fleet Press Corp., 1954), 246.
[54]Memphis at War Collection, (Memphis: Memphis Public Library and Information Center.)

anti-immigrant Ku Klux Klan reached its peak strength. In 1924 the infamous National Origins Act was adopted, placing a ceiling on the number of immigrants and establishing discriminatory national and racial quotas. The effect was striking: in the last decade of the nineteenth century, approximately one hundred thousand immigrants were admitted to the United States each year; in 1924, fifty thousand entered America; in 1925, only ten thousand were admitted. The National Origins Act legitimized anti-Semitism in America until 1948 when the Displaced Persons Act permitted four hundred thousand non-quota immigrants to enter, including nine thousand Jews.

While most of the early immigrants had made the change from working class to middle class with relative ease, their descendants, the native-born, college-bound, faced the first serious obstacles in American Jewish history to social and professional advancement. As they began to enter universities and professional schools in the 1920s they found newly erected quotas. There were now barriers to Jews entering the professions, desirable residential neighborhoods, private clubs, and business and industrial corporations. Some firms did not hire Jews. Henry Ford's newspaper, the *Dearborn Independent*, printed a steady flow of virulent anti-Semitism. In May 1920 Ford began to publish in serialized form The Protocols of the Elders of Zion, the Russian forgery declaring that there was a Jewish conspiracy to rule the world.

Thus, while the American Jewish community was becoming increasingly middle class economically, the path to educational and professional advancement was narrowing. Historian John Higham wrote that the Jews, "alone among European immigrant groups, lost in reputation as they gained in social and economic status."[55]

Viewed against this background of increasing anti-Semitism and nativism in the nation, the calm tolerance of religious minorities in Memphis was unusual. Jewish Memphians continued to be elected to political office. William Bailey Rosenfeld was a member of the Tennessee legislature from 1917 to 1918. Hardwig Peres was chairman of the Memphis School Board from 1919 to 1920. Joseph Hanover was a member of the

---

[55]Coppa and Curran, *Immigrant Experience*, 160; Kennedy, *A Nation of Immigrants*, 93; Judith E. Endelman, *The Jewish Community of Indianapolis, 1849 to the Present* (Bloomington: Indiana University Press, 1984), 111, 117; Alberta Eiseman, *From Many Lands* (New York: Athaneum, 1970), 155; John Higham, "Social Discrimination Against Jews in America, 1830-1930," a publication of the American Jewish Historical Society, 47 (1957) 26.

Tennessee House of Representatives from 1918 to 1919, before accepting the position of Assistant City Attorney. As Democratic floor leader, he led the fight for passage of the Nineteenth Amendment to the United States Constitution granting women the right to vote. Although Crump was a loyal partisan of the amendment, as were John M. Keating, editor of the *Commercial Appeal,* and Rabbi William Fineshriber of Temple Israel, most southerners were opposed to it. Reasons for their opposition varied. Some equated suffragettes with "women of the streets." Some, among them the *Memphis Daily Avalanche,* opposed it because it would double the number of black votes. The liquor lobby was against it because most agitators for temperance were women. By the summer of 1920 thirty-five states had ratified this amendment, but thirty-six were required in order for it to become a part of the Constitution.[56]

One of the people troubled by the issue was Joseph Hanover, who said the question of women's suffrage had bothered him since age seventeen or eighteen. Because he strongly favored women's suffrage, he resolved to work for passage of the amendment in Tennessee. To do so more effectively, he resigned his city position to run for his former position in the state legislature in a special election called by the governor. This action represented a considerable sacrifice for the thirty-year-old attorney. The floor battle was difficult, with strong feelings expressed on both sides of the issue. Hanover received so many letters, phone calls, and threats that the governor assigned a bodyguard to protect him. A three-hour debate resulted in two tie votes before a final vote in favor of passage of the Constitutional Amendment. The Supreme Court of the United States eventually decided that the amendment was ratified.[57]

The 1920s were a time of advancement for women. Not only did they gain the vote, but more of them entered the professions and made their mark in business. Sophie Goldberger Friedman, a pioneer female attorney in Memphis, was also active in the fight for women's suffrage. She was the first woman to participate in annual meetings of Temple Israel, when in 1929 its Board of Trustees invited women to attend. One of the first females to become a pharmacist in the city was Yetta Feinberg (later Yetta Manis)

---

[56]Perre Magness, "Jews Came to Memphis in the 1840's." *Commercial Appeal* (7 April, 1988): 2; *Universal Jewish Encyclopedia,* 484; Grace Elizabeth Prescott, "The Woman Suffrage Movement in Memphis: Its Place in the State, Sectional, and National Movements," M.A. thesis, Memphis State University, 1963: 22-33.
[57]Prescott, 177-178.

who graduated in 1926 from the University of Tennessee. She owned and operated her own drugstore at 751 South Parkway East, where she "combined a philanthropic spirit with her apothecary ability . . . supplying medicine to anyone who needs it, whether they can pay or not." After her marriage, her husband handled the pharmacy's business affairs, while she continued as pharmacist. Mrs. Manis said that her goal in childhood had been to do something to help people who needed medicine they could not afford. She was the only woman in her graduating class and had the highest average of anyone in her group taking the Tennessee Board of Pharmacy examinations.[58]

During the period following World War I, Memphis and its Jewish community enjoyed general economic prosperity. Old businesses profited from favorable conditions, and some notable new ones were established. The Southern Leather Company originated in 1919 when Ira Lichterman married Lottie Loewenberg, and he and brother-in-law William Loewenberg became partners. The company did not begin to grow until about 1929; by 1943 it had grown sufficiently to be divided into three parts: Loewenberg and his son William I. Loewenberg kept the leather company; Ira Lichterman's son Herbert took the shoe division, and his son Martin took the appliance division.[59]

Mayer Myers, who had worked for Otto Metzger's American Paper Company, opened his own Mayer Myers Paper Company in 1919. Farber Brothers, manufacturers of seat covers and car cushions, opened in 1920. M. G. Liberman, who moved to Memphis in the early 1900s, started his Merchants Credit Association in 1920. There were then four large department stores in the city—Goldsmith's, Gerber's, Bry-Block, and Lowenstein's—but none had thought of a central credit bureau until Liberman presented the idea. Within a year, by 1921, the value of the service was established. Later, the name was changed to the Credit Bureau of Memphis, a collection department was added, and the "Red Book," with coded credit ratings, was published.[60]

Gaston D. Strauss bought the Memphis Packing Company and South Memphis Stockyards for the sale and distribution of cattle and meat in

---

[58]Wax, *Our First Century*, 41; *Commercial Appeal*, 25 November 1945.

[59]Interview with William I. Loewenberg, 1991.

[60]Interview with Malcolm Levi, 1991; Eldon Roark, *Memphis Bragabouts: Characters I Have Known* (New York: McGraw Hill Book Co., Inc., 1945); Interview with Ann Marks, 1992.

1928. Brothers Joseph and Leo Levy founded Levy's Ladies Toggery in the 1920s. Herman Adler, wh had operated a tavern in the Pinch, opened the Adler Hotel on Main and Linden in 1925. The hotel was arranged in two sections: the Adler Apartments for long-term residents in the front, and the Adler Annex for travelers in the back. Herman's son Johl opened the Tennessee Hotel in the late 1920s. Milton Allenberg opened the small but thriving Allenberg Cotton Company in 1921. When Eric Hirsch graduated from Cornell, Allenberg hired him; when Allenberg died, Hirsch bought the business but retained the name of its founder. Hirsch built the firm into one of the significant companies on Front Street, "a street with character . . . a club," and Hirsch was an honored member. He was voted Cotton Man of the Year and was the only Jewish member elected president of the Memphis Cotton Exchange.[61]

If Front Street was a club for successful Jews, then Beale Street was a commercial base for those who found a way to make a living there. Beale Street during the 1920s was a mecca for blacks from all over the lower South and was lined with many businesses operated by Jews. A number of businesses were loan shops: Cohen's Loan Office, Sonny's Loan Office with Maynard Epstein, manager, Lipman's Loan Office and Nathan's Loans.[62]

The first Memphis office of Malco Theaters opened in 1929. The company, owned by M. A. Lightman, Sr., and a partner, maintained headquarters in Arkansas until 1944 when its center of operations was relocated to Memphis. The company grew into a large chain of local and regional theaters. Like many other Jews, Lightman embarked upon his business ventures unexpectedly. An engineering graduate of Vanderbilt and Cornell Universities, Lightman had secured government contracts during World War I. After the war he traveled to Sheffield, Alabama in search of other business opportunities in his field. There, he saw people lined up outside what appeared to be an empty building. He soon discovered that inside the building were a projector and screen on which a movie was being shown. Concluding that the desire for entertainment was great and acting upon this observation, Lightman leased an empty building, procured a projector and screen, rented a film, and soon had a large crowd standing in

[61]Hubert Kiersky personal interview; Interview with Bert Wolff, 1991; Interview with Leah Hirsch, 1992.

[62]Alan Singer, "A Self-Guided Tour of Jewish Memphis, Past and Present." (Memphis Jewish Federation Pamphlet, 1980), 13.

line to buy his wares. A new business was born.[63]

Beyond his extensive business accomplishments, Lightman contributed to the welfare of the city by involvement in fund-raising campaigns for the tuberculosis, heart, and polio associations; the Young Men's Christian Association; Crippled Adults Hospital; and Collins Chapel Hospital for Negroes. He served as president of the Variety Club of Memphis which he helped to found. He was Mid-South chairman of the War Activities Committee during World War II and was Shelby County chairman for the United States Service to China campaign. He was president of and an active participant in the Little Theater. At his death in 1958, there were fifty theaters in the Malco chain.[64]

Several Jewish builders "changed the face of Memphis" in the 1920s. Harry Dlugach, with his three sons, Manny, Gilbert, and Ben J., built residences and developed housing subdivisions. Dlugach's brother-in-law Sam Malkin came to Memphis from New York in the 1920s to work as a carpenter, but soon he too entered the construction business. On a lot he purchased facing Crump Stadium on Cleveland Street, Malkin built the first apartment house in the city designed around a courtyard. Because the property originally had been a dump, he received praise for "beautifying an eyesore." He built other houses before going into commercial construction in which much of his work consisted of renovation and restoration of buildings on Main Street.[65]

Dave Dermon was one of the city's major real estate developers, a "key figure in building modern Memphis." Dermon immigrated to Memphis from Kiev, Russia, around 1905, at the age of nineteen. His first job was for the Memphis Power and Light Company, as a layer of electric cable in ditches under the city streets. The job paid six dollars a week, but he had to relinquish it when he became ill with fever and chills. Shortly thereafter, he took fifty dollars from his savings, made a down payment on a lot, later the site of the Chisca Hotel, and opened a tin shop in the old church building standing on it. Two months later he received an inquiry from someone who wished to buy the building. He priced and sold it for eighty-five hundred dollars to complete the first of a series of successful real estate transactions

---

[63]*Commercial Appeal* 15 December 1958; *Press Scimitar* 16 September 1957; Interview with Richard Lightman, 1992.
[64]Lightman interview.
[65]Interview with Rosabel Strauch, 1990.

that were to make the young immigrant "one of Memphis's and the South's best-known realtors."[66]

The boarding house was a popular housing arrangement for many Jewish families from 1915 through the 1920s. Sawrie's, at 572 Poplar, was such an establishment, well-known and well-patronized. Among those who lived at Sawrie's at various times were the Abe Kaufmans, the Leon Beckers, the Lou Kellermans, the Leo Wurtzburgers, the Fred Brenners, sisters Olive and Florence Schloss, the Louis Halles, the Julian Kerns, the Arthur Browns, the Louis Baums, and the Sol Lewises. The Sawrie family, who owned and operated the boarding house, was not Jewish and did not live there. Entertainment was sometimes provided in the evenings. S. L. Kopald Sr., best known as one of the founders of Humko, came from time to time to play the piano and perform magic tricks. It was "a comfortable and pleasant place to live."[67] Another such boarding house was the Hobson Inn, across the street from Sawrie's.

The Rex Club remained a center of social activity for long-established families. Patterning its functions after those of non-Jewish social clubs, it held an annual debutante ball during the fall season. The *Commercial Appeal* described its 1919 ball as "an unusually brilliant event," during which "seven charming girls: Misses Marguerite Lowenstein, Mildred Ehrmann, Florence Gates, Bertha Tobias of Baton Rouge, Mildred Jacobson of Baltimore, Lucille Hiller of Little Rock, and Marjorie Mook were introduced to the two hundred or more guests." It was not uncommon for out-of-town debutantes to be presented at local balls, especially when they had close relatives in the city who wished them to "come out" in Memphis as well as in their home towns.[68] The newspaper described in elaborate detail the decor and the clothes worn by all the women.

In continuing pursuit of philanthropic and social goals, the Memphis Jewish community in 1918 established a local branch of Hadassah, a national Zionist women's organization created to provide resources for

---

[66]*Commercial Appeal*, 23 June 1963; The *Press Scimitar* 27 May 1957.

[67]Interview with Dorothy Davis and Helen Dinkelspiel, 1989.

[68]The Board of Governors of the Rex Club included R. H. Bernhold, president; Dave Halle, vice-president; William Loeb, secretary; I. Dinkelspiel, Milton A. Sternberg, Harold H. Roth, Ike Gronauer, Gilbert M. Schloss, and Milton B. Silberberg. Serving on the Entertainment Committee were Elias Gates, Abe Frank, Louis Roth, Abe Goodman, M. H. Mayer, Henry Halle, Harry Cohn, and A. L. Lowenstein. Also working on the ball were Charles J. Haase, Merrill Brooks, Nathan Wellman, and Leo Goodman.

Palestine. The local chapter was formed by a group composed primarily of Orthodox women, meeting at the home of Mrs. Sam Steinberg. Its members included Pearl Baruchman, Mrs. H. I. Schaffer, and Mrs. Raphael Gold, who was elected president. From its earliest days, Hadassah has felt a special responsibility for the children of the Jewish homeland. An early project adopted by the group was to sew clothes for orphans. From this small sewing circle, the organization grew into a chapter of fourteen hundred women, divided into two groups, which raised over one hundred thousand dollars annually to support its projects. The Memphis chapter of Junior Hadassah was formed in 1925, again in the home of Mrs. Sam Steinberg, with Mrs. Perry Sewel selected as its first president.[69]

The Memphis Arbeiter Farband, a Jewish organization with branches throughout the United States and Canada, was organized in 1920. The Memphis branch's founders were A. Novak, Leon Berger, H. Schechtman, J. Scheinberg, I. Elster, and A. Schneider. The Arbeiter Farband began a fund-raising campaign for Palestine, became interested in literary affairs, and established the previously mentioned Yiddish school. The founders of the school were Hyman Rushansky, J. Scheinberg, Joe Shankman, Leon Berger, A. Novak, and Mr. and Mrs. A. Green. First located in the basement of Beth El Emeth Congregation, the school was later moved to a rented house at 450 Alabama Street. The group established a sinking fund in August 1929; with a sum of six hundred dollars, it organized a credit union with Aleck Pinstein as president; and purchased a house at 638 Alabama Avenue. The house, remodeled, and named the Farband Culture Center, contained modern classrooms for the school, a library and reading room, a kitchen and dining room, and a small theater to promote literature and art. A mother's club of the Farband was created to participate in all activities.[70]

In the summer of 1925, Leo Goldberger, then not quite twenty-two years old, founded a newspaper for dissemination of information about both local and world events affecting Jewish life. He hoped it would unite the diverse interests and factions of the local Jewish community. The *Hebrew Watchman*, now a fixture of the community, was only one of the ways Godberger worked to unite Memphis Jewry. He worshipped at the

---

[69]*Commercial Appeal*, 10 November 1922; Rhea Gross letter to Memphis Chapter of Hadassah 4 December 1990.
[70]Freda Brode, "History of Haddasah," *Southern Jewish Heritage* 3(July 1989): 5-6.

Orthodox Baron Hirsch synagogue, but he belonged to the Reform Temple Israel, was instrumental in starting the Conservative Beth Sholom synagogue, and was active in the founding of the Jewish Community Center.

Goldberger was involved with the printing business for most of his life. The Goldberger family lived ten or twelve blocks away from the Pinch, which became their primary source of business. The Goldberger Press, which Leo operated along with his brothers Emanuel, Sam, and Milton, later became the Tri-State Press, Incorporated. During World War I, Emanuel Goldberger was in the Marines. Until he returned, Leo ran the press.

Originally named the *Memphis Hebrew*, the paper became the *Hebrew Watchman* following a suggestion by Max Boshwitz, a local poet. The new name referred to the prophet Isaiah's question, "Watchman, what of the night?" and his answer, "The Watchman said, 'The morning cometh.'" The paper was edited for twenty-seven years by Leo's uncle, Milton Goldberger, who turned over its management and editing to Leo in 1955. Leo recalled that "Every member of the family worked or helped, especially during the early days." Some of those family members were Leo's brother Emmanuel, partner with Leo in the Goldberger Printing Company and owner of the Tri-State Press; Herman Goldberger and Sam Goldberger, both practicing attorneys; and Leo's wife, Gertrude Scheinberg Goldberger, who sold subscriptions and gathered news. Leo remained the editor of the *Hebrew Watchman* until his son Herman succeeded him in 1970. Leo was one of the founders and an honorary vice-president of the Jewish Press Association. The National Jewish Press Association honored Leo Goldberger in both 1965 and 1975 for his contributions to Jewish journalism.He received the Joseph Polakoff Award for Integrity in Journalism at the assocation's annual convention in 1987.[71]

Leo's interest in Zionism began early in his life when his sister Regina was secretary of the Memphis Zionist group. Since he had born in 1902, he had witnessed the great influx of Jews from Eastern Europe during the latter years of the nineteenth century, and understood that such immigration would not be allowed to continue indefinitely. This was one of the realities that led Leo to espouse Zionism, a cause for which he worked fervently all his life. He joined the first Young Judaean Club, organized in 1917 under

---

[71]Goldberger, 100-101; *Hebrew Watchman Golden Anniversary Edition*, v. 53, No. 38, 1.

the leadership of Pearl Bauchman. He participated in debating and oratory, and edited the *Southern Judaean*, the official organ of the Southern Young Judaean Region. He was also chairman of the Zionist Youth Council, and later of the Memphis Zionist district from 1953-1955; secretary from 1955-1974; a board member for forty years; and chairman of the Memphis Council for many years. He respresented the Memphis district at both regional and national meetings and was a member of the administrative committee and Board of Governors to the southeastern region for a number of years.

The Memphis Zionist District honored Leo on 18 August 1957; he was honored at at Israel Bond Testimonial Dinner in 1970, recognizing his service in every Israel Bond campaign since inception in 1951. The American Committee for Shaare Zedek Hospital in Israel honored him in 1972, and in 1978 established a blood bank and laboratory in the emergency section of the hospital in his honor.[72]

To address the need for a home for elderly and infirm Jews from the area, the B'nai B'rith Home was founded in 1927 by District Grand Lodge No. 7 of B'nai B'rith, which encompassed seven states—Tennessee, Arkansas, Mississippi, Texas, Alabama, Oklahoma, and Louisiana. Rabbi Max Samfield worked for fifteen years to create such a home, a task in which he was aided by, among others, Leo Bearman Sr., and Charles Haase. Haase, a former B'nai B'rith district president, served as first president of the home. Bearman also served as president. Ground breaking took place in 1926 with Charles Wainman, the father of Josephine Burson, among those participating. Members of Boy Scout Troop No. 25 of Temple Israel were official flag raisers for the ceremony. Aaron Brenner, a member of that troop, later became president of the home.[73]

In its first year the home provided sanctuary for twenty-two people. Most early residents entered the home because they were without financial resources, many having been immigrants who had no relatives in this country, and many having been forced from their own homes by the Great Depression. The requirements for entrance included the stipulation that residents had to be well enough to carry their own bags up the stairs and

---

[72]Dottie Goldberger, *Jewish Historical Society Newsletter*, v. 2, No. 3, 1.

[73]Interview with Leo Goldberger, 1989; *Commercial Appeal*, 3 January 1937; Marvin Silver, "History of B'nai B'rith Home." Unpublished Pamphlet, 1952; Charles Burson speech at dedication of Memphis Jewish Home 7 July 1992.

across the threshold since the facility was designed as a "social umbrella of care rather than a skilled health facility." The home was supervised at that time by Matron Mrs. Harry Wolff, who lived there with her husband, Dr. Harry S. Wolff.

Many of the home's residents helped to ensure that it ran smoothly. Sam Olswing, who had operated a tailor shop on South Main Street, became the official tailor for the home where a tiny shop, open just a few hours each day, was set up for him. Olswing and his wife were the first residents of the home. Joseph Fox did heavy work in the kitchen area while Theresa Epstein, Rosa Lazerowitz, and Rebecca Rosenbaum performed lighter chores. Charles Wolf, a retired barber, opened a one-chair barber shop for the other residents. A mending and darning society made up of residents met three mornings a week.

Both Orthodox and Reform services were held regularly in the home's synagogue which housed, for a while, Memphis's only minyan east of downtown. There were monthly birthday parties with readings, dance recitals and musical presentations by a local group, the Beethoven Club. Resident Amalia Ritterban gave operatic concerts. "Grossmutter" Goldstein came to visit every Saturday with $5 worth of pennies for the weekly Keno game. There was much talking, card playing and radio listening. The home was a lively place. Women of the community visited the residents and hosted parties, picnics, and automobile forays for them. The B'nai B'rith Women, Memphis chapter, led by Ida Lipman, sponsored many activities for the home's benefit, including a community-wide canned goods shower.

Although the home was created totally from money raised in the B'nai B'rith district, and although it retained the name B'nai B'rith Home, in the 1950s, it became an independent non-profit entity. By the early 1960s, a new building was erected in order to meet its residents' needs for medical services which had become an increasingly important component of the care offered. Support through the years has come from individuals, The United Way, and the Memphis Jewish Federation.[74]

The first B'nai B'rith Youth Organization of the America Zionist Association (AZA) was founded in Memphis in 1928, although it had existed nationally since 1924. Its purpose was to help young men develop character and lead productive lives. Locally, Julius Bisno, Aaron Brenner, Fred Goldberg, Joe Allenberg, and Morris Fogelman, among others, felt it

---

[74]Silver, "History."

could be a vehicle to bridge the gap between Orthodox and Reform members. Leo Bearman Sr. helped to obtain the group's charter and Joe Allenberg became the first president of the twenty-three member organization.[75] The Memphis Chapter, No. 71, was named the order's outstanding chapter in 1929.

A second chapter, Israel H. Peres, was formed in 1938. When the demands of World War II reduced the memberships drastically, the chapters merged to become Peres No. 71. Another A.Z.A. chapter, formed in 1947, was called Harry Washer Chapter No. 634. Washer, a member of the 106th Infantry Division of the Armed Forces, died at the age of twenty-two in the Battle of the Bulge. Corporal Washer also was honored by the Memphis Jewish War Veterans who established the Harry Washer Post No. 121.

The Dr. Edward M. Fortas AZA Chapter, formed in 1959, honored the memory of a man who died during the period he served as advisor to the boys. A fourth chapter, named in memory of Lester S. Okeon, who had served in many positions of leadership in the youth community, and was killed in a plane crash, was chartered in 1959. A fifth chapter, established in 1963, was named for an outstanding humanitarian, Leo Levy.[76]

The first Memphis chapter of B'nai B'rith Youth Organization for Girls was founded in 1944, sparked by the interest and enthusiasm of Miriam Weiss and Fanny Brenner Asher. Named for "Ma Brenner," in 1946 it became an official member of the international organization. Bluff City B'nai B'rith for Girls (BBG) became Memphis's second chapter in 1947. It was later renamed in memory of Dr. Ben T. Finebaum whose wife, Gloria, had been its advisor. The third BBG chapter, Rose Belz Kriger, which honored the memory of the talented musician and singer who had led the Sunday School assemblies at Baron Hirsch, was chartered in 1955. The fourth BBG chapter in Memphis was named for Cantor Morris I. Levin, who served Baron Hirsch for thirty-two years. This chapter was chartered in 1960. The fifth chapter, Reena BBG, was joined by a sixth, River City, which was established in 1978.

---

[75]Ibid.

[76]Charter members included those mentioned above, as well as Herbert Shainberg, I. G. Goldsmith, Dave Blumberg, Morris Kemp, Sam Wiener, Izzy Karchmer, Henry Vosse, Theodore Folz, Irving Pelts, Nathan Derman, Sam Goldstein, Joe Wiener, Alfred Scharf, Joe Benewitz, Arthur Hutkin, Fred Cohen, Morris Rosenblum, Newton Green and Charles Schwartz.

The Jewish community in the 1920s made significant contributions to the civic well-being of Memphis. Officers of the Federation of Jewish Charities helped organize the Community Chest fund which they joined in 1923 as one of the charter members. Rabbi Harry W. Ettelson of Temple Israel invited an ecumenical group of clergymen to a meeting at the Peabody Hotel in 1925 to organize the Cross Cut Club. In issuing this invitation, he was fulfilling a pledge made in his installation sermon as Rabbi on 3 April 1925, when he said,

> I shall try . . . to establish fraternal relations and the fullest neighborly contacts with the ministers of all denominations. . . . Let us hope that Protestant, Catholic, and Jew, while each loyal to his convictions, shall in all movements for civic communal betterment, constitute a real holy triple alliance.

The purpose of the club was "to interchange views, to promote mutual understanding, cutting across denominational lines and working towards that understanding and good will which would prevent or soften religious or any other prejudices." Ettelson served as first president of the group, a position he held again twenty-five years later. One of his proposals, was an eve-of-Thanksgiving, non-sectarian service that was implemented for a number of years. The group met at the Nineteenth Century Club where in the 1930s, it held an integrated meeting. The following year, it was not invited to return. The work of the Cross Cut Club, preceding by two years the founding of the National Conference of Christians and Jews (NCCJ), laid a foundation for the establishment of the conference's Memphis chapter in 1932.[77]

Hardwig Peres was a valued public servant and civic supporter. In 1921 he was elected to the board of directors of the Memphis Chamber of Commerce. In 1925 Peres gave twenty-five thousand dollars to Southwestern, later renamed Rhodes College, to create the Israel H. Peres Memorial Scholarship in memory of his younger brother. In 1927, as a result of a poll of its readers conducted by the *Memphis Press Scimitar*, Peres was selected

---

[77]Shankman, "History of Zionism"; Interview with Rabbi Harry Ettelson, Memphis State University, Mississippi Valley Collection, Oral History Project, 1967; Harry E. Moore Jr., "The National Conference of Christians and Jews in Memphis, 1932-1989," *West Tennessee Historical Society Papers*, v. 45, 1991 (Memphis): 52.

as the "Most Valued Citizen of the City." His belief in the equality of all men is illustrated by one of his comments: "I have never considered myself better than any man alive, but I neither consider any man alive better than I am."[78]

The first student to receive a Peres scholarship was Abe Fortas, who went on to pursue a brilliant career in law and as a Justice of the United States Supreme Court. Charles Diehl, president of Southwestern, kept a copy of Fortas's senior thesis on his desk. Fortas and his benefactor, Hardwig Peres, began a friendship that was to be important to both men. They corresponded for many years while Fortas was attending Yale on scholarship, again facilitated by Peres, and during Fortas's government service in Washington in the 1930s and 1940s.

While he was a student at Yale, Fortas met and became a protege of William O. Douglas, who was later appointed to the Supreme Court by President Franklin D. Roosevelt. After his graduation in 1933, Douglas persuaded Fortas to come to Washington where his natural ability propelled him into high positions. At the age of twenty-three, he became a lawyer on the staff of the Agricultural Adjustment Administration. He was a member of Roosevelt's "Brain Trust," a talented group of close advisors.

Fortas became Under-Secretary to Secretary of the Interior Harold Ickes in 1942, a time when Interior was one of the major departments in the cabinet. Like other competent New Dealers, Fortas served in many capacities: as a member of the Food Advisory Committee, the Committee of Legal Personnel of the Civil Service Commission, the Special Committee on International Power, the president's committee to study changes in the Organic Act of Puerto Rico; Acting General Counsel of the National Power Committee, Director of the Virgin Island Company, and secretary of the Petroleum Reserves Corporation.

Fortas's formative years in Memphis had made him aware of the "outrages of the Ku Klux Klan directed against Jews, Catholics, and Negroes." Later, during the McCarthyite 1950s, Fortas's influential law firm (of which he was a partner) defended government employees who were under attack. Eventually he was instrumental in forcing an end to the McCarthy-inspired loyalty boards. Fortas left government in 1945 to form a law partnership with Thurman Arnold, another prominent New Dealer.

---

[78]Moore, "National Conference," 53; "Rhodes Alumni News" (Memphis: Rhodes College) February 1991; *Memphis Chamber of Commerce Journal*, v. 4, 1921.

The landmark case of Gideon vs. Wainwright, which established the right of indigents charged with a felony to be represented by counsel in state courts, was successfully argued before the Supreme Court by Fortas.

When the election of Lyndon Baines Johnson for President of the United States was challenged by Coke Stevenson in Texas, Johnson hired Fortas to represent him. He and Fortas established a close relationship that led Johnson to appoint him to the Supreme Court in 1965. Fortas sat for four years on the Court, where he was considered to be not only good at writing opinions, but also valuable at helping justices arrive at consensus. Johnson named Fortas in 1968 to succeed Earl Warren as Chief Justice, a position in which one of his biographers thought he would have been "formidable."[79] But the Senate Judiciary Committee was leery of Fortas's close ties to Johnson, whom he inappropriately continued to advise even after he was serving on the Court. Johnson was at that time in the last months of his term of office, and some senators felt the next President should be able to make that appointment of Chief Justice of the Supreme Court. There was also a question of the propriety of Fortas's acceptance of a speaking fee. After a Senate fillibuster, Fortas withdrew his nomination.

A few months later a financial dealing with a client, some of whose business Fortas had retained while on the Court, reached public attention when the client, Louis Wolfson, was indicted. Fortas then resigned from the Supreme Court. His actions were not illegal, but they were ethically questionable. Although his accomplishments were sufficient to make Abe Fortas a well-known name and an imposing leader in his field, by an unfortunate combination of choices and circumstances, the Supreme Court lost a talented jurist, and Fortas lost an opportunity to fulfill his great potential.[80]

The realization of a long-cherished dream of another Jewish Memphian expanded the city's medical treatment facilities. Financing his enterprise by selling first, second, and third mortgage bonds to his family and friends, Dr. Louis Levy was able to build an eye, ear, nose, and throat hospital for the benefit of the city. Completed in June of 1926, the hospital was located at 1060 Madison Avenue and was built at a cost of three hundred thousand dollars. A donation in 1928 by Abe Plough in memory of his father made

[79]Interview with Grace Marks, Memphis State University, Oral History Project, 1968.
[80]Berkley Kalin, "Young Abe Fortas," *West Tennessee Historical Society Papers* 34 (1980): 99.

possible the opening of the Moses Plough Memorial Hay Fever Clinic within the Memphis Eye, Ear, Nose, and Throat Hospital. Within three years the hospital earned one of the highest ratings in the country from the American College of Surgeons. Despite the superior care it provided, the facility was plagued by a shortage of funds. At one point a group of Memphis's leading physicians, who formed a corporation to underwrite the deficits, gained control of the hospital, but Levy resumed control the following year and retained management and financial responsibility for the facility until the Methodist Hospital bought it in 1943. In January 1946 the *Councillor*, published by the Memphis Council of Social Agencies, printed an article about Levy entitled "Good Medicine for Memphis," which highlighted his contributions to medicine, the arts, and social welfare.[81]

The nucleus of the print collection at the Memphis Brooks Museum of Art, the basis of the Marcus W. Orr Print Room established in 1990, is the collection of etchings, lithographs, and woodcuts donated by Levy to the museum in 1947. Levy's contributions to the arts were not confined to the visual arts; he served more than one term as president of the Memphis Symphony Society, sponsor of the Memphis Symphony Orchestra, forerunner of the present local symphony orchestra.

For more than one term, Levy was president of the Council of Social Agencies, and he was president of the Tennessee Conference of Social Work. He served as president of the Lions Club; as vice-president of the Jewish Welfare Board of Memphis; and he was a longtime member of the Board of the Federation of Jewish Welfare Agencies. He was president of Sam Schloss Lodge No. 35 of B'nai B'rith and president of Congregation Children of Israel from 1930 to 1937. He was also president of the Zionist District of Memphis.

Despite such an impressive list of contributions in civic and religious affairs, both cultural and charitable, Louis Levy's primary interest was the practice of medicine. A graduate of the University of Tennessee Medical School, he began to practice eye, ear, nose and throat medicine while working at a clinic and teaching. As Memphis became an important regional medical center, Levy recognized the need for an Eye, Ear, Nose, and Throat Hospital. He was the organizing force in building such a facility, as mentioned above. For many years, free of charge, Levy contributed his

---

[81]John Harkins, *Metropolis of the American Nile: Memphis and Shelby County, Tn* (Woodland Hills, Cal.: Windsor Publications, 1982), 201.

time and effort to supervise it.

Levy's interest in promoting racial and religious harmony was evidenced by his membership on the board of directors of the local Conference of Christians and Jews. He also chaired the city's Interracial Committee. In addition, he was an organizer of the Mid-South Sight Conservation Association. He died suddenly at the age of sixty-three in 1952.

Other notable Jewish civic officials in the 1920s were Henry Brenner, Assistant Fire Chief of Memphis, and Morris Solomon, the first Jewish detective employed by the Memphis Police Department. Solomon received national recognition for solving the murder of John E. Levy, "the hot tamale king," with the aid of only one clue, Levy's gray felt hat found at the scene of the crime. Solomon was a World War I veteran, belonged to the Veterans of Foreign Wars, and frequently delivered patriotic speeches on local radio stations.[82]

Although throughout the decade Jewish Memphians continued to assume positions of importance in the life of the city, their recognition of serious anti-Semitism both in America and abroad led them to support Zionism in growing numbers. When a southern branch of the United Palestine Appeal committee was formed to encourage Zionist activity, it included Rabbi Ettelson of Temple Israel who, in a reversal of opinion, had become an advocate for the cause; Rabbi Elijah Stampfer of Baron Hirsch Synagogue; and laymen Dave Dermon, and Sam Steinberg, who were appointed to the advisory committee. Hardwig Peres was named chairman of the Memphis district of the organization. Local events promoted Zionist concerns. Hadassah held a benefit show for the United Palestine Appeal, and the National Zionist Organization met in Memphis to protest to the British government atrocities by Arabs against Jews and to demonstrate that American Jewry was "undeterred in its support of a Jewish homeland." Abe Simon and Hardwig Peres organized the meeting and Sam Shankman, Jake Felt, and Milton W. Goldberger were members of the sponsoring committee.[83] Drawing adherents from all branches of Judaism, Zionism, which earlier had emphasized differences within the Jewish community, now began to serve as a unifying force for Memphis Jewry.

---

[82] *The Councillor*, v. 2, No. 3, January, 1946.

[83] Morris Solomon Papers, Memphis Public Library and Information Service, Memphis Room; *Hebrew Watchman*, 23 November 1928; *Hebrew Watchman* 18 November 1929; *Hebrew Watchman* 15 November 1929.

A PHOTO ALBUM

Tombstone of Samuel E. Andrews, 1846, first burial in the Jewish cemetery of Congregation B'nai Israel. Photograph courtesy of Jan Meyer.

Jacob J. Peres, first rabbi of Congregation B'nai Israel, pictured
in 1852. Photograph from Sam Shankman, *The Peres Family*,
used by permission of Peres's great-granddaughter, Kay Myar.

Elias Lowenstein, member of Congregation B'nai Israel and a committee to restore Memphis to the status of a city after the Yellow Fever epidemics. Photograph courtesy of Memphis Public Library and Information Center (MPLIC).

Lowenstein House, built by Elias Lowenstein as his home, late 1800s. Photograph courtesy of Jan Meyer.

The Arthur N. Seessel Grocery Store, opened in 1863. Photograph courtesy of MPLIC.

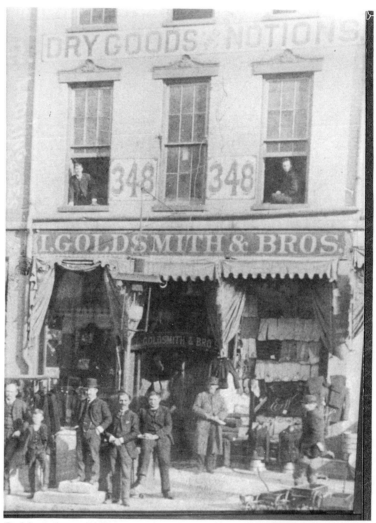

Goldsmith and Brothers Store, opened by Isaac and Jacob Goldsmith in 1870. Photograph courtesy of MPLIC.

Congregation B'nai Israel at 165 Poplar, built in 1883, sold to Beth Emeth in 1917. Photograph courtesy of MPLIC.

Marker for the Pinch Historical District, home for most Eastern European Jewish immigrants. Photograph courtesy Jan Meyer.

Baron Hirsch Cemetery, Abraham Chapel. Photograph courtesy of Jan Meyer.

Abraham Schwab's store—a fixture on Beale Street since 1876. Photograph courtesy of the Center for Southern Folklore (CSF).

Rabbi Max Samfield, leader of Temple Israel, 1871-1915. Photograph courtesy of Temple Israel Archives.

Officers of Temple Israel, at the cornerstone laying of the temple at Poplar and Montgomery Streets, 1915. Photograph courtesy of CSF.

Joseph Newburger home, now the home of Memphis Theological
Seminary. Photograph courtesy of Jan Meyer.

Baron Hirsch Talmud Torah (basic Jewish education class), 1916. Photograph courtesy of CSF.

The Pinch's Baron Hirsch Boy Scout Troop, photographed downtown in the late 1920s. Photo courtesy of the Riki Sachs Collection, CSF.

A. R. CHILDREN'S ORCHESTRA AND TEACHERS

Arbeiter Ring Band and School bus, 1929. Photograph courtesy of CSF.

Doors of Temple Israel, Poplar and Montgomery streets. Photograph courtesy of Jan Meyer.

Baron Hirsch Synagogue, on Vollintine Street, built 1957. Photograph courtesy of Jan Meyer.

Window of Anshei Sphard-Beth El Emeth, on North Parkway, built in 1950. Photograph courtesy of Jan Meyer.

Rabbi Isadore Goodman and unidentified cantor playing the shofar (ram's horn). Photograph courtesy of CSF.

E.I. Segal with his family and employees in front of his delicatessen on Second and Beale Street, c. 1938. Segal Halpern Collection, Center for Southern Folklore Archives

Segal's Delicatessen. Photograph courtesy of CSF.

Rabbi Elijah Stampfer of Baron Hirsch—one of the founders of the
Memphis Hebrew Academy, 1949. Photograph courtesy of CSF.

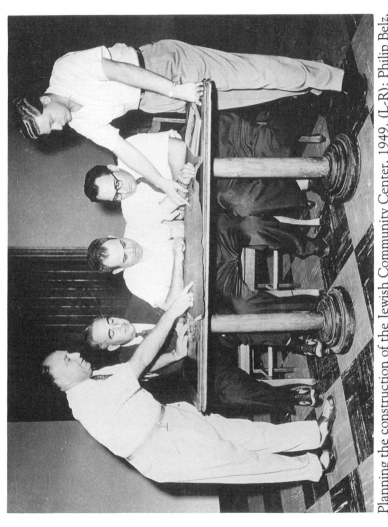

Planning the construction of the Jewish Community Center, 1949. (L-R): Philip Belz, Herbert Kahn, Aaron Brenner, Paul Schwartz, and Jack Belz. Photograph courtesy of CSF.

Louis Levy, M.D., founder of the Memphis Eye, Ear, and Throat Hospital. Photograph courtesy of Evy Levy.

Myra Dreifus, found of the Fund for Needy School Children,
1950s. Photograph courtesy of Jed and Jeanne Dreifus.

Abe Plough, philanthropist and founder of the Plough Company.
Photograph courtesy of his daughter, Jocelyn P. Rudner.

Rabbi James Wax of Temple Israel, civil rights advocate during the 1960s. Photograph courtesy of Temple Israel Archives.

Leo Goldberger, founder of the *Hebrew Watchman*. Photograph courtesy of the Jewish Historical Society of Memphis and the Mid-South.

Nina Katz, Holocaust survivor and proponent of civil rights. Photograph courtesy of the Jewish Historical Society of Memphis and the Mid-South.

Newcomers Club—Holocaust survivors. Photograph courtesy of the CSF.

Belz family and officer of the Belz Corporation. Photograph courtesy of the CSF.

7

SURVIVING THE GREAT DEPRESSION

"The first World War made the Zionist state possible. The second World War made it essential."

—Paul Johnson

The bubble of prosperity that had seemed to be perpetually expanding burst in October 1929. In what has been called "the great crash," shares in the stock market in which many had invested speculatively suddenly plummeted. Millionaires became paupers almost overnight as the possessions they had considered of permanent value became worthless. Real estate holdings changed from assets into liabilities as their owners could not pay the taxes levied on them. It was not uncommon to see formerly wealthy businessmen selling apples on street corners to earn nickels or dimes. Some men committed suicide or left home to wander as stowaways on freight trains because they could no longer support their families.

The disaster was worldwide and it did not spare Memphis. Local businesses experienced declining revenues, a situation that threatened their ability to meet payrolls and other expenses. Already high unemployment increased as most were forced to reduce the number of employees or to pare salaries. Like the general population, many Jewish families suffered through the hard times, struggling just to exist. Some had utilities disconnected because they could not pay their fees and many families had to rely on assistance for the essentials of life.

In the midst of the crisis help came from many sources. As they had in other times of need, Jewish individuals who could do so took care of others who required help. Some grocers, both Jewish and non-Jewish, generously extended credit to enable their customers to avoid hunger. In the Pinch, a neighborly spirit extended beyond religious boundaries. The Catholic Walshes, bachelor brothers John and Anthony, and their sister Marie, provided aid to needy people, including poor Jewish immigrants who needed food, or coal or wood for heating and cooking. The Walshes were cotton brokers who owned a large warehouse at Main and Commerce, as well as a great deal of other property. After they opened the North Memphis Savings Bank, they also offered immigrants business loans. When the husband of an immigrant woman died of cancer, the Walsh family provided free housing for the family; the rest of the Pinch community took up a collection for burial expenses. Leo Goldberger, who delivered newspapers during the Depression to help his family survive the hard times, recalled that the Walshes always paid him a dollar instead of the ten cents they owed him when he collected at the end of the week.[1]

Charitable organizations also suffered the effects of the Depression. As business earnings declined, so did contributions to charities. Like the Walsh family, the *Memphis Jewish Federation* addressed needs that were not purely sectarian even as it remained the chief agency for Jewish assistance. Faced with a deficit, the Memphis Community Fund, the city's umbrella philan-thropic agency, requested in 1931 that the Memphis Jewish Federation reduce salaries and put a moratorium on all but emergency building repairs. The following year a consultant to the Community Fund suggested that the Jewish Federation divest itself of the Jewish Neighborhood House because the Community Fund, with even more limited resources, was no longer able to support it. He made this recommendation in spite of the fact that the Well Baby Clinic was established at Neighborhood House at the suggestion of the Memphis Board of Health to serve both Jewish and non-Jewish women who were not receiving adequate benefits from the clinic at the General Hospital. In order to follow the recommendation of the consultant, yet at the same time to continue the services provided by the Well Baby Clinic, the Jewish Federation established the Worker's Council of Jewish Neighborhood House, a women's group, as a separate entity. The Worker's Council was incorporated on 19 February 1932, by Estelle Goodman, Hortense Jacobs, Vera Block, and Louise Cohn.[2]

A second social welfare organization was born out of Depression-related need. Large-scale national unemployment caused by the Depression created additional problems in the city as many transients, predominantly men, passed through in their wanderings from place to place in search of jobs. The Jewish Federation appointed a special committee in 1930 to discuss ways and means of meeting this new and growing concern. A group of men

---

[1]Schaeffer interview; Goldberger interview.
[2]Minutes of Jewish Federation.

led by Harry Wolf responded to the transients' situation in 1931 by creating the Young Men's Hebrew Relief Organization; its stated goal was "helping transients to help themselves." William Engelberg was elected president. The Community Fund, thirty percent short of its goal in 1933, was again forced to ask for drastic reductions in the Jewish Federation's budget. It specified that salaries were to be reduced to two-thirds of those paid in 1929. The Federation complied, but restored the salary of its executive director, Miss Miriam Goldbaum, out of its reserve funds.[3]

Synagogues suffered also, as their members' reduced incomes forced them to trim their contributions. Some members even felt it necessary to resign. The young Baron Hirsch congregation was heavily strained by the many resignations of Reform members who had been its patrons. Its Talmud Torah suspended operations for lack of funds. Board meetings of Temple Israel centered on finding the means to sustain the congregation financially during the stringent times. Rabbi Harry Ettelson asked that his salary be reduced in 1931, and in 1933 he requested a further reduction. In 1933 Rabbi Morris Taxon of Baron Hirsch, whose five-year contract provided a yearly salary increase, agreed to continue to serve with no increase. The cantor's salary, and the salaries of all other employees, were cut at all synagogues. Many Sunday school teachers taught without pay. Students shared in the hard times that plagued their elders. Many had to postpone or forgo higher education. Those who continued their schooling usually did so at considerable sacrifice for themselves and their families. Leo Burson was typical of many young people who worked selling shoes or waiting tables or in any jobs they could find in order to remain in school. Some, like Abe Fortas, were able to go to college only with the aid of scholarship funds.[4]

Although the economic hard times affected the whole community, most individuals continued to function and outstanding youths of the Depression rose to success. Two became officers of Humko Corporation and played important roles, not only in their primary occupations in the industry, but also in civic affairs. S. L. Kopald Jr., who served as president of Temple Israel, and later as chairman of the Board of Trustees of Hebrew Union College, also became chairman of the Republican Party of Tennessee, vice-

---

[3]Minutes of Jewish Federation, 8 September 1930 and 3 February 1930; *Hebrew Watchman*, 23 April 1930.

[4]Interview with Rabbi Mark Levin, 1991; Sam Shankman, *Baron Hirsch*, 94, 96; Wax, *Our First Century*, 48; Interview with Leo Burson, 1989.

president of the Memphis Chamber of Commerce, a member of the Board
of Directors of the Federal Reserve Bank of St. Louis, and chairman of the
fund drive of the United Way. Sam Cooper began his career with Humko
as an office boy while still in high school, later becoming president of the
company.[5]

Cooper was born in 1911 in New York City. The family moved to
Memphis at the invitation of Cooper's uncle, who had a tailor shop in the
Pinch. Like most other residents of that area, the family was poor. Cooper
went to work as soon as he could, carrying newspapers and selling soda pop
at the baseball park. While in high school at Humes, he took some business
courses, learning typing and shorthand, which led to his being hired by
Humko, which was just getting started. He was hired as an office boy and
a bookkeeper,

> at an office boy's salary of $10 a week. I wasn't worth any more
> because I didn't know how to keep books. Every day at the end of
> business, I would go to night school and take all our papers,
> vouchers, and invoices, and sit down with the professor. He would
> tell me whom to debit and what to credit.

At the end of the month, the professor showed him how to make a profit
and loss statement; this continued until he "got the swing of it"— about
two or three months. From this starting job, Cooper rose to become
president of Humko from 1952 until 1976, when he retired to become
president of Grafco, Incorporated.

When the Federal Reserve Bank dedicated its new building in
Memphis, the president of the Board of Directors was ill, so vice-president
Sam Cooper presided. It was a satisfying moment for him to announce to
the distinguished guests that the new structure was on the very site where
his father's tailor shop had formerly stood. Cooper's commitment to causes
in which he believes and his fund-raising ability won for him President
George Bush's Thousand Points of Light Award, a recognition for outstanding volunteer service. Among his other awards were the Rotary Club's Civic
Award in 1972; Junior Achievement's Master of Free Enterprise Award in
the same year; an honorary Doctorate in Humanities from Christian
Brothers University in 1976; the Sertoma Club's Service to Mankind Award

---

[5]Interview with S. L. Kopald, 1990; Interview with Sam Cooper, 1992.

in 1977. The Jewish National Hospital honored him in 1983. He was named Memphis Volunteer of the Year in 1985. He received the Senior Citizen Award of the Council on Aging in 1990, the year in which he was also awarded the National Society of Fund-Raising Executives Award. He headed the campaign of Shelby United Neighbors (SUN) in 1961, which he agreed to do if SUN would invite blacks to serve on the board of directors, which they did.

Cooper's favorite public service was raising funds for cancer research. The father of four daughters, he and his wife Frankie lost their second-born, Beverly Howard, to the disease when she was a young mother. He has worked to raise money for both the University of Tennessee and St. Jude Children's Research Hospital. A wing of the hospital was named for him in 1976. Cooper was instrumental in St. Jude's decision to remain in Memphis. His friendship with Lamar Alexander, governor of Tennessee, facilitated Alexander's obtaining $25,000,000 of public revenue to upgrade facilities at the University of Tennessee Medical School, which in turn encouraged the hospital to remain in Memphis.

Among other efforts, Cooper worked to create an endowment fund to secure the future of Temple Israel, of which he was president from 1967 to 1972, and was made honorary President for Life in 1983. He was campaign chairman of the Memphis Arts Council in 1966, and served on the board of the Tennessee Arts Commission from 1968 to 1969. He helped to secure a warehouse for the Memphis Food Bank. In 1968 the city named one of its ten expressways the Sam Cooper Boulevard.[6]

Despite the Depression, some new businesses and institutions opened in Memphis. Elkan Hohenberg, recognizing the city's importance to the cotton business, moved his organization from Alabama to Memphis in 1932. Formerly named M. Hohenberg after Morris Hohenberg, one of its founders, the company in 1943 was incorporated as Hohenberg Brothers Company. International in scope, it became in 1975 a subsidiary of Cargill, Incorporated, a large, privately-owned international trading and processing corporation headquartered in Minneapolis. Hohenberg's officers have played a large role in encouraging charitable, artistic, cultural, and religious affairs in Memphis.[7]

---

[6]Interview with Sam Cooper.
[7]John Harkins, *Metropolis of the American Nile: Memphis and Shelby County* (Woodland Hills, Ca.: Windor Press, 1982), 194.

Sam Margolin founded Southern Law School. After graduating in 1929 from night law school at Memphis Law School, he opened a law practice. At the same time, he began to coach a group of students in preparation for their state bar examinations. All of Margolin's students passed. He applied to teach at Memphis Law School, but it declined to hire him. Two years later he decided to open his own law school, modeled on the one he had attended. He operated Southern Law School from its opening in 1931 until it became a part of Memphis State University (now University of Memphis) in 1964. (Memphis Law School had already joined University of Memphis in 1962.) The last class of Southern to graduate under that name did so in 1966, by which time the institution had awarded degrees to 1,000 lawyers.[8] Margolin commented:

> The Southern Law School meant a great deal to me. I knew that there were many others, like me, who would never have the opportunity of becoming lawyers unless they could study in the evenings after working all day. I realized that the standards of evening classes had to be elevated so that the general public would have a greater respect for the graduates.

Another of Sam Margolin's primary interests was the National Mortgage Company, a family-owned concern. The company's origins can be traced to 1945, when Margolin's brothers Ben and Joe left their respective occupations and entered the construction business. Margolin decided to join them. The National Mortgage Company, specializing in home mortgages, was established in 1951 as an outgrowth of the original venture. Ben Margolin died in 1975, followed by Joe in 1985, which left Sam the sole surviving brother. All have descendants, however, who participate in the business.[9]

All three Margolin brothers helped found the Memphis Hebrew Academy in 1949; in 1992 the name was changed to Margolin Hebrew Academy/Yeshiva of the South. Sam Margolin, who served for many years as Chairman of the Board, believed that the Jewish day school movement is an important factor in the relatively large Orthodox movement in Memphis. Margolin was president of Baron Hirsch synagogue in the 1950s.[10]

---

[8] Interview with Sam Margolin, 1991.
[9] David Yawn, *Memphis Business Journal*, 27 April and 1 May 1992.
[10] Margolin interview.

Simon and Gwin Advertising Agency originated in 1936. Milton Simon realized that he had "gone as far as he could go" at radio station WMC, and he convinced a somewhat reluctant non-Jewish partner, Norburne Gwin, to join him in creating a new advertising agency. It was a risky time to embark on such an enterprise and Simon described the difficulties of the era. "It was a period of great frustration," he said. Budgets for advertising were so much reduced, that "for six months we barely existed. Salaries were so low, income so hard to come by. So, all you could do was hold on until better times came." The partners persevered, and by 1939 their efforts were becoming profitable.[11]

That same year Lew Weinberg opened a clothing business. He rented a store at Main and Gayoso for two hundred dollars a month and held expenses down by "doing everything himself." He made a profit of two thousand dollars the first year he was in business. In many ways, Weinberg said, it was a "fortunate time for business to get started because rents were low, people trusted each other, you could get credit, and you could deal directly with the manufacturer." He believes that the World War I soldiers' bonuses, paid out in 1936, gave a boost to the clothing market.

Weinberg's store, which bore his name, was one of the first to cater to customers of all races. Most merchants of the period, including Jewish merchants, would not allow blacks to try on apparel before buying it. Weinberg believed that this policy was inhumane and demeaning, and he made a deliberate effort to welcome blacks. He says he "had a love affair with his customers." For more than fifty years, Weinberg's created many black fashions that were adopted in other sections of the country.[12]

Nat Buring founded the Nat Buring Packing Company in 1937. Producing meats under the King Cotton label, the firm became a successful food company with plants in Memphis, New Orleans, and Arkansas. Growing up in the Pinch, Nat organized a baseball team at Market Square, serving as both manager and third baseman. In 1955 he bought the Memphis Chicks, the city's minor league team. Unfortunately, Russwood Park, where the team played, was accidentally burned to the ground. It was uninsured, so the total loss ended his venture. He remained an ardent sports fan, however, supporting sports programs in the Memphis public schools and at Memphis State University.

---

[11]Interview with Milton Simon, 1991.
[12]Interview with Lew Weinberg, 1992.

Buring's philanthropies included St. Jude's Children's Research Hospital and projects in the primarily black Orange Mound neighborhood. He received the Junior Achievement Master of Free Enterprise Award in 1973. He was honored by Anshei Sphard Beth El Emeth synagogue, which named its educational building for him in its site on North Parkway; the Sylvia Buring Social Hall at the present-day site is dedicated to his first wife.[13]

While some entrepreneurs defied financial hardships of the Depression by starting businesses, others tackled social issues of the era by starting organizations. In an effort to counteract religious prejudice, the Memphis branch of the National Conference of Catholics, Jews, and Protestants met for the first time on 26 May 1932. Its second meeting in June 1993, billed "The Memphis Good Will Meeting," protested the rise of Hitler in Germany and of an American fascist organization known as the Silver Shirts.[14]

On 2 April 1930, twenty-three women met at the home of Esther Kempner to form a local chapter of the National Council of Jewish Women. First organized in 1893 at the Chicago World's Fair, Council, as it was known, allowed Jewish women to work together to accomplish common goals that would not have been possible for them to achieve individually. The organization appealed mostly to German Jewish women. Beatrice Stern was unanimously elected first president of the Memphis Section. In addition, she served on its national board for years. She was a member of the board of directors of the Health and Welfare Planning Council of the Memphis Community Fund (now the United Way), the organization concerned with long-range plans for agencies serving the city's needs. During World War II she was in charge of publicity for the American Red Cross and worked as a volunteer for Family Service of Memphis and for Traveler's Aid.[15]

From the beginning the Memphis Section of Council sought to provide aid to the local community and to further the goals of the parent organization in regard to national issues. It worked by conducting study groups on selected topics, then acting on its findings. Of its first two groups, one was concerned with children, the other with drama. Combining its missions and its interest in children, the chapter undertook as its first project the establishment of a summer playschool for underprivileged children; Sylvia

---

[13] *Hebrew Watchman*, 3 December 1992.

[14] *Hebrew Watchman*, 2 June 1933.

[15] Marcus, United States Jewry, vol. 4, 401. Interview with Dr. Thomas N. Stern

Kremer was its chairman. The chapter later developed the Leath School lunch program, through which daily lunches were provided for forty needy children.[16] The Memphis section also participated in the national organization's program to bring two hundred fifty German Jewish children to live in the United States.

Despite the hard times that might have made them turn inward, Jewish individuals and groups continued to focus their efforts outward to the welfare of the city as a whole. The Regina Health Center, in association with the City of Memphis Health Department, opened the Well Baby Clinic in the Binghampton area of the city in 1931. It was "a very valuable service." Alberta Rudner, was clinic president. Pediatricians voluntarily provided monthly check-ups, immunizations, and tuberculosis tests for children from tubercular families. The clinic also dispensed cod liver oil and milk. In a period of two months, one hundred sixty-five children were treated.[17]

Jewish Neighborhood House also served the community. In addition to providing naturalization classes for refugees, it offered a free kindergarten, access to the Well Baby Clinic, and a variety of youth activities. Among the latter was a Girl Scout troop whose members were from immigrant families living in the Pinch. Dorothy Waldauer and Hazel Seessel served as the Girl Scout Committee of Jewish Neighborhood House.[18] The leader of the troop was a non-Jewish volunteer, Lula Coffey, who wanted the girls to feel responsible for "paying their own way"; consequently, dues were set at two cents a week, a sum all could afford. Under Coffey's guidance, the scouts participated in a city-wide competition for all scouting skills including signaling, first aid, and tree identification. Because the competition took place on a Saturday, scouts who observed the Sabbath had to walk a distance of several miles, from Second and Market Streets to Overton Park Avenue, where the event was held. In spite of the extra hike, the troop from Jewish Neighborhood House won the competition. Its members included Fannie and Dorothy Kipper, Frances and Blema Tennebaum, Miriam Goldstein, Rose and Ethel Salky, and Miriam Siegel.

Clothes for children were provided by The Pauline Levy Circle Dollar Shoe Club, newly organized at Christine School in Market Square as well

---

[16]"History of Memphis Chapter, National Council of Jewish Women."

[17]*Hebrew Watchman*, 23 March 1933; Jewish Federation Minutes 4 July 1933.

[18]Interview with Lula Coffey, 1990.

as by The Pauline Levy Sewing Circle, founded twenty years earlier. Sewing circle members originally met twice a month to sew for charity, but recognizing "an unprecedented demand for clothing" born of Depression-era conditions, began to meet weekly. During the entire existence of the Dollar Shoe Club, Hattie Brooks was president.

The Jewish Welfare Fund was incorporated in 1935. Its mission was to raise money, and it became the second primary agency in the Jewish community, joining the already-established Federation of Jewish Welfare Agencies, the social service arm. Eventually the Federation of Jewish Welfare Agencies changed its name to reflect more accurately its role as the community's central agency for record keeping and planning as well as for service. It adopted the name Jewish Service Agency, then later, Jewish Family Service, in accord with the name used by most similar agencies elsewhere. Over the years this agency has responded to the changing and diverse needs of the Jewish community. It served refugees fleeing the Holocaust, Vietnam veterans, and Russian immigrants. Its programs include its own adoption service, established in 1959, and career planning.[19]

The religious community of Memphis remained active in the 1930s despite the reduced circumstances of the synagogue. Rabbi Harry Ettelson of Temple Israel participated in a 1932 debate entitled "Is Religion Necessary?" at Ellis Auditorium. Ettelson argued for the affirmative against the famous attorney, Clarence Darrow, who took the negative position. Darrow, an atheist, had been chief of the defense in the historic Scopes trial of 1925 in which John Scopes, a school teacher in Dayton, Tennessee, was convicted of teaching the theory of evolution in the public schools of that community. The *Press Scimitar* reported that it was "a poor debate, but a mighty good show." The B'nai B'rith Home received some of the proceeds from the event.[20]

In addition, a small but fervent group continued to work for the aid of Palestine. In 1929 Sam Shankman wrote *The Peres Family*, a book that contained introductions by Abe Fortas and Rabbi Stephen S. Wise. Shankman contributed profit from the book to the Jewish National Fund, to support that organization's planting of trees in the desert of Palestine. In

---

[19]Jack Lieberman speech to Jewish Service Agency, Lieberman personal papers, Memphis, TN.
[20]Richard Morris, *Encyclopedia of American History* (New York: Harper and Row, 1953), 586; *Press Scimitar* 5 January 1932, 1; *Hebrew Watchman*, 21 January 1932.

1932, Zionist Council was formed, with Hardwig Peres as acting president. At a celebration of Peres's eightieth birthday held at Temple Israel in 1939, the two thousand attendees were informed that a colony in Palestine was to be named the Peres Colony in honor of its veteran supporter. Rabbi Stephen S. Wise of New York City, a leader of the Zionist movement and featured speaker for the evening, accepted a check from Peres for fifteen thousand dollars to purchase land for the colony. Abe Plough was named chairman of a campaign to raise an additional $30,000 to fund the Peres Colony.[21]

For the most part, southern Jews rarely thought of themselves as belonging to a distinct people seeking for national existence. Nor did they consider themselves to be members of a separate group called Hebrews. In the first half of the twentieth century, anti-Zionism was probably more prevalent in the South than in other Jewish communities. Of the twenty rabbis on the original board of the American Council for Judaism, the core of organized opposition to Jewish nationalism, a third were from the South.[22]

On the Sunday afternoon in 1930 following Great Britain's issuing of the so-called White Paper limiting Jewish immigration to Palestine, a "well-attended" protest meeting took place at the Menorah Institute. Jewish and non-Jewish community leaders voiced their opposition to what they saw as a betrayal of the Jews, and a committee was appointed to send a telegram to Secretary of State Cordell Hull. In an uncommon gesture of unity, Sam Abraham, Jake Felt, Rabbi Morris Taxon of Baron Hirsch and Rabbi Harry Ettelson of Temple Israel spoke at the meeting.[23]

Although the Depression cast a pervasive shadow over the 1930s, day-to-day life continued much as before for most members of the Jewish community. Over the course of the decade, people became accustomed to hard times and learned to live with the new realities. They continued to marry and have children, attend to their businesses, practice their religion, and participate in the life of the community. Heroic efforts were sometimes required and did occur, but for many, ordinary life went on. For Jewish Memphians, ordinary life included leadership roles in civic endeavors. Even during those difficult years, Memphis's Jews contributed to the larger

---

[21]*Hebrew Watchman*, 2 May 1939; *Hebrew Watchman*, 19 February 1932.
[22]Myron Berman, "Rabbi Nathan Calisch and the Debate over Zionism in Richmond, Virginia," *American Jewish Historical Quarterly*, 62, March 1973, 301.
[23]*Hebrew Watchman*, 21 May 1931.

community in a wide range of fields.

Among those Jewish citizens who occupied positions of leadership in Memphis's civic life was Fletcher Gans Cohn, a prominent attorney and member of the 1930 Tennessee General Assembly. Abe Goodman, who formerly had been a member of the board of directors of the Memphis Park Commission, was elected to the board of directors of Oakville Sanitarium in 1932.[24] David Asher Levy was one of those concerned about the serious problems made worse by the Depression. He was chairman both of the Board of Mendicants and of the Board of Advisors of the Negro Council of Social Welfare Groups.

Edward M. Salomon, president and general manager of Bry's department store and president of the Peabody Civic Club, was honored by the Civic Clubs of Memphis as the most outstanding president of any such organization in the city. In 1930 Salomon worked to solve problems of unemployment as a member of Governor Horton's staff. He was elected Grand Ruler of Memphis Lodge of Elks in 1932. In 1933 Joseph Bearman became Assistant United States District Attorney. In 1935 Will Gerber succeeded Walter Chandler as City Attorney when Chandler was elected to Congress, and Gerber, in turn, was succeeded on the City Commission by Ralph Picard, who trimmed his mustache in honor of the occasion. Joseph Hanover became attorney general of Shelby County in 1939, and attorney Abe Waldauer was appointed by President Franklin D. Roosevelt as collector of customs for the Tennessee-Arkansas district of the United States. Waldauer also served as assistant district attorney and president of the State Board of Elections.[25] Abe Fortas, officially assistant to the secretary of the interior, Harold Ickes, was unofficially a member of President Roosevelt's intimate circle of advisors, the so-called Brain Trust.

Sophie Goldberger Friedman, the sponsor of several bills in the Tennessee State Legislature, was a member of the Committee to Elect Roosevelt in 1933. She was listed in "Who's Who of Clubwomen in Tennessee," as was Raye Gattman, editor of the group's magazine, the *Tennessee Club Woman*, and vice-president of the Tennessee Federation of Women's Clubs.[26]

---

[24]*Hebrew Watchman*, 12 January 1933.

[25]Milton Goldberger, "Loves," unpublished; *Commercial Appeal*, 11 January 1936; *Commercial Appeal*, 1 January 1937; *Bench and Bar of Memphis*, v.3, 239.

[26]*Hebrew Watchman*, February 1937; *Hebrew Watchman*, 7 May 1930.

M. A. Lightman Sr., was re-elected president of the Motion Picture Theater Owners of America in 1932. A banquet on 2 November 1933, honored A. D. Bearman, brother of Joseph Bearman, upon his election as grand master of the Progressive Order of the West. Milton S. Binswanger, Sr., was elected president of the Memphis Natural Gas Company in the same year. Dr. Marcus Spingarn, an instructor at the University of Tennessee Medical School, was elected president of the Memphis Urological Society in 1932. Joseph Altfater, president of the Tennessee Auto Wreckers and Parts Association, became national vice-president of the organization. Isaac (Ike) Myers created Arts Appreciation in the early 1930s to underwrite art productions in Memphis.[27]

Myers's goal was to give Memphis children the opportunity to see, hear, and enjoy the arts. To accomplish this, for twenty-nine years, from 1931 until his death in 1960, by means of Arts Appreciation he brought annual performances of the Metropolitan Opera Company and many other fine artists to Memphis. Myers had been a partner with his brother in a paper and distribution business, Mayer Myers Paper Company. After the partnership ended, Myers formed his own I. L. Myers Paper Company in 1939. As his passion for the arts grew, his business appeared to be for the purpose of underwriting artistic productions for the city. He assisted both individuals and organizations, among them the Memphis College of Music and the Memphis Symphony Orchestra. He periodically brought exhibits of high quality to Brooks Memorial Gallery. For years he was President of the Board of Trustees of the Memphis Art Academy, whose first student yearbook was dedicated to him.[28]

Myers had international connections in the world of art. He received one of the highest of European civilian awards when he was made a Chevalier in the Legion of Honor of France in 1951. This award was given to Myers for his help in the restoration of French art museums after World War II, for arranging four tours of French art centers, and for his "great contribution to a better knowledge of French contemporary painting in the United States."[29]

---

[27]*Hebrew Watchman*, 24 March 1932; Interview with Milton S. Binswanger Jr., ; *Hebrew Watchman*, 15 December 1932; *Hebrew Watchman*, 9 August 1934.

[28] Ike Myers Interview by Berkeley Kalin, 8 December 1968; *Memphis Art Academy Student Yearbook*, July, 1961.

[29]*Commercial Appeal*, 12 August 1946; 23 May 1948; 2 June 1951; 4 September 1960.

Also in the early thirties, Louis Morris became a squire of the Shelby County Court. Ira J. Lichterman was appointed in 1937 to the board of directors of the Memphis Light and Water Commission.[30] Sam Kahn, who traced his roots to the older town of Bolivar, Tennessee, was appointed Sunday editor of the *Commercial Appeal* in 1939.

A. Arthur Halle Sr., the president of Phil A. Halle, the clothing firm begun and operated by his family, served as a member of the Auditorium Commission. Concerned because "the bottom had fallen out of the cotton market," on which Memphis heavily depended, Halle invited his friend Everett Cook, the president of the Memphis Cotton Exchange, and Palace Theater manager Herbert Jennings to discuss ways and means of helping the city recover. By the time the meeting ended several hours later, "the office was ankle-deep in peanut shells, and the Memphis Cotton Carnival was born." Among those on the committee to raise money for the Carnival were Avrome Boshwit and B. W. Hirsch Jr.; Saul Bluestein arranged for the music. Alice Goodman worked on the parade itself; "the Goodman boys"— Charles, Abe Jr., and William—donated piece goods for smocks and costumes. Eric Hirsch and other cotton men also contributed. Hirsch, an accomplished worker in wood, built the carriage for the first queen of the Cotton Carnival. The Memphis Cotton Carnival, conceived to provide a "shot in the arm" for suffering business, became an annual event in the city, leading to the establishment in Memphis in 1938 of the National Cotton Council.[31]

As if the Depression were not enough, the 1937 flood of the Mississippi and Ohio Rivers caused the Mississippi River to crest at a record height of 48.7 feet on February 10, adding to the city's woes. Memphians responded by building levees and piling sandbags, and with the exception of parts of north Memphis, most of the city was spared. But health problems arose as twenty thousand refugees streamed in from flooded areas of Arkansas and Missouri. Of the five thousand persons housed at a refugee center at the Fairgrounds in January, five hundred were ill. Schools became hospitals. The American Red Cross converted Bethany Home, in normal times a residence for unwed mothers, into an emergency maternity hospital. Among

[30]Interviews with Martin Lichterman and Herbert Lichterman, 1991.

[31]Harkins, 131; Everett R. Cook, *Everett R. Cook: A Memoir* (Memphis: Memphis Public Library, 1971) 110-111; Arthur Halle Sr., "History of the Memphis Cotton Carnival," *West Tennessee Historical Society Papers*, vol. 6, 34, 49; Interview with Leah Hirsch, 1992.

those who volunteered to help there was Eulalie Meyer. Baron Hirsch Congregation sponsored a dance for the benefit of flood victims and urged the entire Memphis Jewish community to support its effort.[32]

In the field of medicine Jewish physicians were contributing organizational skills and innovative medical procedures in the 1930s. Dr. Neuton Stern was a founder of the American Heart Association and of the local Heart Association, as well as of the Memphis Academy of Medicine, an organization of internists. He was the editor of the Memphis *Medical Journal* and the author of several books, among them *Physical and Clinical Diagnosis: Rare Diseases, Bases of Treatment*, with son and co-author, Dr. Thomas Neuton Stern. In the 1940s he made a vital contribution to the ability of physicians to make accurate diagnoses when he brought to Memphis the first electrocardiograph machine in the southern United States. To honor his seventy-fifth birthday, his students, friends, and patients endowed a visiting professorship at the University of Tennessee Medical School where he was a clinical professor. The gift provides for an annual lecture by an outstanding cardiologist. In 1992 Stern's son and daughter-in-law, Harriet Wise Stern, endowed the Dr. Neuton Stern Chair of Cardiology at the same school.

Dr. Charles Olim also helped improve medical services in Memphis. From 1937 to 1939, during his internship at John Gaston Hospital, Olim became concerned about patients who bled to death as a result of wounds or surgery. To reduce the risk to patients from loss of blood, Olim organized a blood bank at John Gaston, modeling the facility on one that had been developed at Cook County Hospital in Chicago. It was the first blood bank in Memphis and probably the first in the state.[33]

During the Great Depression some women who had never before worked outside their homes sought jobs to help with family finances. Many became teachers. Among the Jewish women who are fondly remembered by their students are Florence Dreyfous, Eva Hahn, and Rebecca Cohen. Non-Jewish attorney Jerred Blanchard harbors a particular feeling of warmth and gratitude toward Miss Cohen, who taught speech at Central High School, generally regarded as Memphis's college preparatory public school.

---

[32] *Life Magazine*, 8 February 1937; *Hebrew Watchman*, February 1937.

[33] Interview with Dr. Charles Olim, 1991; Marcus Stewart, M.D., William T. Black, M.D., eds. and Mildred Hicks, co-editor, *History of Medicine in Memphis* (Jackson: McComat and Mercer Press, Inc., 1971), 193.

Blanchard was one of her best pupils. One day, toward the end of his senior year, he recalls that Miss Cohen asked him where he intended to go to college. When Blanchard replied that family financial hardships were forcing him to go to work instead, Miss Cohen asked him to see her after school, at which time she took him to see Hardwig Peres who arranged for him to receive a scholarship to Yale University. Blanchard received his degree from Yale and returned to Memphis to practice law. He served as a member of the city council.[34]

One of the pressing issues of the 1930s that aroused concern within the Jewish community was the plight of the laboring man. The Arbeiter Ring established a credit union to provide its members with easy access to loans. In 1933 an important figure in the local labor movement, Jake Cohen, formerly president of the Tennessee Federation of Labor, became president of the Memphis *Labor Review*. In the same year, he supervised a Labor Day celebration in which more than twenty thousand workers paraded down Main Street to Ellis Auditorium to hear an address about combating the Depression by Donald Richberg, chief counsel for the National Recovery Administration and one of President Roosevelt's spokesmen.[35]

Most Memphians and most Jews of the era agreed with Boss Crump's view of labor unions. Crump had fought determinedly to keep the CIO out of Memphis and tolerated the AFL only as long as it behaved in a manner he considered acceptable, which meant that it offered no threat to existing conditions. Police Chief Will Lee was in charge of enforcing Crump's opposition to industrial unions. When the Southern Tenant Farmers Union (STFU), a part of the CIO, conducted strikes against nearby Arkansas cotton planters, it coordinated these protests from its headquarters in Memphis. Lee instructed his men to prevent union organizers from crossing the Mississippi River into Arkansas. Local fears that the STFU was a radical organization were fed by the fact that socialist leader Norman Thomas was one of its founders in Arkansas. Of particular concern to many Memphians, especially to members of other unions, was the fact that the STFU not only accepted black sharecroppers as members, but actually allowed them to hold positions in the union hierarchy. After a ten-year struggle to prevent the establishment of industrial unions in "his" city, Crump declared, "We aren't

---

[34]Interview with Jerred Blanchard, 1992.

[35]*Hebrew Watchman*, 31 May 1932; *Hebrew Watchman*, 7 September 1933.

going to have any CIO nigger unions in Memphis."[36]

In the face of such outspoken opposition, Herman Goldberger courageously agreed to become the attorney for the STFU in Arkansas, a position others had refused. In 1933 Crump henchman, Police Commissioner Clifford Davis, accused Goldberger of being a Communist. Three years later Goldberger drove to Nashville to defend a black man despite his receipt of an anonymous telephone call warning him not to go. He was killed en route in a one-car accident. His family always believed that he was murdered by being forced off the road.[37] The truth is not known, but it is known that Goldberger, like so many Memphis Jews before him, worked to improve the lot of those less fortunate.

During the 1930s all segments of the Jewish community made valiant attempts to alleviate suffering, both individual and communal. In many of these efforts Jews worked closely with Memphians of other faiths. But despite their shared compassion, Jews and Christians remained separate in spheres of religious observance and social life. As the 1930s ended, the Memphis Jewish community itself was also divided, as it had been, between those whose roots were in Germany and those from Eastern Europe. German Jews, for the most part, had enjoyed ascendance. But this status was to change in the next few years as Eastern European Jews, despite a later start, attained or surpassed the business successes of their German counterparts. The ideological division among Memphis Jews, still pronounced, was especially evident at the time in relation to the issue of support for Palestine. With a few notable exceptions, most Zionists were still from the Orthodox community. Change was also to come in this area, as Jews learned from the Holocaust that they were all alike in the eyes of an oppressor.

The entry of the United States into World War II in December 1941 made official American opposition to the Nazi regime and lifted the country out of the Depression. As America equipped itself for the confrontation against Germany and Japan, the economy began to improve. In Memphis, unemployment declined in response to the location in the area of a number of military installations, including the headquarters of the Second United States Army and the naval base at Millington. Several businesses converted

---

[36]Roger Biles, *Memphis in the Great Depression* (Knoxville: University of Tennessee Press, 1986) 108, 119.
[37]Interviews with Harold Friedman and Herman Goldberger, 1991.

to military production creating in the process a more diverse manufacturing base for the city. Cotton sales were high, as people and money began to return to the city from the surrounding areas. The Community Fund allocated $19,280 to the Jewish Federation for fiscal year 1943-1944, an increase of 7.4 percent over the previous year and a reflection of the improving economy. The war also brought loss to the Jewish community as it did to the non-Jewish community. Most Jewish men of appropriate age and health served in the armed forces. As one veteran put it, "Everybody served." Many lost their lives.[38]

Corporal Harry Washer, killed in 1945 in Belgium in the Battle of the Bulge, was one of the war heroes of the Memphis Jewish community. Washer was a member of a unit captured in a surprise attack by German troops who broke through the Allied line dressed as American soldiers. The Germans ordered the captured Americans to remove the tags identifying them as Jewish. Washer, a boy scout leader and a scholar of Hebrew, Torah, and Talmud who had a scholarship to study at Yeshiva University before war was declared and who overseas served as both chaplain and cook, refused to obey the order denying his Judaism and was shot by German soldiers.[39] Memphis Post No. 121 of Jewish War Veterans, established on 4 April 1981, through the efforts of Bernie Leviton is named for Washer.

Sam Weintraub was another who made an important contribution to the conduct of the war. While stationed in the Pacific, he was ordered with finding all Japanese who remained on the island of Tinian after the 1944 bombing and marine invasion that had routed most of the island's nine thousand soldiers and fifteen thousand civilians. Weintraub said that although he and his staff were "hunting Japs, when I was finally in charge, we didn't fire a single shot for three or four months." Through cajolery and persuasion, the Tinian Hunt Club, as Weintraub's group was called, was able to accomplish its task without gunfire. The group's use of psychological warfare offered an effective method of fighting that saved many lives, both Japanese and American. Weintraub became a partner in a national labor law firm based in Memphis.[40]

Air Force Captain Max Halle Mayer, a much-decorated Memphian,

---

[38]Biles, *Memphis*, 121; Minutes of Jewish Federation, 18 November 1945; Franklin interview.

[39] Interview with Morris Washer, 1992.

[40]Anita Houk, *Commercial Appeal*, 14 August 1983.

"flew into flame and steel-splitting mouths of Japanese guns at mast height level." He first earned Air Force medals for each of two eight-thousand-ton transports he bombed and sank. He next won the Silver Star for bombing a Japanese airfield and blowing up two fuel dumps in a sortie that he flew solo, in a disabled plane, in broad daylight, over a heavily armed base, disregarding orders to return home because of bad weather. He was awarded the Distinguished Flying Cross after having flown three hundred five hours in forty-eight missions, almost one hundred hours more than the two hundred sixteen required for the medal.[41]

Some members of the Jewish community, too old for the draft but determined to serve their country, volunteered for the armed forces. B. W. Hirsch joined the army, as did Arthur Halle Sr. Eric Hirsch, who was familiar with water and boats, found that at his age, the only way he could be accepted by the navy was to buy a boat and donate it. With four men under his command, he was sent to New Orleans to intercept vessels that entered the mouth of the river illegally. Other Jewish Memphians aided the war effort as well: Aaron Scharff, Abe Waldauer, Sol Halle, and Sam Taubenblatt were officials of the Selective Service Board and were presented with medals for their vital work in securing personnel to fight the war. Members of Baron Hirsch bought and sold war bonds and women of the synagogue worked for the Red Cross. The synagogue contributed space as well: part of its Menorah Institute was converted into a United Service Organization (USO) operated by the Young People's League; another part of the facility was used as sleeping quarters for servicemen; and the building and grounds, including an area between the synagogue and the Menorah Institute that was paved with concrete for dancing, were put at the disposal of the government.[42]

The Sam Schloss Lodge of B'nai B'rith offered daytime recreation and entertainment to the service personnel in area hospitals, at the naval base at Millington, and at the Fourth Ferrying Group. The Lodge also bought five thousand dollars worth of war bonds and provided gifts for servicemen.[43]

In the early days of the war in Memphis, as in much of the country, the

---

[41]Ibid.

[42] Leah Hirsch interview; *Commercial Appeal*, 15 February 1947; Sam Shankman, *The Peres Family* (Kingsport: Southern Publishing., 1938), 116.

[43]*Press Scimitar* 5 August 1943.

division persisted between Orthodox pro-Zionist and anti-Zionist Reform forces. Stalwart Zionists Hardwig Peres, Abe Waldauer, and Abe Plough sent one thousand dollars to the American Jewish Congress, a contribution for which they were thanked on 20 December 1943 by its chairman, Rabbi Stephen S. Wise. In a telegram to Peres, the Zionist Organization of America announced that it had authorized a special committee to oppose the activities of the American Council for Judaism, "which is waging a relentless attack on Zionism."[44] Peres sent one hundred dollars on 28 December 1943. In the same year a letter from the city's Orthodox leader, Will Gerber, to Reform Memphians "Milton Binswanger, Sr., Fred Dreifus, William Goodman, Avrome Boshwit, et al.," accused them of being "rich, blind, divisive."[45] The shocking revelations of the war which later helped to soften differences within the Jewish community were not yet widely known.

Concurrent with their support for the war effort and their attention to matters related to Judaism, Memphis Jews continued to participate in the life of the larger community. In 1944, M. A. Lightman Sr., president of the Jewish Welfare Fund, served also as vice-chairman of the Memphis and Shelby County War and Welfare Fund Campaign. In 1945 he headed a fund drive for the expansion and operation of a "colored" hospital, Collins Chapel.[46] The end of segregation, although signaled, was not yet a reality.

Members of the Nineteenth Century Club, a cultural, philanthropic, and social women's group, held fund-raising teas to benefit the war effort and provided canteens for soldiers at the Fairgrounds and at the airport. Among the many who participated were Cecilia Felsenthal; Nell Ettelson, who had been president of the Club; and Alice Goodman, a volunteer teacher of speech and physical fitness training, who was cited by the Department of the Treasury for her work during the war. At war's end Memphis became the site of a Veteran's Rehabilitation Hospital, which served many of the wounded. Volunteers who helped the patients recover the desire to go on with their lives included Lybie Adler, Viola Frank, Pat Goodman, Nina Katz, and Jane Seessel.[47]

---

[44]Peres Family Papers, Memphis State University, :Mississippi Valley Collection, No. 232.

[45]Peres Family Papers.

[46]"Duffel Bag" of Temple Israel. Flyer;   Letter to Hardwig Peres, Memphis State University, MSS. No. 232, 15 August 1945.

[47]*Commercial Appeal*, 11 June 1977; *Press Scimitar*, 30 April 1946.

Abe Scharff, president of Kraus Cleaners, worked for civic well-being throughout the period. Scharff was president of the Chickasaw Council of Boy Scouts in 1940, received the council's Silver Beaver Award in 1944, and helped to secure a dining hall for its Camp Currier. He was a long-time member of the Memphis Chamber of Commerce having joined the organization when it was founded under the name of the Business Men's Club. The Club's name was changed when its charter was amended in 1917. In 1947, Scharff, who already had donated "a fine old home at Linden and Lauderdale" for a Negro branch of the YMCA, gave fifty thousand dollars for construction of a new building on South Lauderdale. It was named in his honor.[48]

Dr. Louis Levy was president of the Council of Social Agencies and a member of the Budget Committee of the Memphis Community Fund in 1940. He was also an art collector who gave a collection of one thousand prints to Brooks Museum of Art (now Memphis Brooks Museum of Art). His gift, purchased through Associated American Artists gallery in New York, was one of the most complete series of the gallery's early prints assuring that "works of art on paper would become one of Memphis Brooks's strengths." I. L. Myers, a long-time trustee of the Memphis Academy of Arts, had assumed its presidency during the wartime years. Fund-raising had come to a halt, and it was through Myers's efforts that the academy continued to operate. At its 1947 graduation exercises, the academy's trustees recognized his generosity in granting personal loans and awarded him a citation for "seeing us through the worst of the war years." Also beginning long careers at this time as academy supporters were Benjamin Goodman Jr., and Julie Isenberg, both of whom were trustees in the 1940s.[49]

William Loewenberg's civic work began in about 1946 when he was elected to the Board of Trustees of the Jewish Federation (now Jewish Family Service). While working on the Social Service Committee of the Federation, he became aware of the unmet needs of Jewish old people in the community who were sick.

Along with Leo Bearman Sr. and Abe Wurzburg, he raised the funds to build the B'nai B'rith Home for the Aged, which Loewenberg later headed. He was president of Temple Israel from 1951 to 1954. He headed the

---

[48]Interview with Kathleen Lowenthal, 1992; *Commercial Appeal*, 15 February 1947.
[49]Ruth C. Hazizlip, "The Memphis Academy of Arts, 1936-1949." Memphis. n.d. Pamphlet.

annual drive for the United Way, and contributed and raised funds for St. Jude's Children's Research Hospital.

Loewenberg was chairman of the Jewish Federation's drive in 1948, the year of Israel's independence. Among numerous awards, he received the 1974 Annual Award of the National Conference of Christians and Jews. In the same year, he received the governor of Tennessee's Outstanding Tennessean Award, and the Boy Scouts named him a Guardian member. He received the Hadassah Humanitarian Award for his contributions to Israel. Mason YMCA presented a plaque to him for services to youth, dated 1972-1973; another plaque, from Project Pull in 1975, credits his services to inner-city youth. Loewenberg was instrumental in the development of Metro Memphis Shopping Center for black entrepreneurs, and was honored for this by the Booker T. Washington Minority Economic Development, 1977-1978.

During the 1960s Loewenberg started the Riverview-Kansas Day Care Center with Myra Dreifus and Frances Hooks. With his wife Ruth he established Dogwood Village, a home for troubled children designated by the Juvenile Court. He helped organize Runaway House, providing a temporary home for youths of all ages and creeds.

Although he worked diligently for Jewish causes, the ecumenical nature of Loewenberg's concerns is demonstrated by his gift to St. Francis Hospital of a large part of the land on which the hospital was built. Immediately after making the gift, Loewenberg was to go on an out-of-town fishing trip with some friends. The group usually flew in a private plane on such trips, and Loewenberg was usually late. On the day of this particular trip Loewenberg arrived at the airport so early that he had to wait for everyone else. His explanation to them was that he had just donated half of his property to St. Francis Hospital, and "had to leave town before his Jewish friends demanded equal treatment." St. Francis Hospital named a building for him, and Christian Brothers University awarded him an honorary degree of Doctor of Humanities.

Loewenberg served on the President's Council of Christian Brothers University and of Rhodes College. He was a trustee for the Herbert Herff Foundation, which has provided help to Memphis State University. His children, Frederika Felt, Joan Markell, and William I. Loewenberg have endowed a Chair of Excellence at the University of Memphis in his honor, designating the School of Nursing as the recipient.

In 1963, when Ira Lichterman died, his wife Lottie and Loewenberg donated to the city 12.4 acres of their property, which included a lake and an historic log home. They gave an additional 11. 48 acres in 1978. The rest of the land that would become the Lichterman Nature Center was bought by the city of Memphis with a grant from the United States Department of Housing and Urban Development in the early 1970s. The Lichterman Nature Center, officially opened to the public on 14 April 1983, is one of the few accredited nature centers in the United States, and the only one located in the heart of a large city.[50]

Eugene Bearman, Marvin Brode, and J. Alan Hanover served in the state legislature. Josephine Burson became the first female and the first Jewish member of the Tennessee governor's cabinet upon her appointment by Governor Buford Ellington as state commissioner of employment security and manpower. Burson's first entry into politics was as Women's Chairman for the 1948 campaign of Estes Kefauver as United States Senator from Tennessee. Kefauver was running against the Crump-supported candidate Judge John Mitchell. Kefauver won, marking the beginning of the end of Crump's control of Memphis.[51]

Among Jewish-owned businesses established in the 1940s were Herff Motor Company, a Ford automobile agency, founded in 1943 by Herbert Herff. The agency became Lewis Ford Company upon its purchase by Lawrence Lewis, the son of Herff's partner, Joseph Lewis. Ben Sacharin opened his Nylon Net Company in the 1940s to capitalize on DuPont's manufacture of the product for use by commercial fishermen. Nets made of nylon were an improvement over nets made of cotton or linen because nylon does not rot. Sacharin's business, operating at first out of his father's fish market, eventually became the largest fish net company in the United States, employing five hundred people.[52]

Brothers Guy and Bernard Lansky, stationed overseas during the war, sent money from their salaries home to their brother Irving, instructing him to open a store for them. Irving opened an army surplus store which Guy and Bernard changed to a clothing store when they returned to the States. Their store became the source of clothing for many entertainers, including Jerry Lee Lewis and Elvis Presley, "who knew where to get those chartreuse socks, shiny shoes, and other spiffy duds: Lansky Brothers." Presley began

---

[50]Interviews with William Loewenberg, Martin Lichterman, and Bob Barney, 1991.

[51]Evans 336; Interview with Josephine Burson, 1989.

[52]*Press Scimitar* 2 January 1959; Interview with Ben Sacharin, 1991.

shopping there when he was working at Loew's Theater as an usher in the early fifties and told the brothers at that time, "Whenever I get rich, I'll be back and buy you out." He remained a good customer.[53]

Two businesses destined to become among the largest in Memphis also had their beginnings in the 1940s. Morris Fogelman started a real estate and insurance brokerage concern in 1940 which was to become the South's largest apartment owners' and managers' firm. Another small business with a big future opened in 1942 when Leo Wurtzburger left Memphis Paper Company to start his own business, the Acme Paper Company. Since 1961, the business has been called Cleo Wrap, linking "the most beautiful paper in the world, and the most beautiful woman, Cleopatra."[54]

Brothers Bert and David Bornblum, who had immigrated from Warsaw in 1938, opened a retail men's store in 1949. After two successful years, they opened another store. Because they were the first merchants on Beale Street to employ black salesmen, their stores were spared during the 1968 sanitation strike marches.

Jewish organizations expanded during the 1940s. B'nai B'rith Women formed Chapter 406 as an auxiliary to support the B'nai B'rith Home. Congregation Anshei Mischne organized a brotherhood in 1946. Through the continuing programs of Jewish Neighborhood House, forty-seven children attended kindergarten; twenty-seven studied instrumental music; eighteen learned vocal music; nineteen persons from five countries studied English; and forty-nine who took citizenship classes became United States citizens in December 1946. In addition, the facility maintained a lending library and offered a speech correction program conducted by the National Council of Jewish Women. The Salon Circle sent five girls to day-camp and eleven to full-time camp. Thirty-six doctors and dentists were members of a medical committee that provided free services, and Marx Borod headed a free legal aid committee.[55]

The year 1949 was an important one for the Memphis Jewish community. In that year occurred two milestone events which have exercised a far-reaching impact on Memphis Jewry. The first was the establishment of a Jewish Day School in Memphis. During the 1940s, Orthodox Jews in the United States were concerned about future generations of Jews remaining

[53]*Commercial Appeal*, 7 August 1992, E-15; Interview with Guy Lansky.
[54]*Commercial Appeal*, 20 December 1987; Wurtzburger interview; Harkins, 180.
[55]Minutes of Jewish Federation; Minutes of Jewish Family Service, 1930-1930.

Jewish in the melting pot that was America. In New York, Torah Umesorah, along with the Vaad Hahinuch of Mizrachi helped support Jewish Day Schools in North America. What was unique about the Jewish Day School movement was its creation of schools that gave to the student both a Jewish and general education—all under one system. On 6 September 1949 the first Jewish day school in the South, the Memphis Hebrew Academy, opened with an enrollment of twenty-four children in kindergarten and nineteen in first grade. Rabbi Elijah Stampfer of Anshei Sphard, Rabbi Seymour Kutner, assistant Rabbi of Baron Hirsch, Rabbi Alfred Fruchter of Beth El Emeth and lay leader Louis Epstein were among the founders.

None of the organizers represented their institutions and each acted as individuals on the committee to establish the school. Rabbi Greenblatt, who later became head of the Vaad of Kashruth in Memphis, was the Hebrew Academy's first teacher and Rabbi Fruchter was the school's first director. Although there was opposition both within the Orthodox Jewish community and in the Reform Jewish community to the idea of Day school education, the committee was able to get enough support to start the school. During the early years, tuition was free and some teachers tauught without compensation. Rabbi Greenblatt believes that "the Hebrew Academy has changed the community; it has retained and strengthened the Orthodox . . . Learning is the substance of Judaism. We are people of the Book." The change is reflected in the fact that "it is the young people who are observant." Sam Margolin, who was influential in the school's inception and continued operation, believed that "a day school is the best hope for preservation and advancement of traditional Judaism with its eternal spiritual values and cultural heritage."[56]

Although impetus for the school came from within the Orthodox community, the Hebrew Academy was organized as an independent, chartered institution, not affiliated with any congregation. In its first year, it was housed in the school building of Anshei Sphard. When a second grade was added in 1950, the school moved to the large Menorah Institute, owned by Baron Hirsch. Neither congregation charged rent. By 1952, the school was sufficiently well-established to employ a full-time director. A committee chaired by Sam Margolin hired Rabbi Joseph Nayowitz, an experienced day-school educator. The faculty included Ms. Sheila

---

[56]Interview with Rabbi Nathan Greenblatt, 1990; Memphis Hebrew Academy Third Donors Banquet, 1953.

Abraham, Emmaline Carrick, Ms. Miriam Ross, Mrs. Frank Sykes, William Schwab, and Bob Fisher; Rabbi Nayowitz taught fourth grade Hebrew. The Hebrew Academy eventually built and moved to a separate building at 390 White Station Road.[57] Each year a new grade was added through 8th grade. By 1965 a separate Jewish high school called the Yeshiva of the South was created.

The second milestone event of 1949 was the establishment of the Memphis Jewish Community Center (JCC). Many such centers already existed in the United States, successors of the post-Civil War YMHAs and Jewish settlement houses. Initially, those institutions, consisting of reading rooms and libraries of Jewish books, emphasized literary, cultural, and social life. The YMHA offered to the nineteenth century wave of immigrants a place where they could learn to adapt to American life. By the 1930s, the needs of immigrants had been replaced by the needs of second generation Jewish Americans. Recreation had become the primary concern, with acculturation the goal. During the Depression, the new community centers provided services for the unemployed, and later, during World War II, for servicemen. After World War II, the Holocaust, and the birth of the state of Israel, an emergent third generation of American Jews emphasized Jewish identity. The national Jewish Welfare Board initiated a study in 1945 to determine the relation of welfare boards to their communities. The major recommendation that resulted was that the activities of Jewish centers should emphasize Jewish content.[58]

For many years Memphis had had a YMCA, but it was an institution lacking in direction and adequate facilities. The YMCA shared space with Rex Ridgeway, a private Jewish club, with which it was incompatible, and the arrangement did not last. As a consequence, the Jewish youth in Memphis had to rely on Christian or civic organizations for a place to play ball or to hold a dance or discussion group. In 1928, the year following the organization of the first Memphis chapter of the national Jewish youth organization, the American Zionist Association (AZA), the group hosted an international AZA convention, which included ball games, oratorical contests, and social events. The frustration of members canvassing the city to find suitable facilities for the convention gave rise to their determination to establish an organization to serve the athletic, social and cultural needs

[57]Memphis Hebrew Academy Third Donors Banquet, 1953.
[58]Endelman, 188.

of the Memphis Jewish community. But the Depression and World War II postponed any action for more than twenty years.[59]

When World War II ended, the wish to provide a home for Jewish activities was reinvigorated by Aaron Brenner, Herbert Shainberg, Morris Fogelman, Julius Bisno, Joseph Allenberg, and Dr. Fred Goldberg, the charter members of AZA. They consulted with presidents of all the local congregations and with other leaders including Gilbert Schloss, William Gerber, Leo Bearman, Sr., Israel Kanarek, and Joe Lazarov. Representatives of all branches of Judaism attended these meetings despite the fact that at the time "there was little intermingling of Orthodox and Reform Jews in Memphis." Indeed, boundaries between the branches were so clearly drawn that each group had its own clubs and social organizations. Intermarriage or even joint activity was rare. In establishing a Jewish Community Center, one goal of the founders was to end the hostility among Memphis Jews of differing beliefs and to provide a common meeting ground for all of them. Finally, William Gerber convened a meeting of fifteen to twenty young men at the courthouse. He appointed a committee to write a constitution and by-laws and asked Carl Karchmer, Sy Wener, and Aaron Brenner to raise money. Baron Hirsch was to be custodian of the funds.[60] The group raised fifty thousand dollars, and a few private individuals, Johl Adler among them, pledged enough money to enable the purchase of a piece of property that included the East End swimming pool.

The project was not without opposition, however. Some of the Reform rabbis opposed the center fearing it might herald "a return to a Jewish ghetto"; some of the Orthodox rabbis feared the center's secular orientation; one congregation felt it might divert children from Sunday school attendance. But the committee persevered, believing that the center would create leaders and unite the Jewish community.[61]

At a meeting at the Peabody Hotel on 1 November 1949, application for the Charter of Incorporation for the Jewish Community Center was signed by twenty men. Aaron Brenner, the temporary chairman, appointed the following committee chairmen: Gilbert Delugach, general solicitations; Mel Grinspan, publicity; Julian Allenberg, personnel; Philip Belz, Jack Belz,

---

[59]Jewish Community Center, "Planting for Our Children," pamphlet, Memphis, TN, 1974, 6.
[60]Interview with Aaron Brenner, 1989.
[61]Brenner interview.

and Sol Lipman, building and real estate; I. E. Karchmer, finance and budget; and Herbert Glazer and Aaron Shankman, by-laws.

Paul Schwartz from Dayton, Ohio, was the center's first director. It was he who established the center as a service institution, which it has remained, and who first carried out the center's program policy: "If ten people want to do something, we will do it." The result is a wide variety of programs involving every age group in athletic, social, cultural, educational, and recreational activities.

Far from becoming a Jewish ghetto, the center from its inception involved the whole community. In a somewhat risky move for a new institution, Schwartz opened the center's day camp to the Juvenile Court to benefit children who badly needed a good camp experience, a decision in which he was supported by the Day Camp Committee whose members were convinced that a service like this was "what the Center was about."[62] The center received both United Way and individual funding; it provided space to the Cerebral Palsy Association for a day care center; it served as the early home for Runaway House, a haven for teenagers; and its membership has always included non-Jews.

The Memphis Jewish Community Center achieved its primary objective: it bridged social and religious differences among Memphis Jews. It continues to serve the entire community, opening its many activities to the general public.[63]

---

[62]"Planting for Our Children."
[63]"Planting for Our Children."

8

THE HOLOCAUST AND THE
BIRTH OF ISRAEL

"The event has shaped future generations. It was a watershed. Everything now is different."

—Elie Wiesel

Economic hardship promotes anti-Semitism, and in the United States, the Great Depression produced an attitude that was no exception. Nationwide, Father Charles Coughlin's anti-Semitic radio broadcasts attracted many listeners; black- and silver-shirted groups cloaked their anti-Semitic statements in patriotic terms; and Fritz Kuhn organized his Deutsche Bund of Nazi sympathizers in America.[1] But anti-Semitism in the United States remained private, unsanctioned by law. By contrast, in Germany anti-Semitism was a matter of national policy, building strength as Adolf Hitler gained control in the 1930s and reaching its peak as he announced his intention to achieve "the final solution to the Jewish problem." Because German anti-Semitism was overt, however, those Jews who believed the unbelievable and could manage to escape fled to foreign lands. Some, of course, came to the United States.

Memphis received its quota of immigrants. Their arrival created pressure on the already economically hard-pressed Jewish community that nevertheless was determined, as always, to "take care of its own." Some of the refugees moved into the homes of relatives, crowding families and straining Depression-thinned resources even more. Some members of the Memphis Jewish community, often relative newcomers themselves, felt insecure with the arrival of a new group of immigrants for the city to absorb. The national *Fortune Magazine* survey conducted in 1939 found that eighty-

---

[1]Lecture by Rabbi Mark A. Levin, Memphis State University, Winter, 1991.

three percent of Americans were unwilling to open the doors of the United States to German-Jewish refugees.[2] Memphis Jews believed that most Memphians would mirror the majority of Americans.

The Memphis Jewish community, like many others in the country, was divided about the best way to influence government officials to admit the endangered German Jews. The American Jewish Committee, composed largely of Jews of German origin, favored quiet attempts to plead for their desperate brethren rather than public protests and demonstrations. In general, they adopted the strategy that had been traditional in European Jewish communities since the Middle Ages: wealthy Jews used their influence to persuade non-Jewish leaders to extend kindness toward Jews. The American Jewish Congress headed by Rabbi Stephen S. Wise opposed this approach. Composed mostly of Eastern European Jews, it was founded in 1915 by those, especially Zionists, who wanted to be more public in their Jewishness.[3] Neither of these organizations represented the opinion of a majority of American Jews which fell somewhere in between these two positions.

In Memphis, Jews were accepted with tolerance for the most part but anti-Semitism was clearly present. Some residential areas excluded Jews: Morningside Park and Tuckahoe Lane, for example, were restricted. Although social life for Jews and non-Jews continued to be separate, there were exceptions. Rosalee and Bertrand Cohn were members of the exclusive Memphis Hunt and Polo Club, but they were its only Jews.[4] There were no Jewish students at Miss Hutchison's school, a private academy for girls, and no Jewish teachers at Memphis University School, a private high school for boys. Southwestern College (Rhodes College) also excluded non-Christian faculty members.

When Dr. Arno Schirokauer, a German immigrant and a highly qualified teacher, came to Memphis by way of Havana, Cuba, a group of Jewish Memphians, headed by Bertrand Cohn who chaired the Refugee Committee, paid his salary so that he could teach at Southwestern without breaking its rules. The college's Executive Committee minutes of 3 April 1939, state that "a motion was made and passed to call Dr. Arno Schiro-

---

[2]*Hebrew Watchman*, 6 April 1939.
[3]Richard Breitman and Alan M. Kraut, *American Refugee Policy and European Jewry, 1933-45.* (Bloomington: Indiana University Press, 1987) 105-114.
[4]Rosalee Cohn personal interview.

kauer . . . to the faculty as assistant Professor of German. Dr. Schirokauer comes very highly recommended as a man of excellent character and attainment." The minutes of 17 May 1939 record that Dr. Schirokauer accepted the position, and that his "salary of twelve hundred dollars has been provided by outside sources." Southwestern's 1939 annual report stated that Dr. Schirokauer ". . . will serve as Visiting Lecturer in Medieval Studies." The next year's report noted that Schirokauer read a paper at a meeting of the Modern Language Association of America at Tulane University in December 1939 and another at the German Teachers Association Conclave in New York City in April 1940. From Southwestern, Dr. Schirokauer moved to a position with the research department of the Carl Schurz Foundation of Philadelphia.[5]

Because pockets of anti-Semitism existed in the city, members of the Jewish community feared that any visible increase in the number of Jewish immigrants would trigger a growth in discrimination, a concern probably made more chilling by their awareness of the treatment of blacks in Memphis. Instead of calling attention to themselves by protesting the treatment of German Jews, most Jewish Memphians preferred to rely on the time-honored method of enlisting the skills and talents of such national Jewish figures as Senator Jacob Javits of New York, Supreme Court Justice Felix Frankfurter, and Rabbi Stephen S. Wise.[6]

In spite of heavy German censorship, information from that country continued to reach Memphis. As early as 1932, even before Hitler became Führer, the *Hebrew Watchman* reported that Mendel Fisher, executive director of the Central-Southwest Zionist region, had described the plight of German Jews as desperate and had appealed for help. The same newspaper reported upon his return from an international conference in London, that I. M. Robinow, executive secretary of B'nai B'rith, said that the only way to help German Jews was to get them out of Germany. Headlines on the front page of the *Commercial Appeal* of 13 January 1935, described the worsening situation: "Terrorism Charged Against Saar Nazis, Showdown is Today, Territory's Outward Calm Controls the Tension of Foes: Jew-Bullying is Alleged." Nazis, according to the article, were making

---

[5]Minutes of Southwestern College Board of Trustees, 3 March 1939 and 17 April 1939; Southwestern of Memphis Annual Report, October 1939, 7; October 1940, 7; October 1941, 10.
[6]Levin lecture.

determined efforts to prevent Jews from voting.[7]

Two events in 1938 made even more apparent the precarious position of German Jews. The *St. Louis*, a ship carrying 907 Jewish refugees from Germany, of whom two hundred were children, was refused permission to dock by Cuba, its country of destination. The ship's subsequent attempts to find a port highlighted the indifference of the world to the plight of the Jews. The United States refused to accept any of the refugees. On instructions from Washington, the United States Coast Guard forced the St. Louis to return to Europe, where only a few passengers were admitted to Britain, Holland and France. Many of the refugees on board later died in extermination camps. A *New York Times* editorial of 9 June 1939, commented on the catastrophe: "The crime of the *St. Louis* cries to high heaven of man's inhumanity to man." Reports carried by the *Hebrew Watchman*, the *Commercial Appeal*, and the *Press Scimitar* of America's failure to respond in a humane way to the persecution of Jews by the Nazis document a painful chapter in the history of the Roosevelt administration.[8]

In Germany, the unmistakably savage intentions of the Nazi regime were illustrated by *Kristallnacht*, the night of the breaking glass. On 9 November 1938, crowds of Germans, encouraged by the regime, destroyed Jewish businesses, synagogues, and homes in cities across the country. This barbaric event was fully reported in all newspapers. In an address to the Memphis Rotary Club in September 1939, Robert G. Neumann, a concentration camp survivor, spoke of the horrors and torture prisoners endured at the hands of the Nazis.[9]

Although it was small and divided, the Memphis Jewish community in the 1930s did respond in some ways, if relatively minor ones, to the Hitler regime. The city's rabbis addressed the plight of the refugees and the ominous specter of the spread of anti-Semitism. On 23 March 1933 the Memphis Jewish community participated in national meetings sponsored by the American Jewish Congress to endorse protest by the United States government against persecution of Jews. In 1936 an emergency campaign to raise two million five hundred thousand dollars for the resettlement of six hundred thousand Jews in Palestine set a Memphis goal of three thousand

---

[7]*Hebrew Watchman*, 15 February 1932, 8 March 1932, 8 February 1934; *Commercial Appeal*, 11 September 1936.

[8]*Commercial Appeal*, 13 January 1935, 1.

[9]*Commercial Appeal*, 6 September 1939

dollars. Assistant United States Attorney Joseph M. Bearman chaired the successful drive.[10]

In 1936 the Jewish Welfare Fund sponsored a drive to raise money for relief and resettlement, "especially for four hundred fifty thousand Jews threatened with destruction in Germany." Funds were to be used to help those uprooted from their native lands to establish themselves elsewhere. The Memphis share was set at fifty thousand dollars. The campaign, to be completed within ten days, required the cooperation of two hundred fifty volunteer workers. William Loeb and M. A. Lightman Sr., president and chairman of the campaign, respectively, hoped to raise the entire amount from the Jewish community itself, despite the fact that the fund would also aid Catholics and Protestants "where they are found suffering from dictators." The successful campaign's committee read like a roll call of Memphis Jewry.[11]

The Jewish community responded in other ways as well. The Memphis branch of the Jewish Welfare Fund sponsored a committee, led once again by William Loeb, to help care for the thirty to forty Austrian refugees who had come to Memphis. In observance of Nazi Refugee Fund Day, the Motion Picture Theater Industry of Memphis and the Mid-South set aside 26 January 1939, to donate its profits to groups organized "for the relief of racial, political, and religious refugees of Germany." M. A. Lightman Sr., was largely responsible for the participation of Memphis theater owners. Temple Israel worked with the Recreation Department of the Memphis Parks Commission to provide activities for refugee children and in 1937

---

[10]Rabbi Mark Levin personal interview; *Hebrew Watchman*, 23 March 1933, 9 November 1933.

[11]*Commercial Appeal*, 11 September 1936; *Press Scimitar* 14 September 1936. Serving in the Initial Gifts Division: Lloyd Bensinger, Avrome Boshwit, Dave Dermon, Fred Goldsmith, Arthur Halle, Sr., Hardwig Peres, Aaron Scharff, Gaston Strauss, I. W. Ashner, M. S. Binswanger Sr., Lester Brenner, Sam Fortas, Ben Goodman Jr., Dr. Louis Levy, Ike Myers, W. B. Rosenfield, Abe Simon, J. P. Stuart, Mark Wile; in the Junior Division: Edwin Sapinsley, chairman; Herbert Morris, Buddy Frank, Jay Schwarz, Louis Miller, Louis Greene, Al Roberts, Norine Lehman, J. B. Heyman Jr., Hubert Kiersky, Leon Rose, Alvin Saloman, Morris Strauch, Alec Okeon, Julius Kaminisky, Max Brown, and Herman Appleson; in the General Division: William B. Rosenfield, chairman, ; Ed Felsenthal, Jake Felt, Ike Myers, Sid Felsenthal, Herbert Hieman, and Reggie Wurzburg. The Women's Division captains were: Dorothy Bearman, Celia Behr, Mrs. A. L. Blecker, Mrs. Rob Cohen, Sylvia Dreyfous, Jane Seessel, Selma Goldberg, Mrs. Jeanette Henochsberg, Mrs. I. Ostrow, Mrs. Phil Pearlman, Mrs. Gertrude Weiss, Leah Wile, Mrs. I. R. Haas, Bertha Shankman, and Daisy Spiro.

formed a Red Cross sewing class to provide clothes for them.[12]

The only community-wide effort organized in the city to protest Germany's treatment of Jews was convened not by Jewish Memphians, but by the Episcopal Bishop of Tennessee, James M. Maxon. The meeting, entitled "All Creeds Protest," was part of a country-wide effort sponsored by the National Conference of Christians and Jews in cooperation with the Federal Council of Churches of Christ in America and the Synagogue Council of America. Held on 20 November 1938, at Ellis Auditorium,[13] it drew twenty-six hundred Memphians and an overflow crowd of five hundred others. It was the largest interfaith assembly ever gathered in Memphis. Attendees included representatives of all religious faiths, members of such civic organizations as the Elks and the Moose, and prominent civic leaders. "Boss" Crump was there as were the editors of both daily newspapers, Frank Ahlgren of the *Commercial Appeal* and Edward Meemen of the *Press Scimitar*; Mayor Watkins Overton; Sam Bates of the Irish Club; Father Owens of St. Patrick's Church; and Dr. R. J. Bateman, president of the Protestant Pastors' Association. Black support was demonstrated by the participation of a leading clergyman, the Reverend T. O. Fuller.

Among the speakers at "All Creeds Protest" was Mayor Watkins Overton, who was introduced by attorney Benjamin Goodman Jr. "We hold out our hands," Overton said, "in sympathy to our neighbors across the sea, and we extend sympathy to the Jews in our own city. Many of them have friends and relatives in Germany. There never has been a call for the betterment of Memphis, for its educational institutions, for its Community Fund, to which the Jews of Memphis have failed to respond." Bishop Maxon called on groups to offer prayers for divine intercession for German Jews.[14]

Although response to the Holocaust by Memphis Jews as a group was limited, there were countless examples of efforts by Jewish individuals and families to rescue German Jews. Families with relatives caught in the crisis tried to arrange for their immigration to Memphis, but often were thwarted in their efforts to secure visas by consular officials who were unsympathetic to the desperate need of German Jews to escape. Most German Jews were killed before help could reach them. Many who did not perceive the real

---

[12]*Hebrew Watchman*, 31 March 1938, 18 January 1939, 23 February 1937.
[13]*Press Scimitar* 17 November 1938.
[14]*Press Scimitar* 21 November 1938; *Hebrew Watchman*, 17 November 1938.

nature of the danger they faced refused to leave their homeland even when help was offered.

In the latter category was the family of William Loewenberg, all of whose male relatives died in German gas chambers. Prosperous merchants, they sent their wives and children away to safety while they remained behind, believing that they could continue to weather the storm as Jews had done for centuries until it inevitably subsided. All perished.[15]

Others, recognizing that a terrible situation was growing steadily worse, took steps to save themselves. Dr. Justin H. Adler, a graduate of the medical school of the University of Heidelberg, was an intern in psychiatry in Berlin in 1933 when storm troopers marched into the hospital where he worked and announced that all Jews had to leave. Adler made contact with his uncle, Herman Adler, in Memphis, who arranged for him to receive a visa, and he landed in New York in August 1933. (Herman Adler's father had come to the United States in 1862, and three of his brothers fought in the Civil War.) With the help of another relative, Dr. Gilbert Levy (who served as president of the Memphis and Shelby County Medical Society in 1963) Adler obtained a position at the University of Tennessee Medical School. He next joined the staff of Western State Psychiatric Hospital in Bolivar, Tennessee, then took further training in psychiatry at Johns Hopkins University. Adler returned to Memphis in 1937 to practice his specialty, introducing for the first time "south of the Mason-Dixon line" insulin shock therapy for the treatment of dementia praecox. He later established a treatment center employing the therapy at Western State. Dr. Adler became chairman of the Department of Psychiatry at Baptist Hospital and president of the Tennessee Psychiatric Association.[16]

Dr. Adler recalled that despite the continuing brutality of the Nazis toward German Jews, his father was compelled at his own expense to sign, print, and have distributed abroad a newspaper report and advertisement denying Nazi participation in any anti-Jewish actions. Published in Dr. Adler's hometown newspaper on 30 March 1933, the document read:

Against the Atrocity Propaganda of Foreign Countries: We send the following telegram to Mr. Herman Adler, Adler Hotel, in Memphis, Tennessee, U.S.A. Inform the press and the public that

---

[15]William Loewenberg personal interview.
[16]Dr. Justin Adler personal interview.

stories of atrocities and reports of violence and tumult in Germany are simply lies and are to be denied and rejected. Combat the senseless agitation against Germany.[17]

Herman Adler sponsored other members of the family as well. He facilitated the arrival of his nephew, Ernest, Dr. Adler's brother, in 1934; of his sister and brother-in-law, Ida and Adolph; Dr. Adler's parents, in 1937; and of his other sisters, Dr. Adler's aunts, Fannie Seligman, Matilda Levy, and Hannah Levy. The family lived at first in apartments owned by Herman Adler at 848 Poplar, an address that became home for many of the era's immigrants. Dr. Adler described his uncle Herman, who came to New Orleans in 1889 at age fifteen and worked as a longshoreman, as "a very colorful, stubborn, and powerful man, who remained the head of his family as long as he lived. He had both goodness and strength."

Herman Adler arranged for another of his nephews, Leo Seligman, to come to the United States in either 1937 or 1938. Seligman had served in the German army in World War I and belonged to the Organized Jewish Front-Line Soldiers. Arrested for making anti-Hitler speeches in the 1930s, he was sent to a concentration camp. It was his good fortune that one of the camp's Nazi officials was a captain he had rescued from certain death during WWI. The grateful captain facilitated Seligman's escape from the camp; the Salvation Army helped him return to Frankfurt. From there, with money Adler sent him, he was able to come to Memphis to join his mother who was already living in the city.[18]

After his escape from Germany, Seligman felt he "owed something for his life." Inspired by a radio program, *Up from Parole*, in 1945 he began to work with boys on parole for whom, at that time, there was no rehabilitation program. In order to secure release from jail, a prisoner had to prove that he had a place to live, a sponsor, and a job. With his own money, time, and energy, Seligman made it possible for boys to meet those requirements. He went into prisons and talked with the potential parolees, continuing to counsel them after their release. His files hold records of twenty-two hundred parolees with whom he worked, ninety percent of whom remained out of jail. His influence finally persuaded the Tennessee Department of Employment Security to open a new section in its Memphis branch to

---

[17]Adler interview.
[18]Interview with Esther Seligman, 1990.

secure jobs for parolees. The work Seligman performed continued to benefit many lives long after his death in 1967.[19]

Dr. Justin Adler's future wife, Herta Anfeld, came to the United States in 1940. She had grown up in a small town in Germany, Diez an der Lahn, where her father owned land and cattle. Although the family was "very integrated" into the town's largely non-Jewish society, she remembers boys at her school singing songs with these words: "If Jewish blood runs from our knife, then everything is twice as good," and "Heads are rolling, Jews are howling." After Hitler came to power, her school was converted into a training institution for future leaders of the Third Reich.

In 1938 Herta lived in Frankfurt, the wealthiest city in Germany, near the Friedberger Anlage, considered the most beautiful synagogue in the city. On 9 November 1938, having heard that the synagogue was burning, she ran out of her house to see for herself what was happening and was stunned to find that the fire department was not trying to extinguish the fire, but instead, was simply protecting the rest of the neighborhood from the conflagration. Thus she became a witness to *Kristallnacht*, an event she called "a great shock, totally unbelievable." As she watched the fire, she remembered overhearing a man in the crowd say that he hated to see what was occurring because he knew many good Jews; and she remembered hearing the man's female companion answer, "A Jew is a Jew, like a herring is a herring." After *Kristallnacht*, all stores, restaurants, and offices were forced to place signs in their windows informing passers by that "Jews are not wanted here." Herta believed that the German population was encouraged to kill Jews with no fear of recrimination.

Herta and her friends were confident that if Americans knew of the danger faced by the German Jews, the United States would save them by establishing refugee camps. To this end, Herta and others sent telegrams to Jewish organizations in the United States, but they received no response. She returned to her home town of Diez to say good-bye to her parents' lifelong non-Jewish friends who told her that they loved her but that they were convinced that Hitler would conquer the world.

Later questioned about her lack of bitterness in the face of her experiences, Mrs. Adler explained that her attitude changed during a trip to Germany in the mid-1950s. Landing at a German airport, she saw an El Al airplane on a nearby runway and a sign advising travelers to "Spend your

---

[19]Seligman interview.

spring in beautiful Israel." Then, she said, she knew the world had changed, and she was able to change along with it.[20]

Anna and Julius Frank were among those who realized relatively early the seriousness of the situation they were in and made plans to flee. The Franks had lived comfortably in Hamburg, where Julius was a banker and a director of the stock exchange. One day, Anna overheard soldiers in conversation beneath her open window. One said to the other, "When my knife runs with Jewish blood, I will be content." Anna Frank determined at that moment that "it would not be *my* Jewish blood." She and her husband tried to convince the rest of their family to leave Germany with them, but were only partially successful. They emigrated to New York in 1937, and were brought to Memphis the following year by attorney Bertrand Cohn, who headed the Memphis Refugee Committee. Cohn and his wife Rosalee also used their home as an informal reception center for refugees, many of whom lived with the Cohns before moving on to their own homes. At a party for twenty businessmen hosted by the Cohns, the Franks met Herman Bensdorf, whose business Julius Frank joined.[21]

Eric Cornell arrived in the United States in 1938. Like many others in the early days of Hitler's rule, Cornell had considered the Führer "a joke in the country of Schiller, Goethe, and all the other mental giants of German culture" and believed he could not long survive. A vacation spent in Switzerland "changed my mind and cleared my head." He returned to Berlin only in order to make plans to leave. Cornell went first to New York where he had family. Believing that he would never become truly American unless he left New York, he went to the New York office of the National Council of Jewish Women just as a letter arrived from Leo Levy, who offered to hire a German refugee at Levy's Ladies Toggery in Memphis. Later, Cornell recalled his thoughts about the placement: "With my limited amount of English . . . I had no idea what a 'toggery' dispensed, I thought it was something like a place selling accessories for horses."[22]

In Memphis, Cornell met Bertrand Cohn who introduced him to Leo Levy, owner of Levy's Ladies Toggery, known simply as Levy's. Levy took

---

[20]Interview with Herta Adler, 1992; Skip Howard, "*Kristallnacht*—Eyewitness to History," *Jewish Historical Society of Memphis and the Mid-South Newsletter*,v. 2, #2, 3.
[21]Interview with Mrs. Julius Frank, 1992; Interview with Rosalee Cohn, 1992.
[22]Eric H. Cornell, "The Lord Is My Shepherd: My Story: Analysis of an Escape." Unpublished Pamphlet.

him first to the Tennessee Hotel, owned by his brother-in-law, Herman Adler, who installed Cornell in a small room on an upper floor; then to lunch at Ridgeway, the Jewish club, and finally to the store where he would work, to meet two of its executives, Irving Freudberg and Eugene Lerner.[23]

It had been Cornell's impression that he had been offered a job because of his personal experience and qualifications, but he found that Levy, who had come from Germany as a child, had made the job available because "he just wanted to help someone." Starting at the bottom in the receiving department of the store, Cornell spent forty years at Levy's, rising through the ranks to head a department.[24]

The refugees who came later, after the terror of the death camps, endured experiences totally different from the ones recalled by those who escaped before the worst of the Holocaust. It is not possible for Jews who spent lives in safety in Memphis truly to know or to understand the psychic cost of such experiences. One marvels at the lack of vindictiveness of those who were so traumatized. Although the concentration camp experience has been well documented, the reality becomes sharper when the stories are told by people who live in one's own community. The history of Jews in Memphis would be incomplete without including what happened to those Jews who became Memphians after they survived the camps.

The life of Nina Katz is testimony to what William Faulkner once called human "capacity to prevail." Nazi tanks arrived in her city in Poland on 4 September 1939, capturing city hall. Nazi soldiers knocked on individual doors, screaming, "Out, Jews, out!" After the crowd was rounded up, there were random shots, and the Jews were forced to dig graves to bury their dead. Katz's parents and seven-year-old, pig-tailed sister, Helen, were sent to Auschwitz where they all perished. Nina, a strong twelve-year-old, was sent at first to a work camp. She was always haunted by having observed a Nazi soldier tear a baby from its mother's arms and kill it by smashing its head against a brick wall. Nina spent four years in a labor camp, from 1939 to 1943; two years in a concentration camp, from 1943 to 1945; and four more years in a camp for displaced persons, from 1945 to 1949. Ten years of her young life were stolen from her.

Katz said of her years in the labor camp, that she was "starved, beaten, and humiliated without a shred of humanity." Of her years in the concen-

---

[23]Ibid.
[24]Ibid.

tration camp, she comments that of three thousand inmates, eight hundred were still alive on 7 May 1945, when the camp was liberated. Many of the newly freed prisoners were too weak to survive, but Katz was rescued by the American Red Cross, hospitalized for ten days, given crutches, and told to "walk out to freedom."[25] Nina's search for freedom gave purpose to her survival. She returned to Poland, only to hear the Poles shouting, "The Nazis did not do a good enough job. We will finish it." There, she visited the grave of her grandfather, only to discover that it had been desecrated, and she knew she had to leave a place that offered no freedom or future for her. She married Morris Katz, her childhood sweetheart, also a concentration camp survivor, and together they crossed the border into Czechoslovakia where they renounced their Polish citizenship. They lived for three and a half years in a displaced persons camp before gaining entry to the United States at New Orleans.

The choices they made about what belongings to bring with them—due to a weight limit of some six or eight pounds—reveal much about the young couple: a candelabra so that they could observe the tradition of lighting the Sabbath candles; a featherbed, which had to be sent back when they reached the United States; and an encyclopedia of philosophy, music, religion, and art. The encyclopedia was bound in leather; in order to comply with the weight limit, they tore off the leather covers which, Nina assured her husband, could always be replaced when they arrived in their new home. Nina remembers clearly the words of the Bishop of New Orleans who greeted the immigrants: "I don't know what the future holds for you," he said, "but one thing I can promise you. You will be free."[26]

Nina Katz discovered that indeed she did have rights and freedom in the United States, but, to her surprise, she also discovered that these opportunities did not exist for all Americans. Realizing that "you cannot change history," she decided to help shape the future by fighting against discrimination and for freedom and justice for all, by devoting her life to service. Katz remained in the forefront of the cause of human rights. She worked for the National Conference of Christians and Jews at both the local and national levels and served for many years as Public Relations Director for the Memphis Literacy Council, receiving its Literacy Luminary Award in 1991 for recruiting more than five thousand volunteer tutors and adult

---

[25]Interview with Nina Katz, 1992.
[26]Katz interview.

students. She once said:

> I can't help but feel that I have a mission. I've always wondered why some survived that horrible chapter in history called the Holocaust, why some were given a second chance at life. I believe that I was given a second chance so I could help others earn the right to call themselves Americans.[27]

Other refugees who found homes in Memphis described their experiences under the Germans. Ruth Diamond remembers being herded into a ghetto with one room for the five people in her family. There was no work; food was rationed. Meyer Kelman recalls the ghetto in Bialystock where he and others fled to escape the Germans who invaded their small Polish town in 1939. Food was so scarce that he and his companions sold their possessions to obtain it. Jews were forced to wear yellow patches on the left side of their chest. When the Bialystock ghetto was liquidated in 1942, Kelman was sent to Treblinka, euphemistically termed a labor camp. Helen Kibel was forced into the ghetto in Lodz, Poland, in 1941. There, she says, "People were dying. Children got swollen. There were three streets, with thousands of people. Children with big eyes wore a star, a *yuda*, on their sleeves. There were no bathrooms, no way to wash or to clean clothes. And no way to receive information." In 1942 Kibel was sent to Auschwitz by wagon.[28]

Jacob Kilstein lived in Tribunaski, near Lodz, a town of sixty to seventy thousand people of whom forty thousand were Jews. People there "lived poor." Most were tradesmen, tailors, shoemakers, cabinet makers, roofers, plumbers. On Sundays, people threw rocks at Jews. One Yom Kippur, the Germans came to town. They forced the Jews, who were fasting and praying with *tallit* on, from the shuls. They put them on trucks and carried them to Cracow and cut their beards. They were put into a ghetto, and any Jewish person found outside it was shot. Kilstein remembered

---

[27]Ibid.

[28]Interview with Ruth Diamond, Center for Southern Folklore Holocaust Interviews, conducted by Judy Pelser, Memphis, TN, 11 August 1987; Interview with Meyer Kelman, Center for Southern Folklore, Holocaust Interviews, conducted by Rachel Shankman, 13 March 1987; Interview with Helen Kibel, Center for Southern Folklore, Holocaust Interviews.

a lady went outside the ghetto to get some bread. She had a child in her arms, and a German officer walked over to her and shot her and didn't shoot the baby. The baby was climbing on her and blood was going all over. It was horrible . . . I saw it because I had customers who gave me papers so I could get out and . . . do tailor work for them. I carried the work out of the ghetto and delivered it to them. They couldn't come into the ghetto.

From 1939 to 1940 the Nazis forced Kilstein to do heavy work all day without food. One day he did not feel well and sent his brother to work in his place, a transgression for which he was beaten the next day by four members of the Gestapo. One held his head while he was undressed and three "knock[ed] me with heavy whips, one hundred twenty lashes. I was bleeding all the way down, could not walk, sleep, or sit down. They kicked you and got pleasure from it." He and others in the ghetto worked underground, digging with their hands, two persons carrying out two hundred one-pound containers, one hundred loads a day. He became ill, suffered a broken spine, but the Gestapo would not release him from his work assignment. They beat and kicked him so severely that he became paralyzed and had to be sent to the hospital where he remained for seven or eight months. His doctor's brother-in-law got him out just before the Nazis shot everyone remaining in the hospital.[29]

Sam Weinreich described the ghetto where he lived with his family as a place of starvation and death. He and others were so eager to escape that they became easy prey for the Germans. Unable to imagine anything worse than the ghetto, they went willingly to the concentration camp. Disillusionment came quickly. On the train ride to Auschwitz, there was one bowl of soup for seven people and no spoon. Everyone was hungry. The first one who got the soup gobbled as much as he could to alleviate his pain. Weinreich explained, "When you are hungry, you are an animal. You don't care if it is your brother or father. The next people in line got very little, and half of it was spilled."[30]

In 1944 Weinreich's wife Frieda and her family were sent to Auschwitz where her mother was selected for the gas chamber, as was a young mother

---

[29]Ibid.

[30]Interview with Sam Weinreich, Center for Southern Folklore , Holocaust Interviews, Memphis, TN, 10 March 1988.

with a baby, and "a lady with a hunchback." The women's heads were shaved; they were undressed and given heavy clothes but no underwear or shoes. Frieda Weinreich further narrated:

We lay like animals spread out, ten on bottom, ten on top, on wood planks. Once a day they took us to the bathroom. There was one bowl of soup for five people without a spoon. After three days we went to a selection by Dr. Mengele, then to a bath. There we were given different clothes, a slip and wooden shoes. There was one cover for fifteen people. The Germans wanted that fun, (to see) how we struggled for that cover.[31]

Ruth Diamond confirmed what happened to women at Auschwitz: "All clothes were taken, and they shaved us completely like men. . . . I didn't recognize my sister, and she didn't recognize me." She recalled that "there were rows in groups of twenty, multiplied by five, which equaled one hundred. This made it simple for one man on a horse to ride through and count the people quickly." Meyer Kelman recalled that in Auschwitz in 1944, three thousand gypsies were liquidated to make room for Jews. When you were marching "if you gave out, they shot you." One march lasted three weeks, without food, "rain or shine." Of the three thousand prisoners who began, only three hundred were left at the end. Kelman, who weighed one hundred forty pounds when he entered the camp, weighed seventy-five or eighty pounds when he was liberated. At Auschwitz Helen Kibel recalled that she was "always hungry. You could not talk, or you would be slapped in the face."[32]

Leah Kaufman told of a death march to the Ukraine that lasted one month. On the march, people were thrown over a bridge, and "their cries for help never left my ears." Everyone was ordered onto a ferry; many were, on a whim, pushed off and drowned. Her father was shot. Jacob Kilstein and his younger brother also were sent to Auschwitz. One day, by a fluke, Jake somehow got enough to eat. Then, he said, he began to cry because, "when you can stop being so concerned about food, you can look around, and how

---

[31]Interview with Freida Weinreich, Center for Southern Folklore, Holocaust Interviews, Memphis, TN, 10 March 1988.

[32]Diamond interview; Kelman interview; Kibel interview.

not cry?"[33]

Sam Weinreich was sent from Auschwitz to another camp in Germany where airplane hangars were built. Weinreich had to carry fifty-pound sacks of cement on his back. He described an experience one very cold winter:

> I put on one sack from the concrete because all I had on me was a little uniform. I put that sack on me to keep warm. When we went back into camp, the Germans stood near the gate and hit you with that little stick to find out what you had under that uniform. [They] found that sack. That's why I got seven teeth knocked out .... At that time I got my number assigned. I had my number under my uniform . . . I lost my name and all I had is a number.... A lot of people committed suicide. They threw themselves into the wet concrete. They could not withstand the happenings.[34]

Meyer Kelman came to Memphis by way of New York, where he spent only one night because he was "scared of the big buildings in New York and got away." In Memphis he went to school in the evenings to learn English. In the beginning he

> didn't feel to talk about anything. Our past was kind of depressing because this was something we just tried to get out of our systems, out of mind, because it was not easy, until later in the years. It doesn't bother me any more right now. . . . In the beginning, we had a lot of nightmares about the whole thing . . . we never will get it out of our minds. . . . If you live in a country where freedom exists, and you do whatever you desire, as long as you have your ambition, you can always come to a better future.[35]

Jacob Kilstein was liberated from Auschwitz by the Americans. In 1948 he and his wife registered to come to the United States and in 1949, were able to immigrate. They "didn't have a penny . . . didn't have anything." Arriving in Memphis by train from New York, they were met by Ruth Marks, a social worker with the Jewish Welfare Fund, who placed them in

---

[33]Kilstein interview.
[34]Weinreich interview.
[35]Kelman interview.

Herman Adler's Tennessee Hotel. But because "it was hot, and there was no kosher food," the Kilsteins arranged to stay with the Kaplans on Parkway and Manassas for two months, then with Mrs. Aaron Dubrovner for eighteen months. Kilstein found employment as a tailor with the firm of Julius Lewis. Mrs. Kilstein was pregnant. Ruth Marks offered to have a baby shower for her explaining that guests would bring presents, but Mrs. Kilstein, misinterpreting the custom, cried for three days because she did not want any charity. Later, she says, she "found out that this is the way."[36] Mrs. Kilstein attended classes at Neighborhood House for five years to learn to speak English and to meet the requirements for naturalization.

Sam Weinreich and his wife also were given lodging at the Tennessee Hotel. They were met upon their arrival in Memphis by Sonya Alperin of the Jewish Federation and were assisted as well in settling into the community by Yetta Kapelow and Anna Gruber. The Federation provided the couple with a food allowance. The Weinreichs moved to an apartment at 688 Jefferson, and Weinreich found employment as a furniture refinisher for Joel Friedman. Later, he got a job refinishing fine furniture for Charlie Schaffler. Once, he remembered, he finished an antique so beautifully that it looked new. He was told,

> It's no good if the [finish] is too pretty. I said I never heard [that] something too good is bad . . . so, it broke my heart that I had to take an ice pick, punch holes in it, take a piece of steel wool, dull it down, and rub umber in [the] little holes to make it look old again, but this is America. You expect the unexpected.[37]

Leah and Moishe Kaufman were liberated in 1945 from Bergen Belsen and came to Memphis by way of a camp for displaced persons. They were married in the camp. Of their wedding, Leah remembers that her outfit was a blue skirt with a blouse; there was a cake made from crackers; and she made a meat loaf. There was no challah to celebrate the occasion. For their first nineteen months in Memphis, the Kaufmans lived in a private home, for which their rent was paid by the Jewish Welfare Fund. "Mrs. Herman Bluthenthal taught us and took care of us. Mr. Makowsky taught my husband the trade of butchering." Later they were able to buy a little house

---

[36]Ibid.
[37]Weinreich interview.

on McNeil.[38]

Adapting to life in Memphis was easier for those who came when they were young. Max Notowitz was twenty years old when he arrived in New York in 1947. Born in Breslau, Germany, his family moved to Poland, and it was in Poland in a ghetto where he observed his Bar Mitzvah. His father died in Auschwitz and the rest of his family, in Belzec. But Notowitz, with forty-eight others, managed to escape from a labor camp in Poland in which fifty thousand prisoners perished. Of the forty-nine who escaped, eight survived, a feat they accomplished by hiding in the forest, "emotionally going into a freeze," and smuggling German marks on the black market. In 1948, at the invitation of a distant cousin, Estelle Friedman, Notowitz came to Memphis for Passover. Recognizing his ability, the family arranged for him to stay in Memphis to attend Christian Brothers High School where one of his subjects was a speech course taught by one of the brothers. Notowitz recalled that because he studied the dictionary, "whatever I could not do with pronunciation, I compensated [for] with vocabulary."

His determined approach led to academic success. Entering a state essay contest on the topic, "I Speak for Democracy," sponsored by the Chamber of Commerce and the American Legion, Notowitz won at the state level and placed fourth nationally. He received a Founders Scholarship to Vanderbilt University where he graduated Phi Beta Kappa five years after arriving in the United States with only a rudimentary knowledge of English. After the Korean War, Notowitz entered the United States Army and was sent back to Germany for a year and a half. He observed during his tour of duty that, in general, the Germans were repentant, an observation that helped him make the decision to "regain his humanity" after concluding that one cannot live in the past.[39]

Anti-Semitism, more than any other factor, underlay American inaction toward refugees before, during, and after the Holocaust. A majority of Americans feared that the refugees would overwhelm the United States. Only seventeen percent of those polled in 1938 favored admitting a larger number of German Jewish exiles. Even after *Kristallnacht*, the number of Americans who wished to relax existing immigration laws to admit more German Jews increased to only twenty-one percent.

---

[38]Leah and Moishe Kaufman interviews, Center for Southern Folklore, Holocaust Interviews, 14 September 1982.
[39]Interview with Max Notowitz, 1992.

Government officials did little to help German Jews or to modify existing restrictive immigration policies. State Department officials often prevented distribution of visas to Jews who might otherwise have qualified for admission under the large and largely unused German quota. When Franklin D. Roosevelt became president in 1933, he did not change the established procedures. Instead, he hid behind laws, public attitudes, and bureaucratic resistance, claiming that he could do little alone. He was unwilling to risk alienating congressmen and senators whose votes he might need by pushing legislation to aid refugees. Secretary of State Cordell Hull, although married to a woman of Jewish birth, did not interfere in immigration matters.[40]

The difficulty Jews had in gaining admission to the United States would not have been catastrophic except for the fact that no other nation would accept them. In 1938, at an international conference in Évian, France, on the plight of refugees, no nation offered them haven. Rational people continued to discount the rumors and reports they heard about Nazi Germany. The editor of *Christian Century* doubted the accuracy of Rabbi Stephen Wise's charge that Hitler was buying Jewish corpses to be "processed into soap fats and fertilizer," saying that the allegation was reminiscent of the propaganda of World War I.[41]

During the 1930s, American Jewish leaders had been too fearful of heightening anti-Semitism at home to demand government help for the refugees, but Nazi atrocities emboldened them to speak out in 1942. Once again, crisis united an otherwise disorganized American Jewish community.

Nearly every Jewish organization in the country supported the demand for a Jewish homeland in Palestine. Anti-Semitism, even in relatively hospitable America, convinced most Jews that they would not feel safe until they had a place to which they by right could go. Only the predominantly wealthy German American Jews, members of the American Jewish Committee and its offshoot, the American Council for Judaism, resisted the call for a Jewish homeland. Because the American Jewish Committee, the most prestigious Jewish organization in America until World War II, always sought acceptance from the larger, non-Jewish American community, it did

---

[40] Arthur Hertzberg, *The Jews in America: Four Centuries of an Uneasy Encounter* (New York: Simon and Schuster, 1989), 292.

[41] Judith Endelman, *The Jewish Community of Indianapolis, 1849 to the Present* (Bloomington: Indiana University Press, 1984), 235; Hertzberg, *Jews in America*, 292.

not support a Jewish homeland in Palestine until 1946.[42] The latter organization, the American Council for Judaism, was established in 1943 to counter endorsement of Zionist demands by the American Jewish Conference.

By 1948 a large majority of the members of Congress favored the rapid amendment of the Displaced Persons Act to admit more refugees. But the revision was blocked by Nevada's senior senator, Pat McCarran, the influential chairman of the Judiciary Committee. His vote was at least in part influenced by the fear of communism that dominated the United States in the late 1940s and 1950s, a fear fed by widespread acceptance of Nazi arguments that had often characterized Jews as communists and by such other major events as the Alger Hiss trial, the "loss" of China, and the Soviet Union's 1949 detonation of an atomic bomb. Xenophobia had always been a part of the American psyche; now Jews and foreigners were especially suspect in the atmosphere of heightened nativism that prevailed.[43]

Another popular anti-Semitic stereotype connected Jewish bankers to American economic problems. Henry Ford's belief in the existence of an international conspiracy was shared by millions in the United States. This attitude provided justification to those who limited the admission of Jews to institutions of higher learning, and who barred them from positions in many businesses and from many desirable residential neighborhoods throughout the country.[44]

The bill to amend the Displaced Persons Act in order to liberalize immigration finally was approved in 1950. It was signed into law by President Harry S. Truman, who commended it as "a corrective measure to the discrimination inherent in the previous act of 1948." But McCarran's opposition to the revision had taken its toll. He had succeeded in demoralizing the Displaced Persons Council and in holding down the number of Jews admitted. Fewer than one hundred thousand Jewish displaced persons were able to come to the United States as a result of the Truman Directive

---

[42]Paul Johnson, A History of the Jews (New York: Harper and Row, 1987), 506; Hertzberg, Jews in America, 310.

[43] Richard Breitman and Alan Kraut, American Refugee Policy and European Jewry, 1933-1945 (Bloomington: Indiana University Press, 1987), chaps. 11 and 12; Hertzberg, Jews in America, 308.

[44]Hertzberg, Jews in America, 309.

and the Displaced Persons Act.[45]

More than two hundred of the survivors of European devastation settled in Memphis after World War II. In addition to the usual problems encountered by all immigrants—learning the language and the customs, finding a means of making a living, and adjusting to the specific characteristics of a southern city—the survivors brought with them the painful weight of the horrors they had endured. The stories of survivors related here are not comprehensive, but only a representation of the whole.

In spite of what they suffered, most of those who came to live in Memphis were able to put their memories behind them and establish a satisfactory life. Many turned their bitter experiences into positive contributions to the lives of others. The survivors often expressed a determination to discover a purpose for their being spared. For some, it was to be witnesses, to be the voice for those no longer able to speak for themselves. For others, it was simply to make their lives, miraculously saved, count for something in the world.

The most important event of the late 1940s for the Memphis Jewish community occurred halfway around the world: the official proclamation of the state of Israel. Declaring its independence on 14 May 1948, Israel was immediately granted de facto recognition by President Harry Truman.[46]

Although its existence was destined to be embattled, Israel had an enormous impact on Jews everywhere. In Memphis, Jews manifested pride in the accomplishments of their coreligionists, and many traveled to see the new country, returning with appreciation for the Israelis' hardships and admiration for their successes. One source of pride was Israel's ability to make the land bloom. Historically not workers on the land because property ownership had long been denied them, Israelis in the infancy of the state became farmers, transforming the desert into productive, fertile land. Another source of pride was Israel's military prowess. Set down in the midst of hostile Arab regimes, Israel realized her precarious position and required military service for all her eligible young people. Although traditionally known to despise war and seek peace, when wars came, Israelis were prepared. Tested again and again by attacking neighbors, excellent, efficient fighters were fierce in defense of their land.

Support for the state of Israel helped erode the divisions between the

---

[45]Breitman and Kraut, *American Refugee Policy*, 113.
[46]Johnson, *History of the Jews*, 525.

branches of Judaism. Nurture of the new state was now the almost universal concern of all Jews, who began to work together to accomplish this singular purpose. In Memphis, most Jews considered it their obligation to support the Jewish Welfare Fund, an attitude whose adherents appeared to agree with author Leonard Woolf, Jewish husband of non-Jewish Virginia Woolf He wrote that before World War II he was not a Zionist, but after the war he could not be anything else. In the Jewish community, worries about divided loyalties no longer prevailed. Attorney Herschel Feibelman, an active member and former president of Temple Israel, spoke for many when he said he was a Jew and not a hyphenated Jew.

The Holocaust also promoted Jewish unity. As the war's end brought disclosure of the scale and scope of the Nazi genocide, it brought as well the shocking recognition, that assimilation, long thought by many to be the panacea for anti-Semitism, was, in fact, no protection against discrimination. Like nothing else in the history of Jews in the United States, the Holocaust brought together Jewish communities that were formerly divided over social, theological, economic, and cultural matters. In Memphis, the lines of separation blurred between Orthodox and Reform Jews.

9

BETWEEN WAR AND
SOCIAL UPHEAVAL: THE 1950S

"In the years following the traumatic experiences of the Depression and
World War II, the American Dream was to exercise personal freedom not
in social or political terms, but rather in economic ones."

—David Halberstam

Despite United States involvement in the military conflict from
1950 to 1953 between North and South Korea, the decade of the
1950s was a period of respite between World War and the social upheaval
of the 1960s. For most citizens the era was stable and focused above all on
concern for business and prosperity. The radical student idealists of the
1930s and 1940s had become part of "the establishment," engaging
themselves in earning a living. Conservatism spread from the Eisenhower
White House throughout all of American. In Memphis the death of political
boss Edward Hull Crump brought many changes. In the absence of Crump's
leadership, people unaccustomed to being in charge of their own government now had to make their own political decisions.

The urbanization of the South that began with the farm depression of
the 1920s continued through the 1930s. Mechanization led to consolidation
of farms and New Deal subsidies paid farmers not to plant. By 1938 one-half
of farm land was out of production and tenant farmers had to move. At the
same time, the New Deal provided jobs in cities, building parks, play-
grounds, and other public facilities.

The influx of people into Memphis from the surrounding small towns
that began in the twenties increased after World War II and continued into
the 1950s. Like the rest of the country, Memphis was enjoying the
economic boom created by the war. Young people from the countryside,
stimulated by the good economic times, and exposed to a wider world by the
war, sought the more exciting life of the city.

The migration of which they were a part was the beginning of the end of a chapter in the history of southern Jewry. For the most part, the grandparents and parents of these post-war Jewish migrants had settled in the small towns of the South, opening and operating stores, developing a comfortable way of life, and creating a Jewish community. They had built synagogues and other institutions, and had practiced their religion as well as they could, given the constraints of such a predominantly non-Jewish environment and the demands of the Orthodox way of life. It was difficult for small-town Jews to observe the Sabbath because most operated stores and Saturday was the preferred shopping day for farmers. It was also difficult to observe the dietary laws because kosher food was unavailable in rural areas. In order to attend religious services, small town Jews sometimes had to travel miles to the nearest town with a synagogue. And there were few other Jews with whom to socialize. Despite these obstacles, Judaism survived and even flourished in the small towns. Jews were often among the towns' leading citizens, owning stores, holding public office, and contributing to the general welfare.

A yearning for education was a significant cause of both Jewish and non-Jewish migration from the small towns, and professional opportunities exerted a powerful pull to the city. Encouraged by their families to acquire as much education as they could, young people graduating from professional schools often had little interest in carrying on the old family business or living in the small towns. Eli Evans wrote: "The story of the Jews of the South, at least a major part of it, is the story of fathers who built businesses for their sons who did not want them."[1]

Although Memphis served as a magnet for Jews from the surrounding area, the size of the city's Jewish population did not change appreciably, except for a temporary increase in the 1940s. Its growth was limited in part by a low birth rate, by intermarriage, and by the move of native Memphis Jews away from the city, factors which have held the Jewish population of Memphis stable at around ten thousand from 1930 until the present day.

Although their numbers did not grow significantly, Memphis Jews remained dependable supporters of their congregations. Memphis is a city where Jews, like their Christian counterparts, are affiliated with a religious institution. During the 1950s, increased affiliation was a national trend,

---

[1]Paul Johnson, *A History of the Jews* (New York: Harper and Row, 1987), 526; Eli Evans, quoted in Peter Applebone, "Jews Seek Survival in the South," *Commercial Appeal*, 28 November 1992, 12.

with church and synagogue rolls expanding to unprecedented numbers. Indeed, from the 1930s through the 1950s, the population of the United States rose forty percent while church and synagogue membership rose fifty percent.[2] For Memphis as for the rest of the country, the 1950s were a period of recovery from Depression and war, a period of building.

The prominence of the original German settlers continued to be challenged by the descendants of more recently arriving Eastern Europeans, many of whom prospered in the post-war boom. Sometimes the change in economic status of the Orthodox Jews was reflected in a change in their religious affiliation. As Orthodox Jews became more affluent, they sometimes joined the Reform congregation or held dual synagogue memberships as a step to higher social status. (At this time there was no Conservative organization in Memphis, although this was to change in 1955.) This practice conforms to the tendency of Protestants to join more prestigious denominations as they accumulate wealth: Methodists might become Episcopalians, for example. The Jewish congregations, responding to their members' new affluence, followed them to the suburbs, expanding their facilities eastward. In 1950, Anshei Sphard held a ground-breaking ceremony for its new synagogue at North Parkway and Bellevue. Harry Cooper was chairman of the building fund. The Nat Buring Educational Building was dedicated in 1955, at the end of the congregation's ten-year building program.[3]

Temple Israel dedicated its new school building in 1951 and began to make plans for a celebration of its hundredth anniversary in 1954. Temple President during the planning phase for the centennial was Leo Bearman Sr., who with Ben Goodman Jr., and Mildred Haas, chaired the celebration. President of the Temple in 1954 was William Loewenberg. To commemorate the occasion, Rabbi James Wax and his wife Helen wrote a history of Memphis Jews entitled, *Our First Century, 1854-1954*. The temple sponsored an All Day Institute for Christian Clergy, Religious School Teachers, and Theological Students in Memphis and the Mid-South with Dr. Louis L. Mann, Rabbi of Chicago's Sinai Congregation as featured speaker. The retirement of Dr. Harry W. Ettelson and his induction as

---

[2]*Yearbook of American Churches*, 1950, quoted in *Hebrew Watchman*, 19 September 1957.
     [3]Murray Radin and Cantor D. W. Skopp interview, Memphis State University Oral History of Jews in the South Project, 1968; *Hebrew Watchman*, 20 January 1955.

Rabbi Emeritus was honored by a service whose participants included Dr. Nelson Glueck, president of Hebrew Union College as principal speaker; Dr. Marshall Wingfield representing Memphis clergy and Walter Chandler, former mayor of Memphis, representing the community. Dr. Abba Hillel Silver traveled to Memphis to address those assembled for the Centennial Banquet, at which Frank Clement, Governor of Tennessee, and Frank Tobey, Mayor of Memphis, also spoke. The final event of the celebratory year was the formal installation of Dr. James A. Wax as sixth rabbi of Temple Israel; Dr. Julian Morgenstern, President Emeritus of Hebrew Union College, and Dr. Ferdinand M. Isserman, rabbi of Temple Israel, St. Louis, were the principal speakers for the occasion.[4]

Baron Hirsch dedicated its new synagogue on November 29 through December 1, 1957. The sanctuary held twenty two hundred permanent seats and enough space for an additional thousand.[5] The idea for the new facility was first discussed during William Gerber's presidency of the congregation when it became apparent to Gerber and other leaders that the membership no longer lived downtown where the old synagogue was located. Land was acquired in 1945, and a building fund established. Rabbi Isadore Goodman was the spiritual leader of Baron Hirsh. Philip Belz was chairman of the building committee and president of the congregation when the new facility was dedicated.

Yet another dedication in the 1950s was that of Beth El Emeth's remodeled synagogue at 165 Poplar. The oldest synagogue building in the city, it had been constructed by Congregation Children of Israel in 1883 and sold to Beth El Emeth when the former congregation moved in 1917 to Poplar and Montgomery.[6]

The first Conservative congregation in the city, Beth Sholom, House of Peace, celebrated its first service on 11 February 1955, at the B'nai B'rith Home. Prayers were led by lay rabbi Jack Langer. Helen Samuels was appointed chairman of a building fund committee. Rabbi James Wax of Temple Israel, who believed strongly that Memphis needed an institution where those who wished to practice Conservative Judaism could worship, was helpful in raising funds for the new congregation and provided its first Torah. Permanent officers were installed on 24 May 1955, by Rabbi Arthur

[4]Wax, *Our First Century*, 57-58.
[5]*Hebrew Watchman*, 3 October 1957.
[6]*Hebrew Watchman*, 16 June 1957.

Hertzberg of Nashville. The Beth Sholom Sisterhood was formed in March 1955 with Jeanette Katz as acting chairman. [7]

Rabbi Herbert Berger was selected as the first rabbi for the new congregation. Services were moved from the B'nai B'rith Home to the Pink Palace in Chickasaw Gardens where a stage was converted into a pulpit, and a boarded-over swimming pool accommodated seats. Property on South Mendenhall was purchased, and in October 1956 the existing house on the property was dedicated by a new rabbi, Meyer Passow. In 1959 Passow resigned to move to Israel and Rabbi Arie Becker became the congregation's spiritual leader.[8]

In 1952 three Orthodox synagogues established a Talmud Torah for the purpose of teaching Hebrew. Available to all their members who wished to attend, classes were held in the afternoons after school and opened with an enrollment of 153 students. The Jewish Welfare fund allocated ten thousand dollars for the year to facilitate the project. The Talmud Torah functioned until 1972 when most eligible students were enrolled at the Memphis Hebrew Academy, and enrollment at the Talmud Torah declined.[9]

Jewish individuals remained active in civic, professional, and cultural affairs. Henry Loeb II, secretary of Loeb's Laundry and Cleaners and future mayor of Memphis, won the 1950 Junior Chamber of Commerce Distinguished Service Award. Leo Seligman was named Optimist of the Year by the Optimist Club for his work with juvenile parolees. Dr. Jacob Plesofsky served as president of the Ninth District Dental Society in 1950.[10] Dr. Morton Tendler was elected president of the Memphis Surgical Society in

---

[7]Interview with Dr. Abraham Bass, 1990; Shankman, *History of Jews.* Other offices were held by Gertrude Altfater, Ruby Bass, and Sarah Yukon, vice presidents; Minnie Kisber, treasurer; Lillian Bluestein, corresponding secretary; Rena Shankman, recording secretary; Fannie Starr, parliamentarian; Thelma Appleson, chaplain; and Rosa Lee Abraham, Adeline Feldman, Bebe Gordon, Hilda Langer, Flora Samuels, Miriam Schnierer, Phyllis Wahl, and Jean Levin, Board of Directors.

[8]Staff of Beth Sholom in *Southern Jewish Heritage*, v. 3, #2, 6; Shankman, *History of Jews.*

[9]Dr. Ben Schaeffer was president of the Board of Directors which included Sol Friedman, Dr. Sam Green, Dave Engelberg, I. R. Engelberg, Harry Evans, Al Ballin, Nathan Engelberg, Robert Udelson, Meyer Kipper, Dr. Harold Cohen, Herman Lubin, Kalman Katz, Nathan Thomas, Dave Kaplan, Nathan Loskovitz, Isaac Loskove, and Morris Franklin; Talmud Torah Minutes.

[10]*Hebrew Watchman*, 7 December 1950; 11 March 1954; 13 September 1951.

1951. In the same year, Rabbi James Wax was re-elected president of the Memphis and Shelby County Mental Health Society. Arthur Halle Sr. was president of the Retail Merchants Association; Jimmie Brett was president of the Tennessee Association of Public Accountants. Harris Scheuner, president of the Memphis Retail Association, was elected vice-president of the Tennessee Restaurant Association. M. A. Lightman Jr. served as president of the Motion Picture Theater Owners of Mississippi, Tennessee, and Arkansas, and of Allied Independent Theater Owners of the Mid-South. Frank Romeo Jr. became president of a sixty-eight store retail organization, Associated Independent Merchants, in 1953.

In the service organization and community agency sector in the 1950s, Ben Goodman Jr. was president of the Memphis chapter of the Red Cross; Irvin Bogatin headed the United Service Organization; S. L. Kopald Jr. was on the Shelby County Planning Commission. Abe Scharff served as 1954 chairman of the Blues Bowl, an annual competition between black baseball teams for the benefit of charity. Blues musician W. C. Handy entertained at the half-time intermission. Ida Lipman led the Women's Round Table of the National Conference of Christians and Jews as president. In the late 1950s Julius Lewis was appointed to the governing board of the Memphis Housing Authority.[11]

In support of the arts, Herbert Herff headed the Memphis Symphony Society in 1950 and founded a History Lecture Society at Memphis State University in 1953. Isabel Goodman became a member of the Board of Trustees of the Memphis Art Academy (now Memphis College of Art) in 1951, a position she was to hold for many years, chairing the Library Committee. During this period Morrie and Lillian Moss began to donate works of art from their varied collection to Brooks Memorial Art Gallery (now Memphis Brooks Museum of Art). They had begun to donate to the Memphis Art Academy in the 1940s, a practice they continued and expanded, and in the 1970s and 1980s, they gave also to Dixon Gallery and Gardens.[12]

Berl Olswanger's career as a pianist can be said to have begun in 1921 when, at the age of three, he was able to play recognizable tunes. While still

---

[11]*Press Scimitar*, 31 December 1966 and 27 January 1967; *Hebrew Watchman*, 13 September 1951; *Hebrew Watchman*, 15 February 1951.

[12]Interview with P. K. Seidman, 1992; Morrie Moss, personal interview and *Memphis College of Art News*, August-November 1992.

in high school, he led a band that entertained at dances and other social functions. After college and military service in World War II, he returned to Memphis and presented a well-received concert of both classical and popular music at Ellis Auditorium. Olswanger accepted the position of piano player and arranger for the nationally prominent orchestra of Jan Garber, brother of Memphian Myron Garber, owner of Garber's Ice Cream Company. But traveling and being away from Memphis were not satisfactory to the young musician. He came home and began his own entertainment business, becoming the best-known popular pianist in the city. Olswanger also opened a music store where he sold instruments and equipment and taught instrumental music and theory.

The Memphis Sinfonietta became the Memphis Symphony Orchestra in the early 1950s. Second president of the new organization was P. K. Seidman, who led the group from 1954 to 1960. During his tenure, the Symphony League was organized as a support group, and the first annual Symphony Ball was held in 1959. Co-chairing the ball was Trude Weil. The successes of the league and the ball helped to put the symphony on a sound financial basis.[13] Seidman also was president of the Memphis Little Theater (now Theatre Memphis) in the 1950s.

Jewish Memphians who received honors included thirteen-year-old Jack Goldsmith Jr., who earned the Boy Scouts' highest lifesaving award for rescuing two men whose boat had capsized on nearby Horseshoe Lake. Eugene Bespalow, vice-president of Choctaw, Inc., was chosen to fill two posts for the federal government. Bespalow was named a member of the Concrete Pipe Industry Committee of the National Production Authority and of the Engineering Manpower Commission of the Manpower Office of the National Resources Board.[14]

Memphians also filled leading roles in regional and national Jewish organizations. Abe Waldauer was appointed to the Board of Trustees of Brandeis University in 1952. Sam Shankman was named Honorary Vice-President of the Southeast Region of the Zionist Organization of America. Leo Burson, appointed to the National Administration Committee of the Zionist Organization of America in 1951, later became one of the organization's one hundred thirty citizen delegates to the Atlanta Congress for

---

[13]Seidman interview.

[14]*Hebrew Watchman*, 19 November 1951; 15 March 1951; 12 April 1951; 3 January 1952; 25 October 1951; 17 July 1933; 4 August 1958; 15 December 1956; 25 October 1951.

NATO Cooperation. Marx Borod became the first non-resident of New Orleans to be elected vice-president of the service board of the Jewish Children's Home.[15]

Encouraged by the economic climate, Jewish businessmen began new enterprises in the 1950s. The Cooper Companies was organized by Louis Cooper in 1954 to manage property and develop hotels. Catherine's Stout Shoppe was opened in 1959 by Ralph Levy Jr. Levy had worked in the family business, the Landres Company, where he discovered that the demand for large-sized clothes was far greater than the supply. Levy and his wife Jo bought the Catherine's name from the original owner for two hundred fifty dollars and recapitalized the business with two thousand dollars. Levy says he gained success by cultivating the large-sized customer while department stores were ignoring her. Aaron Scharff, retiring as president of the then large department store, Lowenstein's, was succeeded by Stanley Fried.

As the decade of the 1950s ended, Memphis Jewry continued its pursuit of activities consistent with prosperity, stability, and with its concern for Jews worldwide. The Jewish community which had provided aid to refugees from Hitler in the 1930s and to Holocaust survivors in the 1940s, in the late 1950s, responded to the need to rescue fourteen thousand Jews from Poland, Hungary, and North Africa. At a mass meeting held in 1957, part of a national drive, the community accepted as its quota the sum of six hundred sixty thousand dollars. But the period of relative calm that characterized the 1950s was harboring seeds of turmoil and change. As the 1960s began, problems present but unacknowledged in the previous decade could no longer be ignored.

---

[15]*Hebrew Watchman*, 31 January 1952; 15 October 1951; 29 November 1951; 7 May 1959; Leo Burson interview; *Hebrew Watchman*, 14 June 1951.

10

THE SIXTIES

"... a watershed in the cultural history of the United States."

—Morris Dickstein

Restlessness and re-evaluation were the tenor of the 1960s. Long accepted values, formerly unquestioned, were subjected to scrutiny and doubt. Change was the order of the day—in politics, culture, values, even in forms of entertainment. Memphis rock-and-roll singer Elvis Presley personified many aspects of the revolution. With his new combination of traditional rhythms and black gospel, Presley achieved international fame. With the introduction of sexual suggestiveness into his performances, he overturned old taboos. Popular music has never been the same.

But a number of other changes in the decade were violent in nature. The Vietnam conflict, one of the most unpopular and divisive military engagements in American history, was escalated by the nation's leaders, eroding public confidence in them. The decade's assassinations of John Kennedy, Martin Luther King Jr., and Robert Kennedy shocked the world.

Much of the decade's turmoil was reflected in the civil rights movement. The changing nature of race relations in the country was validated by the United States Supreme Court's landmark decision in the 1954 case of *Brown v. Board of Education*. The ruling outlawed segregated schools, but implementation of the ruling was not pushed until the 1960s when it became part of a larger movement for desegregation in all areas of life. The Memphis branch of the National Association for the Advancement of Colored People (NAACP), aware of the local racial climate, moved slowly. It filed its first civil rights suit in 1955 to force Memphis State College (later renamed the University of Memphis) to admit black students, an action the school finally implemented in 1959. The NAACP filed desegregation suits for the use of the public libraries in 1958, and for the use of the zoo and parks in 1959, but did not sue the Memphis Board of Education until 1960.[1]

Jews traditionally had been in the forefront of national movements for the advancement of civil rights, and Jewish Memphians were no exception. But in the South, those whose roots had been deepest in southern land often, paradoxically, felt the least secure, the least willing to risk the aftermath of the demands of Judaism and of conscience. In the immediate aftermath of the *Brown* decision, civil rights activist Rabbi Jacob Rothschild of Atlanta found that the "scions of old, established families well settled in the South for generations ran for cover first. It was they who claimed to be completely accepted by the Gentiles in their communities and they who insisted that for them Judaism was a religion only."

When in 1958 another southern rabbi urged prudence, Rothschild replied, "How can we condemn the millions who stood by under Hitler or honor those few who chose to live by their ideals when we refuse to make a similar choice now that the dilemma is our own?" Nevertheless, several Jews led the local movement in the 1960s. The Memphis Committee on Community Relations, formed in 1959, included on its prestigious board of directors Rabbi James Wax of Temple Israel and Lester Rosen, an insurance executive. Its goal was to achieve voluntary progress toward equal treatment for all citizens of Memphis rather than wait for court orders that would mandate equal justice. It planned to work without publicity to attain its ends, convinced that quiet, behind-the-scenes pressure could achieve desegregation without dire consequences. Once desegregation was accomplished, the committee members believed there would be a precedent for building a more equitable future.

During Rosen's tenure on the Memphis Committee on Community Relations, blacks were picketing restaurants and being picked up and jailed by the police. Rosen went to see Police Commissioner Claude Armour, who was aware that in other Tennessee cities, restaurants were being quietly desegregated. Armour met with restaurant owners and urged them to integrate their businesses, assuring them that the process could be conducted peacefully.

Lester Rosen had a long history of involvement in the fight for equality. For twenty years beginning in 1949 he was a member of the board of directors of the Urban League whose main purpose was to gain employment

---

[1]David Tucker, *Memphis Since Crump: Bossism, Blacks, and Civic Responses, 1948-1968* (Knoxville, University of Tennessee Press, 1980), 118.

for blacks. In the late 1950s, Rosen had an experience that heightened his consciousness of the omnipresence of prejudice. He was invited to speak at a convention of the Million Dollar Roundtable, an international life insurance organization. During the convention, his host told him he would like to take him to his club, but members were forbidden to invite Jewish guests. Returning home, Rosen realized that he, too, belonged to a club that discriminated, the Summit Club. Determined to try to change that situation, and having first alerted the club's manager to his intentions, Rosen invited his friend, the Reverend Henry Starks, a black minister, to lunch with him at the Summit Club. The club manager urged him not to follow through with his plan because "members from Mississippi would not like that." But Rosen would not be dissuaded and the lunch took place. No one resigned from the club.

Mayor Henry Loeb appointed Rosen in the late 1960s to the Memphis and Shelby County Human Relations Commission. Working with Judge Benjamin Hooks, who later became national head of the NAACP, the Human Rights Commission was able to bring a measure of calm to a sit-in by black students at Memphis State University.

Shortly after he moved to Memphis in 1963 to practice medicine, Dr. Lawrence Wruble had a black patient who required hospitalization and who requested admission to Baptist Hospital. Wruble called the hospital asking that his patient be admitted and informing hospital officials that his patient was black. The response, "We refuse no one," facilitated admission of the hospital's first black patient. Although Wruble was a newcomer to the city, his wife, Diane Leach Wruble, was a native Memphian. They both understood that this event set a new precedent. Wruble received anonymous threatening phone calls, and some of his colleagues, mostly other Jewish doctors, questioned his actions. The complaints led Baptist Hospital to examine all of his records in an attempt to find some reason to remove him from its staff, but nothing was found to justify such action. The hospital's decision to desegregate its facility later placed it in compliance with federal regulations.[2]

After years of escaping responsibility by entrusting race relations to politicians and economic leaders, in 1968, the Memphis Ministers Association decided to organize its own Race Relations Committee to work with the Memphis Committee on Community Relations. Rabbi Wax was

[2]Interview with Diane Wruble, 1992.

president of the Ministers Association at that time, as well as an active member of the Race Relations Committee. He proposed that the Ministers Association issue a statement in the form of a paid advertisement in the city's two major newspapers. When the suggestion was adopted on 2 January 1968, it produced the first such public statement ever made by ministers as a group in Memphis. The association's "An Appeal to Conscience" urged that "anyone who loves God must also love his brother . . . therefore, prejudice and discrimination are sinful according to the Judeo-Christian ethics." Public reaction to the ministers' unusual candor on social issues was generally unfavorable. The ministers were advised to "let the mayor run the city" and to focus their attention instead on religion.

Rabbi Wax's pleas for social justice often were delivered from the pulpit at Temple Israel, despite the fact that his sermons defied popular opinion in the city and indeed in his own congregation. Under his leadership, the Ministers Association continued to work to improve race relations. Although it failed in its efforts to bring about a settlement between labor and city leaders during the sanitation strike that began on 12 February 1968, Rabbi Wax continued to be an example for all Memphians of the manner in which people true to the tenets of Judaism and Christianity should behave toward each other. Threatening letters, phone calls, and dangerous incidents did not stop him from his tireless crusade against prejudice.

As a national officer of the American Jewish Committee who came to Memphis to visit, Lester Rosen recognized the possibility of bitter outcome during the sanitation strike. Rosen took Rabbi Wax with him to see Mayor Loeb, where they tried to convince Loeb that unless the strike were settled, violence would result. The attempt was unsuccessful.[3]

As the strike continued and tensions mounted in the city, Martin Luther King Jr. came to Memphis to lend his prestige to the conflict, to prevent violence, and to lead sanitation workers in their quest for union recognition, better wages and decent working conditions. The workers' slogan, "I Am a Man," was a summation of the civil rights movement, challenging the taken-for-granted inequality of life for blacks in the city and in the nation. The strike united the black community as never before. Supporters of the strike were rallied by their religious leaders and influenced by the militant non-violent methods of King and by contemporaneous civil

---

[3]Interview with Lester Rosen, 1991.

rights efforts in other areas of the country. On the evening of 4 April 1968 King was assassinated.[4]

The entire community was stunned, not only by the event itself, but by the fact that it had happened in Memphis, a city that thought itself more progressive than the "Deep South," that believed it was making progress on desegregation, albeit slowly. The following day, the Ministers Association marched from St. Mary's Episcopal Cathedral to City Hall to plead again with the mayor to settle the strike. Rabbi Wax, who had always considered himself to be a man of words, took the unusual action of marching, choosing to do so alongside "his black brother, the Reverend Henry Starks." Reaching City Hall, Wax, as president of the Memphis Ministers Association, addressed Mayor Henry Loeb, who had been one of his congregants until Loeb married an Episcopalian and joined his wife's church.

The mayor's position, repeatedly stated, was that the city would not deal with striking municipal workers who were forbidden by law to strike. He insisted that the city's position was about legality, not race. When Loeb continued to cling to the same posture, even after King's murder, Wax spoke words that were reported throughout the country. "Your Honor," he said, "there are laws higher than the laws of Memphis and Tennessee, and those are the laws of God."[5] Several years later, a Methodist minister said that on that day God had spoken through Rabbi Wax.

Jimmy Wax had intended to become a lawyer until he heard a sermon delivered in St. Louis by Rabbi Ferdinand Isserman. Isserman's description of the social justice message of Judaism touched such a responsive chord in Wax that he decided to become a rabbi. During his installation as rabbi of Temple Israel he told the congregation,

> This pulpit shall ever be concerned with the problems of life. Whatever effects human beings, children of God, shall be of utmost concern. . . . By that I mean that one lives according to the old virtues and cares about others; to help alleviate the conditions of poverty and discrimination that deny individuals the opportunity to live a fuller, richer life.[6]

---

[4]Selma Lewis, *Diversification and Unity A History of MIFA, 968-1988* (Memphis: Metropolitan Inter-Faith Association, 1988).

[5]Joan Beifuss, *At the River I Stand* (Memphis: B and W Books, 1987), 320.

[6]Joy Hall, *Commercial Appeal*, 26 February 1978, 6.

He adhered to the standard he set himself, convinced that religion and morality are synonymous.

Wax's service to the community also included significant work for the mentally ill. Governor Frank Clement appointed him to the state of Tennessee's first Mental Health Commission; he was reappointed by both Republican and Democratic governors. The Activities Building of the Memphis Mental Health Institute was named for him. He was a founder and president of the Memphis Mental Hygiene Agency, the forerunner of the Mental Health Association of Memphis and Shelby County.

In 1956, long before it was popular to be a civil rights advocate, Memphis's black newspaper, the *Tri-State Defender*, honored Rabbi Wax for promoting harmonious race relations. County Commissioner and long-time civil rights activist Dr. Vasco Smith spoke of Wax as "one of the very early individuals in the city of Memphis concerned with human relations."

Among many honors, Wax received the Distinguished Citizen Award of the Newspaper Guild of Memphis; the Outstanding Citizen's Award by the Veterans of Foreign Wars; the Service to Mankind Award in 1967 by the Sertoma Club; the Human Relations Award in 1978 by the National Conference of Christians and Jews; the Public Service Award by the Jewish Chatauqua Society in 1978; and the Ministerial Alliance of Memphis and Shelby County's Outstanding Award in 1978.

Wax's parishioners remember his challenging sermons punctuated by a long, bony forefinger, exhorting them to live up to the best ideals of Judaism, encouraging them to make the world a better place for all its people. It is for this conception of religion, that "it has to be related to the issues of life and society . . . with . . . how we treat one another as human beings," that he is often remembered.

Rabbi Wax revealed his love of learning and respect for history by helping to found the Jewish Historical Society of Memphis and the Mid-South. He was himself the author of *The Jews of Memphis, 1860-1865*, and *Our First Century, 1854-1954*, a history of Temple Israel written with his wife, Helen Goldstrum Wax. Wax's intention had been to write a history of all the religions in Memphis after he retired. He felt it would be an appropriate gift for him to make to the city that had been so kind to him.

Unfortunately, illness kept him from that task.[7]

When he died in October 1989 an editorial observed that Wax had been

> in the forefront of every community effort to bring tolerance, understanding, and problem-solving into the maelstrom of intolerance, division, and misunderstanding. He has never been afraid to take the risks that such leadership demands . . . . Nobody is more a part of the fabric of the community than James Wax.[8]

The strike ended on 16 April 1968. Its settlement had been facilitated by the intervention of President Lyndon Johnson who sent Undersecretary of Labor James Reynolds to Memphis, and by the philanthropy of Abe Plough who gave the city enough money to grant sanitation workers an increase in pay.

Rabbi Arie Becker of Beth Sholom also took a strong stand for civil rights during the 1960s. A refugee from the Hitler regime, Becker believed that God had left him on earth to accomplish something; he could not live with himself if he did not act. In early May 1963, Becker was in upstate New York attending a meeting of the Rabbinical Assembly of Conservative Judaism while King was in Birmingham leading the infamous protest marches during which the police, led by Birmingham Police Commissioner "Bull" Connor, used attack dogs, cattle prods, and fire hoses to disperse the marchers. The rabbis at the assembly, moved by these events, by memories of the Holocaust, and by the obligations of their religion, decided that they could not remain silent in the face of such atrocities. A phone call to Birmingham inquiring if it would be useful for a group of rabbis to join the marchers met with an immediate positive response. They were told that they would be sincerely welcomed, and that "the time to come is now." The assembly voted to send representatives at once to Birmingham and provided funds for the trip. Nineteen rabbis volunteered to go, Becker among them.

When the rabbis arrived in Birmingham they were met at the airport by two delegations. One, from the Southern Christian Leadership Conference, welcomed them and escorted them to the only integrated motel in the city, the Gaston, where King's headquarters were located. The other delegation,

---

[7]Interview with Helen G. Wax. 1990.
[8]*Commercial Appeal*, 19 October 1989.

members of the local rabbinate, worried about the effect on them and on their congregations of the participation of the rabbis in the march, urged the group to turn around and return home. The nineteen were worried about the situation as well, but chose to follow through on what they had decided was right. They proceeded to march back in Memphis. Becker received death threats as a result of his participation in the march.[9] His son remembers moving to a hotel for a while and even spending several months in Philadelphia in order to be safe. Becker spoke often from the pulpit about the need for equal rights for all. His congregants had ambivalent feelings about what he was doing. They were frightened for him, and probably for themselves as well, but they were also proud of what he said and did.[10]

Josephine Burson was another of the city's Jewish leaders who exhibited an unwavering commitment to civil rights. In her capacity as head of the Democratic Party's Women's Division for the Kennedy-Johnson ticket, during the presidential campaign of 1960 she planned a reception for "Lady Bird" Johnson at Ellis Auditorium. The auditorium's management told her that she had to plan two events, one for white women, the other for black. Burson "didn't think this was right, since we had worked together on the campaign," and refused to hold segregated receptions. Because it was an unusually large and lucrative affair for the auditorium, its management altered the rules and, for the first time, allowed its space to be used for an integrated party. "It was a beautiful affair, with no picketing," Burson says, "and only a couple of women on the committee quit in protest."[11] Since then, integrated political functions have become routine in Memphis.

Burson remained active in politics after 1960. She had refused to support Buford Ellington's gubernatorial race in 1958 because she found him to be an "old-fashioned segregationist." However, in 1966 he asked her to be chairperson of his women's campaign for governor. Ellington convinced Burson that he had changed his position on segregation and she accepted the task. When Ellington won, he credited her with his victory, and invited her to join his cabinet. She served as Commissioner of Employment for the next four years. She introduced ideas to prepare minorities to pass basic civil service examinations. The resulting program,

---

[9]Harriet Stern, "A Southern Rabbi in Martin Luther King's Court, *Southern Jewish Heritage* 8 (Winter, 1995): 3-4, 7.
[10]Telephone interview with Dr. Daniel Becker and Sarah Yukon, 1995.
[11]Interview with Josephine Burson, 1991.

called GREAT (Government Recruitment, Education, and Training) proved to be effective. Under Burson's administration, Tennessee became the first state to inaugurate a federally-funded work incentive program.

As a senior citizen herself, Burson went to work in the Public Relations Department of Senior Citizens Services, offering her experience and knowledge of another agency whose purpose it is to help people improve their lives. In addition to her career as a public servant, Burson was recognized for a more traditional role when she was selected National Mother of the Year on Mother's Day, 1975. She is the only Jewish woman to receive this award.

Upon his succession to the presidency in 1963, Lyndon Johnson proclaimed a national War on Poverty. Every city was told to create a community action agency charged with the responsibility of devising its own anti-poverty program. Mayor William B. Ingram named the Memphis response the War on Poverty Committee (WOPC) and asked twenty-five agencies already involved in providing social services to participate. Lester Rosen was the Urban League's representative on the WOPC; attorney Herschel Feibelman represented the Jewish Community Center.

An acting chairman led the WOPC's for its first six months, after which Herschel Feibelman was elected chairman, a post he held from 1966 to 1969. Feibelman describes those turbulent years as "a time of anguish and action," not only nationally, but locally as well. The agency saw as its role the stimulation of new projects to attack poverty on as many levels as possible. Feibelman believes that while the WOPC never achieved its ambitious aim of eliminating poverty, a judgment that has been made of the national program as well, it did achieve some "marginal success." He points to the proven value of the Head Start and Legal Services programs. He recalls losing a few clients from his law practice who did not approve of his involvement in the project, and remembers a few unpleasant phone calls. One caller was particularly abusive. "You nigger-loving s.o.b.," said the voice, " why don't you people go back where you came from?"

But Feibelman was not influenced by comments of this kind. What did exert a lasting effect on him was an experience in a Head Start class in which a teacher was explaining the way primary colors can be combined to create a new color. As an example, she showed the children an orange, whose color is a blending of red and yellow. As he watched, Feibelman realized that one of the children had never seen an orange before. He fled from the classroom into his car and wept. Although the WOPC was "inept," he says, "it had good intentions to make things better for those in poverty." He does not regret his involvement.[12]

Other programs begun in the 1960s targeted hunger. The federal government ran a lunch program for needy children. As it included only one thousand children and more than forty thousand Memphis school children lived in poverty, the federal lunch program fell far short of the city's need. A discussion of the program's inadequacy at a meeting of social workers in 1964 prompted Myra Dreifus to see for herself. Visiting a school at lunchtime, she was horrified. She observed that while some children had money to go through the lunch line and purchase a lunch and others brought sack lunches from home, some children had neither option. Surrounded by the sight and smells of food, these children remained unfed, often putting their heads down on their desks to wait out the time.

Recently returned from a trip to India, Dreifus and her husband had seen poverty that not only dismayed them, but that left Myra feeling hopeless and powerless. Here in America, she believed, people of good will could correct injustice. Gathering a biracial group of ten or twelve women, Dreifus set about ending the intolerable condition of hungry children in Memphis. With determination and persistence, fighting against community disbelief and bureaucratic satisfaction with the status quo, she explored every method at hand to combat hunger in Memphis schools.

Dreifus's philosophy, reflected on a button created for her by one of her volunteers, was that "You cannot educate a hungry child." The Memphis Board of Education was initially deaf to this point of view, believing that its responsibility was only to educate children, not to feed them. The two positions were incompatible until an aroused public, alerted by this diminutive but determined woman, influenced the Board of Education to agree that the ability to learn was tied to freedom from hunger. Finally, she convinced the community that hungry children cannot be educated, and that allowing children to remain unfed when a remedy was available was a scandal.

By the time the community was sufficiently aroused to want to end hunger in its schools, it was difficult to find a source of funding. Federal funds already had been allocated for the year; the budget of the City Council had been set. The Shelby County Quarterly Court, the funding agent for the county, was the only public agency whose annual budget had

---

[12]Interview with Herschel Feibelman, 1993.

not yet been passed. Dreifus and her committee lobbied the members of the county court to pass a special tax to finance school lunches for the rest of the year, until federal funds could be requested for the following years. Against many odds, but with no thought of defeat, the women persuaded the group to levy an extra five-cent tax to be used to provide lunches for needy school children.

The school lunch committee, originally called Food for Fitness, was renamed Fund for Needy School Children to reflect more accurately the multitude of needs addressed by the group. Among the Jewish women who were members of the original committee were Marjean Kremer, Harriet Stern, Linda Kaplan, Grace Katz, Stella Menke, Selma Simon, and Selma Lewis. The committee eventually numbered some four hundred Jewish and non-Jewish, black and white, male and female volunteers who performed varied services in the public schools.

The summer of 1968, the year of King's assassination in Memphis, saw possible danger for the city if teenagers had no jobs or time-consuming useful activities. Working with the Fund for Needy School Children Steering Committee, Dreifus determined to provide jobs for some young people and scholarships for training for others. With assistance from guidance counselors from the schools, needy young people were identified. But raising money to fund the program was a daunting prospect. Dreifus believed that the city and county should allocate the money, deeming it a valid expenditure of public funds because it would demonstrate the concern of government for the welfare of its people. After several weeks of lobbying, members of the City Council and County Court granted a sum of $200,000 to fund the program. Unlike many other cities across the nation, Memphis remained quiet over the long summer.

Dreifus received many awards, among them the Humanitarian Award by the National Conference of Christians and Jews, and an honorary doctorate from Southwestern (Rhodes College), where she served on the President's Council. Her actions and ideals inspired the community as a whole and her own children in particular. After his since retirement as President of the Dreifus Jewelry Company, her son Jed devoted much of his life to being a board member and President of Lemoyne-Owen College, a black institution in Memphis. He created a program called Memphis Volunteer Placement Committee whose purpose was to guide talented, needy, college-bound young people into future careers through counseling, tutoring, employment advice, and scholarships to fine eastern prep schools.

Dreifus also arranged weekly meetings at which invited leaders of the black and white communities discussed racial problems in the city and ways to solve them. These gatherings, built on the close personal friendship of Dreifus and black attorney Benjamin Hooks, were called the Ben Hooks Breakfast Club. For many years, they have provided a valuable forum for the examination of important local issues.

Jeanne Dreifus was president of the Memphis Branch of the National Council of Jewish Women, and served on its national board. Both she and her mother-in-law received that organization's prestigious Hannah G. Solomon Award.[13]

Jocelyn Dan Wurzburg was inspired to fight against "attitudinal racism" after hearing an emotional message delivered by Mary Collier Lawson, an eloquent black teacher, at a mass meeting called "Memphis Cares" following King's assassination. Recalling the influential work accomplished in Little Rock by a Panel of American Women, Wurzburg recruited a group of women, some black, some Catholic, some Protestant, and some Jewish, and organized them into a Memphis Panel of American Women. Among other Jewish women involved were Bernice Cooper and Marilyn Weinman. Wurzburg became the executive director. The women spent a year of "consciousness raising" during which they educated each other about their differences. In 1969 they began to take their message before all sorts of organizations throughout the city. The panel eventually dissolved as the women found other social interests, particularly the newly burgeoning feminist movement. Wurzburg says "everyone started going back to school." She went back as well and earned a law degree.[14]

The task of desegregating Memphis business in which Jewish business-men played a central role was underway before the King assassination. The role of merchants in the South during the 1960s was not an easy one, caught as they were between pressures from the established, segregated order and the new demands for equality. Accepting that integration was inevitable and hoping that violence could be averted, Jack Goldsmith, president of Goldsmith's department store, and Mel Grinspan, head of public and personnel relations for the Shainberg stores, began to meet in the early 1960s. They wished to formulate a plan by which stores in the city would move collectively and voluntarily toward integration, to create a

---

[13]Interview with Myra Dreifus, 1995.
[14] Interview with Jocelyn Wurzburg, 1992.

climate in which none would become a target.

Grinspan, who represented a firm that maintained a home office in Memphis but that also operated properties outside of the city, was pleased to have the opportunity to become involved in something he believed in, and "because it was the right thing to do." Goldsmith, who had a "broad and liberal outlook," called upon a respected negotiator from Dallas, Sam Bloom, to help develop the plan. Adept at public relations, Bloom was retained by Federated Stores, which had bought Goldsmith's from the local Memphis family. Eventually, step by step, individual contact by individual contact, Goldsmith, Grinspan, and Bloom arranged a meeting of the managers of all the large downtown stores on 6 March 1964. Although only a handful attended, those present agreed that there was a need for all to work together.

The store managers who did not come to the meeting probably stayed away for a number of reasons: some feared becoming involved in something that would lose business; some were not in favor of integration; and some were encouraged by their regional offices not to meet with the group.[15] The managers group decided that it would move together, within a period of a week to ten days, to place black salespeople on the sales floors.

Goldsmith and Grinspan received threats, both to their stores and to themselves personally, leaving them fearful but undeterred. Grinspan worked hard to convince the Shainberg's store manager in Memphis to follow the plan already employed by the chain's stores elsewhere. The process took a period of months during which there were many meetings to develop acceptance of the plan. When he met with store managers at Shainberg's Mississippi locations—Tupelo, Columbus, Kosciusko, and Jackson—Grinspan "snuck into town" at night. In carrying out his role in the integration process, he endured threats; bombs; a lecture from the mayor of Jackson, Mississippi, telling him to stop interfering with the southern way of doing business; and menacing messages from the White Citizens Council, "the elitist Ku Klux Klan," informing him that two people were not welcome in Mississippi: Grinspan himself and Rabbi James Wax. Eventually, however, integration was accepted; and although some businesses experienced days or weeks of poor sales, business was never seriously affected overall.[16]

---

[15]Mel Grinspan interview.
[16]Ibid.

Grinspan served as vice-president of the Memphis Chamber of Commerce for a number of years in the 1960s and 1970s. Working closely with the other leaders of the chamber, he continued his efforts to help build minority business and to achieve economic equality in the city. Grinspan was co-founder with John T. Fisher of the Greater Memphis Urban Development Corporation, a manufacturing company with black management and employees. He was founder as well and first chairman of the Minority Regional Purchasing Council, an organization that brought together representatives of larger companies who could give contract business to minority-owned firms. "Lots of people took risks to accomplish something positive." The council is still operating and "doing well."[17]

By the early part of 1963 Memphis theater owners had met with members of the Memphis Committee on Community Relations to plan for desegregation of their theaters. The process had begun when an executive of United Artists in New York City invited Richard Lightman, an owner of Memphis's Malco Theaters, to Washington for a meeting with Attorney General Robert Kennedy. Along with some one hundred fifty other owners of theaters, restaurants, hotels and motels, Lightman heard Kennedy and his deputy, Marshall Burke, tell the audience that danger in the country could be averted only by breaking down old barriers. Ten days later, Lightman and the others were asked to return to Washington, this time to meet with President Kennedy and Vice-President Johnson, as well as the Attorney General. The President asked them to desegregate their facilities. Although some grumbled, most agreed to comply. Lightman returned to Memphis to begin the desegregation of all Malco theaters.[18]

Other leaders of the Memphis community, both white and black, also worked diligently in the 1960s to make desegregation a reality. Lucius Burch, a white Christian attorney, and Jesse Turner, a black banker, both civil rights activists, conceived of the idea of forming a social club for young white and black professionals in order to promote better knowledge and understanding among them. Marvin Ratner, a partner in the prestigious law firm of Heiskell and Donelson, joined, as did black attorney Russell Sugarmon. The two men had been acquaintances, but the new association provided an opportunity for friendship to develop. They and their wives became best friends, "visiting in each other's homes and clubs." They also

---

[17]Ibid.
[18]Interview with Richard Lightman, 1992.

became political allies, supporting liberal candidates.

Their friendship led to another kind of collaboration. When Louis Lucas, who was with the United States Justice Department, came to Memphis and proposed the idea of an integrated law firm to Russell Sugarmon, it was logical for Sugarmon to recruit Ratner. Although he knew it was a risky venture financially, Ratner, with the full support of his wife, left his old law firm to form a new, integrated one. The first such firm in the city, it opened on 15 July 1967, and included two other white attorneys, Russell Thompson and Louis Lucas, and another black attorney, A. W. Willis. Joining them as associates were Walter Bailey, who is black, and Irvin Salky, who is white and Jewish.[19]

Announcement of the establishment of the new law firm generated a few harassing phone calls to Ratner in the middle of the night, but the calls represented less trouble than he had anticipated. His old clients remained loyal, bringing in fees that paid most of the bills of the new firm. Although civil rights work was usually unprofitable, Ratner's satisfaction in providing a place where blacks could obtain good legal advice from skilled professionals compensated for the lack of revenue.

The partners specialized in fighting discrimination, whether in the field of housing or employment or education, a mission to which they displayed a special sensitivity and dedication. As head of the city's Better Schools Committee and vice-chairman of the state organization, Ratner was particularly aware of the differences in educational opportunities available to blacks and white. During the fifteen years of the firm's existence, it recruited many idealistic law students as clerks. One, a young Jewish law student from Berkeley, California, wanted to work with the group, but his mother was reluctant for him to live in the strife-torn South of the 1960s. She relented when she read the firm's letterhead, because she recognized that "Sugarmon was such a good Jewish name."

Ratner says he has never regretted his experience as a partner in the area's first integrated law firm. It made life "fuller than ever before. When you are working for an unpopular cause, there is a feeling of camaraderie and warmth because of sharing common beliefs." He believes that he had an opportunity to put the goals of equal justice and equal education above the goal of earning money, and he is proud that he chose to do so.[20]

---

[19]Interview with Marvin Ratner, 1992.
[20]Ibid.

In addition to the external civil rights issues it addressed in the 1960s, the Temple Israel congregation faced an internal dilemma when its Sunday school population outgrew its facilities. In order to accommodate the overflow, the board of trustees decided to divide the student body. Most would continue to attend on Sunday mornings; but 122 children, whose families had only one child in Sunday school classes, were assigned to attend on Saturday mornings. A group of parents with "Saturday" children complained that their children would be prevented from participating in such "normal" non-Jewish Saturday activities as birthday parties and athletic events. When the board refused to compromise, the rebellious parents established their own Sunday school on Sunday mornings. They rented a room at a conveniently located bank on Perkins Avenue Extended and took turns conducting classes.

The alternate Sunday school lasted for approximately three years, until Temple Israel built new facilities that enabled the prodigals to return to the fold. There was some resentment on both sides of the issue: the parents felt that the board had been intransigent in refusing to consider any other solutions; the board felt that the parents had demonstrated an unwillingness to appear Jewish to the non-Jewish world. However, peace was finally restored. One humorous incident resulted: when six-year-old Louise Wolf, daughter of Joanne and Herbert Wolf, went to her school's library to check out books relating to Chanukah, the librarian asked where she attended Sunday school. Louise replied, "I go to the National Bank of Commerce."[21]

Clearly, civil rights was a dominant theme of the 1960s. But the Jewish community was active in other pursuits as well. Concerned about the growing number of incidents of crime in the community, Ira Lipman established a security business in 1963. With an investment of one thousand dollars, Lipman founded a guard service which he named Guardsmark in honor of his father, Mark. Lipman's first office, a small room in the basement of a building in downtown Memphis, has grown to become the national headquarters of one of the country's largest security services. By the end of the 1960s eight branch offices served eighteen states.[22]

To enhance the cultural advantages of the city, P. K. Seidman, a partner in the accounting firm of Seidman and Seidman, established the Seidman Memorial Town Hall Lectures in memory of his brother M. L.

---

[21] Interview with Joanne Brod, 1994.
[22] Interview with Ira Lipman, 1992.

Seidman, who died in October 1963. The series, which features talks by
authorities in the fields of business, world affairs, and current events, was
presented originally at the University of Memphis. It is now held at Rhodes
College where it is coordinated by Mel Grinspan, former Rhodes professor
and civil rights activist.

Members of the Jewish community held political office in the 1960s as
they had in other decades. Philip Perel, executive vice-president of Perel
and Lowenstein, who was serving a second term as president of the
Downtown Association of Memphis, was elected a member of the first
Memphis City Council in 1966. A. Arthur Halle Jr., elected in 1968 to
represent District 3 as a squire of the Shelby County Quarterly Court,
defeated his opponent by a margin of 12,252 votes. Jane Seessel was elected
to the Memphis Board of Education in 1963.[23]

Joseph Exelbierd established a self-help organization for Holocaust
survivors in the early 1960s. Called the New Americans Club, the group
met monthly at Temple Israel, where its members enjoyed a meal and
dancing. Many members of the organization described it as a "lifesaver"
because it provided a "sense of family" for the survivors, many of whom had
lost their own immediate families in Europe, and because they felt most at
home with people who had shared similar experiences and memories. With
the money raised from the dances and dinners, the New Americans planned
to build a monument to the memory of the six million victims of the
Holocaust. But they used the money instead to buy an ambulance that was
urgently needed by Israel during the 1967 war. Paul Lewis of Dallas offered
to complete the group's original project and built a monument to the
Holocaust victims on the grounds of the Jewish Community Center.

The New Americans disbanded in the 1970s as its members became
acculturated and felt more at home in their new city. The Jewish Welfare
Fund cares for the Holocaust memorial.[24]

Memphis Jews continued in the 1960s to support the city's philanthropic efforts, to occupy their traditional roles as merchants, and to join
the ranks of the professions in ever-larger numbers. Jewish names were
prominent among patrons of the arts, often listed as contributors in
programs and brochures of musical offerings in the city. Doctors Thomas
Stern and Sheldon Korones served on the Board of Directors of the

[23]Interview with Margaret Halle, 1992; Interview with Jane Seessel, 1992.
[24]Interview with Joseph Exelbierd, 1991.

Memphis Symphony Orchestra. Jane Seessel was the president of the Memphis Symphony League from 1962 to 1963.[25] Continuing their work for the benefit of youth, Myra Dreifus and Selma Lewis headed the symphony's concerts for children.

In 1967 Richard Lightman and his non-Jewish partner, Cary Stanley, organized Concerts International to bring outstanding chamber music groups from all over the world to perform in the city. With the exception of one brief interlude, the organization has continued to add to the musical richness of the community.[26] Dr. Joseph Parker established Artists Ascending, a series that features young Jewish artists performing in the sanctuary of Baron Hirsch synagogue. With help from other members of the congregation, including Donna Hanover, the Philip Belz family, and Rabbis Chaim Seiger and Raphael Grossman, and attended by music lovers form the entire community, the series presented such artists as Itzhak Perlman, Mischa Dichter, and Pinchas Zuckerman on their way to outstanding careers.[27]

Jews were actively involved in the theatrical life of the city. Alfred Alperin, a founder of the Front Street Theater, was its president from 1964 to 1968, when it was the first theater in Memphis to cast blacks in leading roles.[28] Harvey Pierce was on the board of the Memphis Little Theater; Eugene Katz and his wife, Donna Davis Katz, acted in Memphis Little Theater productions and served on its board. Bea Miller, a mainstay of the Little Theatre Board, was president from 1963 to 1965 and has served as business manager. Audrey and Hubert Lewis both acted on the stage of the theater and served on its board, as did Jeanne and Richard Lightman.[29] In the late 1960s, Linda Burson Lewis became president of Stage Set, a women's support auxiliary.

The participation of Jews in the civil rights movement of the 1960s, however, particularly marked Memphis Jewry's coming of age. The courage required to support an unpopular cause is evidence of the Jewish community's commitment to the commandments of Judaism and of its willingness to take a public stand. It is evidence that the discrimination against Jews

---

[25] Seessel interview.
[26] Lightman interview.
[27] Interview with Dr. Joseph Parker, 1992.
[28] Interview with Alfred Alperin, 1992.
[29] Interview with Bea Miller, 1992.

diminished in the United States after World War II. And it is evidence that Jews had achieved a feeling of security and comfort that permitted them the freedom to act in accordance with their conscience instead of conforming to the standards of the larger community. Although the Jewish civil rights activists took stands often criticized by others, given the chance to choose again, none of those interviewed would have performed in any other way.

EPILOGUE

As the 1960s ended the successes of the state of Israel exercised a profound effect on the Jewish community of Memphis. Even in this corner of the South, so remote from Israel's borders, Jews stand a little taller and feel united as never before in common support of a homeland for their once-homeless brethren. Largely because of their pride in the Jewish state, Jews register a new willingness to be recognized as a family and to champion values that make them a people as well as a religious group.

The problems of the world, always mirrored in Jewish life, were reflected in the plight of Russian Jews, oppressed by Communism and denied the freedom to practice their religion. Successful efforts to facilitate their departure from the former Soviet Union resulted in a new wave of Jewish immigrants to Memphis. As always, in the spirit of K'lal Yisroel, the oneness of Jews, and wary of a repetition of the hostility of Governor Peter Stuyvesant, the Jewish community has accepted the responsibility of caring for its own. While the welcome accorded Jewish immigrants to this country is no longer dependent upon the whim of a governor or any individual, the practice of assuming responsibility for fellow Jews has endured. Enshrined in the people's memory, reinforced by example, the tradition is honored in Memphis where now as in the past the Jewish community supports newcomers until they become self-supporting, helping them to develop their own skills and talents and thus enabling them to make their own contributions to the city.

A new wave of Russian Jewish immigrants have been allowed to enter the United States since the late 1970s when New Jersey Senator Frank Lautenberg attached a human rights amendment to a trade treaty with the Soviet Union. At that time, very few of the new immigrants had family connections in America, so local communities accepted responsibility for them. The doors closed again between 1978 and 1986 when a few families arrived from Russia and the Ukraine. Russian immigration to Memphis peaked in 1990 and 1991 with the total newcomers reaching between 250 and 300. The Memphis Jewish Federation bore the financial responsibility for the immigrants and Jewish Family Service became the agency responsible for their resettlement. Except for a few who because of handicaps were incapable of learning the requirements, all became citizens of the United States. Eventually all were gainfully employed and were able to take care of their families. While the adjustment was not easy, the Russian immigrants tenaciously sought to make the change work. Many volunteers helped them learn English, find jobs, obtain medical and legal help when needed, and generally to help them adapt to new ways of doing almost everything.[1]

In the final years of the twentieth century, a search for spiritual fulfillment was discernible throughout the nation. Indicative of this was the phenomenal upsurge in the publication of books concerned with faith and spirituality. In response to this demand for spiritual sustenance, national Jewish Reform leadership added more traditional elements to its worship services. Courses in Hebrew, Basic Judaism, and the study of Torah were attended by growing numbers of Temple Israel members. The Hebrew language became a more integral part of Reform services, where some men returned to the wearing of yarmulkes (skull-caps) and tallisim (prayer shawls) and the Torah was increasingly paraded through the congregation by the rabbis. Many of these rituals had been abandoned by the Reform movement, but enjoying a rebirth as the new millennium approaches. At the same time, some signs of assimilation, such as the use of Christmas trees in Jewish homes, declined sharply.

Another national change has been the increase in the membership of fundamentalist religious institutions and a corresponding drop in membership in the so-called "mainline" churches. The emotional, evangelistic organizations continue to gain ground as the more restrained, formal ones are losing adherents. For example, small as is the percentage of Jews in the American religious spectrum, that of Episcopalians is even smaller. The turn to the right is reflected in Memphis Jewish institutions as well. Strong in Memphis since the early 1900s, Orthodoxy remains vigorous, in part because of the influence of its parochial day schools, the Margolin Hebrew Academy/Feinstone Yeshiva of the South. In the Conservative branch of Judaism, Solomon Schechter Day School is attracting students not only from Beth Sholom synagogue, but from other branches of Judaism as well.

Contributing to Jewish education of both young people and adults is the Lemsky Fund, created in the 1990s by a bequest from Abe Lemsky. Relatively unknown in the community, Lemsky was a bachelor whose parents had been immigrants and whose his father operated a shoe repair shop on McLemore Street. One of the first graduates of a lumber inspection school held in the 1920s at the William R. Moore School, Lemsky became

---

[1]Telephone interview with Henrie Marcus, 27 April 1998. Marcus, an employee of Jewish Family Service, was the officer most directly responsible for their resettlement.

general sales manager of the Anderson Tully Lumber Company in Memphis. He also became the editor of an influential publication, the *Hardwood Lumber Report*, a weekly paper that quoted prices for lumber. Lemsky's large bequest to the Memphis Jewish Federation is administered by Jewish Family Services and is used to bring cultural events for all ages. The gift also helps build bridges between the Memphis Jewish community and the state of Israel, and to help oppressed Jews go to Israel to live. The Lemsky Fund thus effectively foster the knowledge of Jewish heritage.[2]

A movement in philanthropy, begun in Jewish communities across the nation in the 1960s, was implemented in Memphis in 1996. The Memphis Jewish Foundation was conceived as an endowment fund to ensure the stability of Jewish organizations for future generations. Created by the Memphis Jewish Federation, the Memphis Jewish Home, the Memphis Jewish Community Center, and Jewish Family Service, the Foundation was joined immediately by the four synagogues and the two day schools. Formation of the Foundation was necessitated by decreasing federal support for such organizations. The Foundation uses tax savings as a technique. In addition to soliciting donations by the use of estate planning, it also allows donors to establish philanthropic funds and to advise the Foundation about how these should be used.[3]

Observable throughout the United States is the incidence of intermarriage between Jews and non-Jews. Once a rarity, current patterns of intermarriage are more like a stampede than a trend. Although there is no demonstrable correlation between intermarriage and divorce, the rate of divorce involving Jews is rising rapidly, as it is in the general population. Both intermarriage and divorce point to the degree of assimilation Jews into the larger community. Both of these trends are alarming to many who fear the further diminishing of Judaism's numbers, already weakened by the loss of six million Holocaust victims. Thus the Jewish community of Memphis is presented with a paradox: once the cherished goal of many Jews, assimilation may now be a threat to their very survival.

On a more positive note, however, the acceptance of Jews by non-Jews has occurred despite Jews' apparent willingness to be recognized as what they are. For the first time, there is now a Jewish member (albeit with a non-Jewish wife) of the Memphis Country Club, formerly a Christian

---

[2]Telephone interviews with Gerald Slavney and Robert Udelsohn, 27 April 1998.
[3]Telephone interview with Paul Jacobson, 27 April 1998.

bastion. Jews seem willing to acknowledge that while they share common human characteristics with non-Jews, Judaism is in many respects different from other religions.

At the end of the twentieth century, the Memphis Jewish community occupies a comfortable position in the city, integrated into its political, economic, cultural, artistic, philanthropic, and religious life. Tangible evidence of this feeling of belonging is the fact that of the city's ten major thoroughfares named in honor of local individuals, three bear the names of Jewish Memphians: Abe Plough, Sam Cooper, and Avron Fogelman.

But the comfortable position of Memphis Jewry is relative, not absolute. Since the middle of the 1980s, an upsurge in the number of anti-Semitic incidents has been reported not only globally, but also locally, a resurgence explained in part by economic downturns that continue to occur and that continue to produce a dismayingly predictable response: when a scapegoat is needed, the Jew is the usual target. Neo-Nazism has arisen in Europe and has encouraged imitators. Skinheads in Memphis have painted swastikas on the Jewish Student Union at the University of Memphis. Synagogues have been defaced. Yet the newly found unity of the Jewish community allows it to answer such incidents in an organized, measured way. While its answers may not satisfy every member of the community, its risen collective voice can speak more effectively than individual voices. Complacency is not an option for Jews who better than most recognize that the price of freedom is eternal vigilance.

It would be presumptuous to predict the future of the Memphis Jewish community. Whatever occurs, however, it seems likely that for Jews, a biblical people in the heart of the Bible Belt, the future will continue to include a commitment to take care of their own and to be responsible contributors to a city in which they have been unusually secure.

SELECTED BIBLIOGRAPHY

A. BOOKS AND ARTICLES

Adler, Cyrus, ed. *The American Jewish Yearbook*. Philadelphia: The Jewish Publications Society of America, 1901.

Alexander, Thomas B. *Political Reconstruction in Tennessee*. Nashville: Vanderbilt University Press, 1950.

Allison, Judge John, ed. *Notable Men of Tennessee, Personal and Genealogical*. Vol. 2. Atlanta: Southern Historical Association, 1905.

American Jewish Historical Society Archives. Cincinnati: Hebrew Union College.

American Jewish Yearbook. American Jewish Committee and Jewish Publication Society of America.

Anshei Sphard—Beth El Emeth Congregation Dedication Booklet. Memphis, 1970.

Art University Press, Supplement to House Warming Edition of The *Evening Scimitar*. Memphis, 1903.

Banks, Richard. "In the Heat of the Night." *Memphis Magazine*, June 1990: 71-79.

"Baron Hirsch Congregation, 1864-1964." Dedication and Family album, Memphis, 1988.

Becker, Babette. "Chronicle of the Congregation." N.p. N.d.

Beifuss, Joan. *At the River I Stand*. Memphis: B and W Books, 1977.

Bejach, Judge L. D. "The Taxing District of Shelby County," *West Tennessee Historical Society Papers* 4 (1950): 5-27.

Bejach, Judge L. D. Interview by Charles Crawford. *Significant People in the History of Memphis* series. Memphis, 1967.

Beth Sholom Staff. "Beth Sholom Synagogue: The Conservative Movement in Memphis." *Southern Jewish Heritage*, 3 (May 1990): 5-6.

Biles, Roger. *Memphis in the Great Depression*. Knoxville: University of Tennessee Press, 1986.

Blumberg, Janice Rothschild. *One Voice: Rabbi Jacob M. Rothschild and the Troubled South*. Macon: Mercer University Press, 1985.

B'nai B'rith Quarterly Report of Euphrates Lodge, 1866.

B'nai B'rith Women of Memphis, Chapter No. 406. *What's Cooking in Memphis*, 1953.

Breitman, Richard and Alan M. Kraut. *American Refugee Policy and European Jewry, 1933-1945*. Bloomington: Indiana University Press, 1987.

Brode, Freda. "History of Hadassah," *Southern Jewish Heritage* 2 (July 1989): 5.

Brooks, Hattie. "History of Pauline Levy Sewing Circle." Unpublished pamphlet. Memphis: March, 1948.

Brownstone, David M. and Irene M. Franck, eds. *America's Ethnic Heritage Series*. New York and Oxford: Facts on File Publication, 1988.

Bruce, Andrea and Thomas S. Fitzgerald. "A Study of Crime in the City of Memphis, Tennessee." *Journal of the American Institute of Criminal Law and Criminology* 19 (1928), 14.

Bruesch, S. Rubin. *Yellow Fever in Tennessee*, 1978. Nashville: Tennessee Medical Association, 1979.

Bureau of Immigration and Naturalization of the United States of America, Department of Commerce and Labor.

Buring, Daneel. "Seessel's: The Development of a Memphis Business, 1859-1986." Master's thesis, Memphis State University, 1986.

"Buring, Nat: A Man and His Business." N.p. N.d.

Burson, Charles. Speech at dedication of the Jewish Home, Memphis, TN, June 14, 1992.

Caffrey, Margaret and Judy Peiser. Lecture, Memphis State University, 1990.

Capers, Gerald. *Biography of a Rivertown*. New Orleans: Tulane University Press, 1966.

Clark, Thomas D. "The Post Civil War Economy in the South." *Jews in the South*. Edited by Leonard Dinnerstein and Mary Dale Pahlson. Baton Rouge: Louisiana State University Press, 1973.

Congregation Children of Israel v. Jacob J. Peres. Jackson, Tennessee, April Term, 1866.

Cook, Everett R. *Everett R. Cook: A Memoir*. Memphis: Memphis Public Library and Information Service, 1971.

Coppa, Frank J. and Thomas J. Curran. *The Immigrant Experience in America*. Boston: Twayne Publishers, 1976.

Coppock, Paul R. *Memphis Sketches*. Memphis: Friends of Memphis and Shelby County Libraries, 1976.

Corlew, Robert E. *Tennessee: A Short History*. Knoxville: University of Tennessee Press, 1981.

Cornell, Eric H. *The Lord is My Shepherd: My Story: Analysis of an Escape*. Memphis, n.d.

Cowan, Neil M. and Ruth Schwartz. *Our Parents' Lives: The Americanization of East European Jews*. New York: Basic Books, 1989.

Crawford, Charles W. *Yesterday's Memphis*. Memphis: E. A. Seeman, 1976.

Davidson, David. "A Biographical Sketch of Jacob Goldsmith, 1850-1933." Unpublished manuscript commissioned by the family, nd.

Davidowicz, Lucy S. *On Equal Terms: Jews in America 1881-1981*. New York: Holt, Rinehart, and Winston, 1982.

Davis, James D. *The History of the City of Memphis*. Memphis, n.d.

Dimont, Max. *The Jews of America: The Roots and Destiny*. New York: Simon and Schuster, 1978.

Dinnerstein, Leonard. *American Survivors of the Holocaust*. New York: Columbia University Press, 1982.

_____ and Mary Jane Pahlson. *Jews in the South*. Baton Rouge: Louisiana State niversity Press, 1973.

Duffel Bag. Memphis: Temple Israel, n.d.

Duffy, John. *The Sanitarians: A History of American Public Health*. Urbana and Chicago: University of Illinois Press, 1990.

Durham, Louise. "The Old Market Street School, 1872-1920." *West Tennessee Historical Society Papers* 7 (1953): 57-71.

Dykeman, Wilma and Carol Lynn Yellin. *Tennessee Women Past and Present*. Nashville: Committee for the Humanities, 1977.

Eiseman, Alberta. *From Many Lands*. New York: Athenaeum, 1970.

Endelman, Judith E. *The Jewish Community of Indianapolis, 1849 to the Present*. Bloomington: Indiana University Press, 1992.

Evans, Eli N. *The Provincials*. Kingsport: Kingsport Press, 1973.

Fakes, Turner J., Jr. "Memphis and the Mexican War." *West Tennessee Historical Society Papers* 1 (1948): 135-7.

Falsone, Anne Marie McMahon. "The Memphis Howard Institute: A Study in the Growth of Social Awareness." Master's thesis. Memphis State University, 1968.

Federation of Jewish Agencies Minutes.

Feibelman, Herschel. Lecture, Memphis Jewish Community Center, 12 January 1992.

Fein, Isaac M. *The Making of an American Jewish Community: The History of Baltimore Jewry from 1773-1920.* Philadelphia: The Jewish Publication Society of America, 1971.

W. McK. Fetzer. Letter to Ben Goodman Sr. 18 February 1919, Ben Goodman Jr. Personal Papers.

Fifty Years of Faith: Anshei Sphard Golden Anniversary, 1906-1956. Memphis, 1956.

Fortas, Abe. Letters. Mississippi Valley Collection, Memphis State University.

Frank, Fedora, S. *Beginnings on Market Street: Nashville and Her Jewry, 1861-1901.* Nashville: Np., 1976.

_____. *Five Families and Eight Young Men: Nashville and Her Jewry, 1861-1901.* Nashville, 1976.

Frankland, A. E. *Kronikals of Our Times.* Cincinnati: Hebrew Union College/Jewish Institute of Religion. Vol. 9, No. 2, October 1957.

Glanz, Rudolph. *The Jewish Woman in America: Two Female Immigrant Generations, 1820-1929.* Vol. 1. *The Eastern European Jewish Woman.* Series. KTAV and National Council of Jewish Women, 1976.

Goldberger, Joseph. *Goldberger on Pellagra.* Edited by Milton Ternes. Baton Rouge: Louisiana State University Press, 1964.

Goldberger, Milton and Joseph L. Malamut, eds. *Southern Jewry: An Account of Jewish Progress and Achievement in the Southland.* Memphis: The *Hebrew Watchman*, 1933.

Goldberger, Milton. *Loves.* Memphis: N.p., n.d.

Golden, Harry. *Our Southern Landsmen.* New York: G. P. Putnam's Sons, 1974.

Goldsmith Civic Garden Center Program for Opening, 22 March 1964.

Goltman, Max. Letter to S. McK. Fetzer. 6 March 1919.

Gross, Rhea. Letter to Memphis Chapter of Hadassah, 1990.

Haizlip, Ruth C. *The Memphis Academy of Arts 1936-1949.* Memphis: N.p., n.d.

Hall, Jay. "A Man for All People." *Mid-South Magazine* 26 (February 1978): 6-10.

Halle, A. Arthur Sr. *History of the Memphis Cotton Carnival.* Memphis: N.p., n.d.

Handlin, Oscar. *A Pictorial History of Immigration: A Dramatic Story of the Building of America from Prehistoric Times to the Present.* New York: Crown, 1972.

Harkins, John E. *Metropolis of the American Nile: Memphis and Shelby County.* Woodland Hill, CA: Windsor Press, 1982.

Hebrew Watchman Golden Anniversary Edition, Vol. 53 (29 May 1975).

Hertzberg, Arthur. *The Jews in America: Four Centuries of an Uneasy Encounter.* New York: Simon and Schuster, 1989.

Heskes, Irene, *Jews in Music.* New York: Block Publishing Company, n.d.

Higman, John. "Social Discrimination Against Jews in America, 1830-1930." *American Jewish Historical Society* 47 (1957): 26.

History of Memphis Chapter, National Council of Jewish Women. Memphis: N.p., n.d.

History of Tennessee from Earliest Time to the Present. Nashville: Goodspeed Company, 1887.

Hoffman, Eva. *Lost in Translation: A Life in a New Language.* New York: E. P. Dutton, 1989.

Holmes, Jack L., ed. "Documents: Joseph A. Gronauer and the Civil War in Memphis." *West Tennessee Historical Society Papers 22* (1968): 148-158.

Holocaust Series. Center for Southern Folklore. Memphis, 1987.

Howard, Skip. "*Kristallnacht*—Eyewitness to History." *Southern Jewish Heritage 2* (February 1989), 3-4.

Hutchins, Fred. *What Happened in Memphis.* Kingsport: Kingsport Press, 1965.

Jackson, Donald Dale. "Who the Heck Did Discover the New World?" *Smithsonian* (September 1991): 76-79.

Jackson, Kenneth T. *The Ku Klux Klan in the City, 1915-1930.* New York: Oxford University Press, 1967.

Janowski, Oscar J., ed. *The American Jew: A Reappraisal.* Philadelphia: The Jewish Publication Society of America, 1972.

Jewish Service Agency *Minutes.*

Jick, Leon A. *The Americanization of the Synagogue, 1820-1870.* Hanover: University of New England Press, 1976.

Johnson, Paul. *A History of the Jews.* New York: Harper and Row, 1987.

Kaganoff, Nathan and Melvin T. Urofsky. *Turn to the South: Essays on Southern Jewry.* Charlottesville: University of Virginia Press, 1979.

Kalin, Berkley. "Young Abe Fortas." *West Tennessee Historical Society Papers* 34 (1980): 96-100.

Karp, Abraham J., ed. *The Jewish Experience in America: Selected Studies for the Publications of the American Jewish Historical Society.* New York: KATV, 1968.

Katz, Nina (Mrs. Morris). Lecture. Memphis State University, 1989.

Keating, J. M. *History of the City of Memphis and Shelby County, Tennessee.* Syracuse: D. Mason and Co., 1888.

_____. *History of the Yellow Fever Epidemic of 1878 in Memphis, Tn.* Memphis: The Howard Association, 1879.

Kennedy, John F. *A Nation of Immigrants.* New York: Harper and Row, 1964.

Killian, Lewis. *White Southerners.* Amherst: University of Massachusetts Press, 1965.

Korn, Bertram W. *American Jewry and the Civil War.* A Temple Book. New York: Athenaeum, 1970.

_____. *The Early Jews of New Orleans.* Waltham: American Jewish Historical Society, 1960.

Landau, Herman. *Adath Louisville: The Story of a Jewish Community.* Louisville: Herman Landau and Associates, 1981.

Lanier, Robert A. *Memphis in the Twenties: The Second Term of Mayor Rowlett Paine, 1924-1928.* Memphis: Zenda Press, 1979.

LaPointe, Patricia. *From Saddlebags to Science: A Century of Health Care in Memphis, 1830-1930.* Memphis: University of Tennessee Center for the Health Sciences, 1984.

Lash, Jeffrey N. "The Federal Tyrant at Memphis: Gen. Stephen A. Hurlburt and the Union OccUniversity Pressation of West Tn., 1862-64." *Tennessee Historical Quarterly*, Spring, 1959.

Lettes, Louis. "On the Verge of Extinction: Small Town Jewish Communities in the Deep South." Master's thesis, Princeton University, 1986.

Lewin, Mark A. Lecture, Memphis State University. 1993.

Lewis, Anthony. *Gideon's Trumpet.* New York: Random House, 1964.

Lewis, Selma. *Diversification and Unity: A History of MIFA.* Memphis: Metropolitan Inter-Faith Association, 1988.

_____. *A History of the Temple Israel Cemetery.* Memphis: Temple Israel, 1990.

Lieberman, Jack. Speech to the Memphis Jewish Federation, February 1983.

Lowenstein, Steven. *The Jews of Oregon, 1850-1950.* Portland: Jewish Historical Society of Oregon, 1987.

Marcus, Jacob Rader. *American Jewry: Documents Twentieth Century.* Cincinnati: Hebrew Union College Press, 1959.

————. *Memoirs of American Jews, 1775-1865.* Philadelphia: The Jewish Publication Society of America, 1955.

————. *United States Jewry, 1766-1985.* 4 vols. Detroit: Wayne State University Press, 1989.

Memphis As She Is: Rambles in the Path of Industrial and Commercial Circles. Memphis, Pittsburgh, and London: Historical Descriptive Publishing Company, 1887.

Memphians at War. Memphis: Memphis Public Library and Information Service, 1974.

Memphis Cotton Exchange Directory and Book of Reference. Memphis: Henry Hatten, 1897.

Memphis Hebrew Academy Third Donor Banquet, 1952.

Memphis Jewish Federation *Minutes.*

Memphis Federation of Jewish Welfare Agencies. *This Is Your Jewish Community: Directory of Jewish Organizations and Agencies.* Memphis: 1956.

Memphis Jewish Community Center: Planting for Our Children. Memphis, 1974.

Memphis Jewish Community, 1840-Present. Memphis: Center for Southern Folklore, 1987.

Memphis Merchants Exchange Officers, Board of Directors and Standing Committees for 1887. Memphis, 1887.

Memphis Press Scimitar Sesquicentennial Edition. Memphis. 28 May 1960.

————. *Special Edition,* "75 Years of Progress Achieved," 12 October 1955.

Memphis Zionist District: A Brief History. Unpublished article, 1962.

Meyers, Lawrence. "Memphis Jews and Civil War Issues." Unpublihsed paper, Memphis State University, 1961.

————. "Evolution of the Jewish Service Agency in Memphis, Tn., 1847 to 1963." Master's thesis, Memphis State University, 1965.

Miller, William D. *Memphis During the Progressive Era, 1900-1917.* Memphis: Memphis State University Press, 1957.

————. *Mr. Crump of Memphis.* Baton Rouge: Louisiana State University Press, 1964.

Mitchell, H. L. . *Roll the Union On.* Chicago: Charles H. Kerr, 1987.

Mooney, C. P. J. ed. *The Mid-South and Its Builders*. Memphis Mid-South Biographic and Historical Association, 1920.

Moore, Deborah Dash. *B'nai B'rith and the Challenge of Ethnic Leadership*. SUNY Series in *Modern Jewish History*, Paula E. Hyman and D. D. Moore, eds. n.d.

Moore, Harry E. Jr. "The National Conference of Christians Jews in Memphis, 1932-1989." *West Tennessee Historical Society Papers* 45 (1991).

Morris, Richard. *Encyclopedia of American History*. New York: Harper and Row, 1953.

Ornelas Struve, Carol M. and Joan Hassell. *Memphis, 1800-1900*. Vols. 1 and 2. New York: Nancy Powers and Co. A Pink Palace Museum Book, 1982.

Ornish, Nathalie. *Pioneer Jewish Texans: Their Impact on Texas and American History for 400 Years, 1590-1900*. Dallas: Texas Heritage Press, 1989.

Pieser, Judy, ed. *Baron Hirsch Congregation Family Album*. Memphis: Baron Hirsch Congregation, 1988.

Peres Family Papers. Memphis: Memphis State University, Mississippi Valley Collection, No. 232.

Plesur, Milton. *A Life in Twentieth Century America: Challenge and Accommodation*. Chicago: Nelson Hall, 1982.

Plough, Inc. Annual Report for 1962.

————. *Facts and Information Pamphlet*.

Plunkett, Kitty. *A Pictorial History of Memphis*. Norfolk: Darning Co., 1976.

Postal, Bernard and Lionel Koppman. *American Jewish Landmarks: A Travel Guide and History*. 3 vols. New York: Fleet Press, 1954.

Prescott, Grace Elizabeth. "The Woman Suffrage Movement in Memphis: Its Place in the State, Sectional, and National Movements." *West Tennessee Historical Society Papers* 18 (1964): 70-86.

Prominent Tennesseans, 1796-1938. Lewisburg: Who's What Press, 1940.

Rauchle, Robert. "Biographical Sketches of Prominent Germans in Memphis, Tennessee in the 19th Century." *West Tennessee Historical Society Papers* 22 (1968): 73-85.

Rhodes Alumni News. Memphis: Rhodes College, 1991.

Ridgeway Country Club Rules and Membership Roster.

Roark, Eldon., *Memphis Bragabouts: Characters I Have Known*. New York: McGraw Hill, Inc., 1945.

Roper, James. *The Founding of Memphis, 1818-1820*. Memphis: Memphis Sesquicentennial, Inc., 1970.

Rothenberg, Joshua. *The Jewish Religion in the Soviet Union*. New York: KRAC Press, 1971.

Russell, Albert R. *U. S. Cotton and the National Cotton Council, 1938-1987*. Memphis: National Cotton Council, 1987.

Sachar, Howard M. *A History of the Jews in America*. New York: Alfred A. Knopf, 1992.

Saharovici, Leonid. "Contributions to the History of Jewish Immigration: "The First Holocaust Survivor Family Settling in Memphis Forty-Three Years Ago," *Southern Jewish Heritage* 2 (October 3, 1989).

Saltzmann, Rachel. "Shalom Y'All." *Southern Experience*. Durham: Institute for Southern Studies. September-October 1983, 28-36.

Sarna, Jonathan O. "Jewish Community Histories; Recent Non-Academic Contributions." *Journal of American Ethnic History* 6 (Fall 1986), 64.

Scales, Dabney. *In Memoriam*, Frederick Wolf. Memphis, 1908.

Schmier, Louis, ed. *Reflections of Southern Jewry: The Letters of Charles Wessolowsky*. Macon: Mercer University Press, 1982.

Schultz, Joseph P. *Mid-America's Promise: A Profile of Greater Kansas City Jewry*. Jewish Community Foundation of Greater Kansas City and the American Jewish Historical Society, 1982.

Seessel, Henry. *Memories of a Mexican Veteran, 1822-1911*. Memphis: N.p., 1891.

Seiger, Chaim. *Immigration, Settlement, and Return: Jews of the Lower Mississippi Valley, 1865-1880*. Master's thesis, Memphis State University, 1970.

Sewel, Lester. Address to Jewish Historical Society of Memphis and the Mid-South. Winter, 1991.

Shankman, Sam. A History of the Jews of Memphis. Unpublished manuscript.

_____. *A History of Zionism in Memphis*. Unpublished manuscript.

_____. *One Hundred Years of B'nai B'rith*. Memphis: Sam Schloss Lodge No. 35 of B'nai B'rith, 1958.

_____. *The Peres Family*. Kingsport: Southern Publishing Company, 1938.

Shapiro, Normand. "Our Rabbis and Their Times." Unpublished paper, 1990.

Shelby County, Tn. Marriage Bonds and Licenses, 1850-1865. compiled by Bettie B. Davis. Memphis: Richard Harris. n.d.

Sigafoos, Robert A. *Cotton Row to Beale Street: A Business History of Memphis.* Memphis: Memphis State University Press, 1979.

Silberman, Charles E. *A Certain People: American Jews and Their Lives Today.* New York: Summit Books, 1985.

Silver, Marvin. *History of B'nai B'rith Home.* Unpublished pamphlet, 1992.

Singer, Alan. *A Self Guided Tour of Jewish Memphis, Past and Present.* Memphis: Memphis Jewish Federation, 1957.

Sloan, Irving J., ed. *The Jews in America, 1621-1977.* Dobbs Ferry: Oceana Publishing, Incorporated, 1978.

Solomon, Morris. *Papers.* Memphis: Memphis Public Library and Information Service.

Southern Consulting Services. *The 1977 Census of the Jewish Population of Memphis, Tn.* Memphis: Southern Consulting Services, 1977.

Southwestern College Board of Trustees Minutes. Memphis, 1939.

Speer, William S. *Sketches of Prominent Tennesseans.* Nashville: Albert B. Tavel, 1888.

Standard and Poor: Statistical Service. New York: Standard and Poor Corp., 1988, 76.

Stavely, Anne Leach. "The Newburger Mansion of Memphis, Tn; Founders Hall of Memphis Theological Seminary," 1992.

Sterling, Eleanore O. "Anti-Jewish Riots in Germany in 1819." Edited by Guido Kirsch. *Historic Judaica.* New York: Historia Judaico. 13 October 1950, part 2, 105-142.

Stern, Harriet W. "A Southern Rabbi in Martin Luther King's Court," *Southern Jewish Heritage* 1 (Winter 1995): 3-9.

Stern, Steve. "Echoes of the Pinch." *Memphis Magazine.* Memphis. March 1984.

Sternberg, Irma O. "Memphis Merchant for More than 60 Years: My Father, 'Uncle' Ike Ottenheimer." *West Tennessee Historical Society Papers* 35 (1981).

Stewart, Marcus and William T. Black, eds. and Mildred Hicks, co-ed. *History of Medicine in Memphis.* Jackson: McCowat and Mercer Press, 1971.

Strauch, Irving. Lecture. Memphis State University, 1992.

Talmud Torah Minutes.

Temple Israel Dedication, September 17-18, 1976.

Thomas, Richard K. "The Residential Distribution of Immigrants in Memphis, Tennessee." Master's thesis. Memphis State University, 1970.

Tobias, Henry J. *The Jews in Oklahoma: Newcomers in a New Land.* Norman: University of Oklahoma Press, 1980.

Tracy, Sterling. *The Immigrant Population of Memphis. West Tennessee Historical Society Papers* 4 (1950).

Tucker, David. *Memphis Since Crump: Bossism, Blacks, and Civic Responses, 1948-1968.* Knoxville: University of Tennessee Press, 1980.

Tennessee Historical Records Survey Cemetery Checklist.

Shelby County Tennessee Will Book, No. 3 E, 1855-1862. January 1830-May 1847; June 1847-July 1855.

Turitz, Leo E. and Evelyn. *Jews in Early Mississippi.* Jackson: University of Mississippi Press, n.d.

Twyman's Business Directory and General Merchandise Advertiser for 1850. Memphis, 1850.

Universal Jewish Encyclopedia. New York: The Universal Jewish Encyclopedia, Inc., 1948.

Vedder, O. F. *History of the City of Memphis and Shelby County.* Vol. 2. Syracuse: O. Mason Co., 1888.

Wax, James A. and Helen G. *Our First Century, 1854-1954.* Memphis: Temple Israel, 1954.

Wax, James A. "The Jews of Memphis, 1860-1865." *West Tennessee Historical Society Papers* 3 (1949): 38-89.

Washburne, E. B. *Memphis Riots and Massacres.* U.S. 39th Congress, 2nd. session. House of Representatives 101. 1866. Memphis Association, 1969.

Wenger, Beth S. *Jewish Women and Volunteerism: Beyond the Myth of Enabler.* American Jewish Historical Society. Autumn 1989.

White, Mimi. *Yellow Fever.* Centennial Edition of the *Commercial Appeal,* 31 October 1978.

Whitfield, Stephen J. "Jews and Other Southerners." In Kaganoff, Nathan and Melvin T. Urofsky. *Turn to the South: Essays on Southern Jewry.* Charlottesville: University of Virginia Press, 1979.

Who's Who in America. 39th ed. Marquis Who's Who: New Providence, NJ: 1985.

Wingfield, Marshall. *The Literature of the Egyptians.* Read at a meeting of the Egyptians Club, Memphis, 15 January 1942.

Wrenn, Lynette. "The Impact of Yellow Fever in Memphis: A Reappraisal."
    Memphis: *West Tennessee Historical Society Papers*, 12, 1987.
Yearbook of American Churches. 1950. Nashville: Abingdon Press, 1950.
Young, J. P. *History of Memphis, Tn.* Knoxville: H. W. Crew and Co., 1912.

B. PERIODICALS

American Israelite
American Jewish Spectator
[Memphis] *Commercial Appeal*
Jewish Spectator
Life Magazine, 8 February 1937.
Memphis Chamber of Commerce Journal, 1921.
Memphis College of Art News, 1992.
Memphis Daily Appeal, 1860-1865.
Memphis Daily Bulletin, 1860-1865.
Memphis Medical Journal, January 1925.
Memphis Press Scimitar
New York Times, 19 November 1972.
Newsletter, Jewish Historical Society of Memphis and the Mid-South. (Later
    called *Southern Jewish Heritage*.)
Press Scimitar
Press Scimitar Art Suppement.

C. INTERVIEWS

*Unless otherwise indicated all interviews were conducted by the author in
Memphis, Tennessee.*

Adler, Dr. Justin and Mrs. Herta, 1992.
Alabaster, Sam. Interview by Steve Stern, Center for Southern Folklore
    Archives, Memphis, 25 July 1983.
Alperin, Alfred, 1992.
Ballon, Dave, February, 1992.

Bass, Dr. Abraham, January, 1990.

Becker, Dr. Daniel, 1995.

Binswanger, Milton S. Jr., 1990.

Blanchard, Jerred, 1992.

Blockman, Asher, 1989.

Bornblum, Bert, 1989.

Boshwit, Buck, 1992.

Brenner, Aaron, 1989.

Brod, Joanne (Mrs. Raymond), 1994.

Brooks, Lakee. Interview by Center for Southern Folklore, Memphis, Tennessee, conducted by Steve Stern, 27 June 1983.

Burson, Leo and Josephine, 1989.

Coffey, Lula (Mrs. Ben), 1990.

Cohn, Rosalee (Mrs. Bertrand), 1992.

Cooper, Polly (Mrs. Robert M.), 1992.

Cooper, Sam, 1992.

Davis, Dorothy (Mrs. Dudley) and Helen (Mrs. Henry) Dinkelspiel, 1989.

Ettelson, Harry. Interview by Berkely Kalin, Memphis State University Oral History Project, 30 November 1967.

Exelbierd, Joseph, 1991.

Feibelman, Herschel. Telephone interview by author, 1993.

Fineshriber, William. Interview by Bekley Kalin. Memphis: Memphis State University Oral History Project. December 1967.

Frank, Anna (Mrs. Julius), 1992.

Frank, Henry C. Interview by Berkley Kalin, Memphis State University, 26 March1968.

Franklin, Abe, 1992.

Friedman, Harold, 1991.

Gerber, Hal, 1991.

Goldberger, Herman, 1991.

Goldberger, Leo, 1989.

Goodman, Charles, 1990.

Goodman, William. Interview by Berkley Kalin, Memphis State University Oral History Project, 5 May 1968.

Greenblatt, Nathan, 1990.

Grinspan, Mel, 1992.

Gronauer, Mr. and Mrs. Joseph. Interview by Berkley Kalin, Memphis State University Oral History Project, 20 September 1968.

Gruber, Anna (Mrs. Herman), December 1989.

Halle, Margaret, 1992.

Hanover, I. E., 1982 and 1987.

Hirsch, Margaret (Mrs. B. W., Jr.), 1991.

Jacobson, Paula, 27 April 1998.

Katz, Nina, 1992.

Kiersky, J. Hubert, 1991.

Kopald, S. L. Jr, 1990.

Kramer, Ethel (Mrs. Lewis), 1989.

Lansky, Guy, 1992.

Lee, Ernest, Sr, February 1989.

Levi, Malcolm, 1991.

Levin, Mark A, 1991.

Levy, Bob, 1992.

Lewis, Jack, 1992.

Lichterman, Herbert, 1991.

Lichterman, Martin, 1991.

Lightman, Richard, 1992.

Lipman, Ira, 1992.

Loewenberg, William, 1991.

Lowenthal, Kathleen (Mrs. J. C.), 1992.

Marcus, Henrie, 27 April 1998.

Margolin, Sam, 1991.

Marks, Ann (Mrs. Julius), 1992.

Marks, Sylvia (Mrs. Edwin), 1992.

Marks, Grace (Mrs. Joseph). Interview by Berkley Kalin, Memphis State University Oral History Project, 18 March 1968.

Miller, Bea, 1992.

Moss, Morrie, 1992.

Myers, Ike. Interview by Berkley Kalin, Memphis State University Oral History Project, 8 December 1968.

Notowitz, Max, 1992.

Olim, Charles, 1991.

Parker, Dr. Joseph, 1992.

Perel, Philip. Interview by Berkley Kalin, Memphis State University, 1968.

Phillips, Anne (Mrs. Louis), 1990.

Radin, Murray. Interview by Berkley Kalin, Memphis State University Oral History Project, 4 December 1968.

Ratner, Marvin, 1992.

Rosen, Lester, 1991.

Sacharin, Ben, 1991.

Samelson, Ira, June 1991.

Schaffer, Fagie (Mrs. Ben), 1990.

Seessel, Jane (Mrs. Arthur, Jr.), 1992.

Seidman, P. K., 1992.

Seligman, Esther (Mrs. Leo), 1990.

Shendelman, George, 1990.

Simon, Milton, 1991.

Skopp, D. W. Interview by Berkley Kalin, Memphis State University Oral History Project, 4 December 1968.

Slavney, Gerald, 27 April 1998.

Stern, Dr. Neuton S. Interview by Berkley Kalin, Memphis State University Oral History Project, 2 February 1968.

Stern, Dr. Thomas N., 1992.

Strauch, Rosalie (Mrs. Irving), 1990.

Udelsohn, Robert, 27 April 1998.

Waldauer, Mr. and Mrs. Abe. Interview by Berkley Kalin, Memphis State University Oral History Project, 1968.

Washer, Morris, 1992.

Weinreich, Sam. Interview by Judy Pelser and Rachel Shankman, Center for Southern Folklore Holocaust Interviews, 10 March 1988.

Weinberg, Lew, 1992.

Wolff, Bert (Mrs. Arthur), 1991.

Wruble, Diane (Mrs. Lawrence), Memphis. 1992.

Wurtzburger, Charles, 1990.

Wurzburg, Jocelyn, 1992.

Yukon, Saran (Mrs. Stanley), 1995

INDEX

Abraham, Rosalie, 68, 99

Abraham, Sam, 137

Abraham, Sheila, 152

Acme Paper Co., 150

Adelphi Theater, 13

Adler, Adolph, 161

Adler, Ernest, 161

Adler, Herman, 114, 161, 162, 165, 171

Adler, Herta, 163

Adler Hotel, 114

Adler, Ida, 161

Adler, John, 114, 153

Adler, Dr. Justin, 106, 161

Adler, Lybie, 146

Agricultural Adjustment Act, 123

Ahlgren, Frank, 160

American Federation of Labor, 142

Alexander II, Czar, 63

Alexander III, Czar, 64

Alexander, Rabbi Joel, 26

Alexander, L., 26

"All Creeds Protest," 160

Allenberg Cotton Co., 114

Allenberg, Joe, 120, 121, 153

Allenberg, Julian, 153

Allenberg, Milton, 114

Alperin, Alfred, 202

Alperin, Ike, 102

Alperin, Dr. Jake, 94

Alperin, Sonya, 171

Altfater, Joseph, 139

American Council for Judaism, 137, 173

American Heart Association, 94

American Jewish Committee, 156, 158, 173, 188

American Jewish Conference, 174

American Jewish Congress, 156, 158

American Legion, 106

American Red Cross, 166

American Zionist Association, 152, 153

Ancient Order of United Workmen, 50

Andrews, Joseph, 8, 21, 22, 24

Andrews, Sally, 8

Andrews, Samuel E., 9

Anshei, Galicia, 74, 76, 78, 79

Anshei, Mischne, 74, 78, 150

Anshei Sphard, 78, 134, 151, 179

Anti-Defamation League, 107

"Appeal to Conscience, An" 188

Arbeiter Ring, 71, 98, 99, 142

anti-Semitism, 42, 108, 109, 111, 155, 156, 157, 158, 172, 173, 176

Armour, Claude, 186

Arnold, Thurman, 138

Artists Ascending, 202

Arts Appreciation, 139

Asher, Fannie Brenner Chapter of B'nai B'rith Youth Organization for Girls, 121

Ashkenazim, 4, 6

Asher, D., 48

Ashner, B. H., 84

Ashner, I. W. 84
Associated Charities of Memphis,
     97
Atlanta, 107
Auschwitz, 167, 168, 169, 170,
     172
Austria, 5

Bach, Nathan, 50
Bacharach, Herman, 102
Bachman, Nathan, 106
Bailey, Walter, 199
Ballon, David, 105
Bamberger, Moses, 9, 24
Baptist Memorial Hospital, 93,
     187
Baptists, Southern, 2
Barinds, A., 9, 44
Barnett, J., 26
Baron Hirsch Synagogue, 71, 76,
     77, 89, 90, 118, 129, 132,
     141, 145, 151, 180, 202
Baron Hirsch Benevolent Soci-
     ety, 103
Baruchman, Pearl, 100, 117, 119
Baruchman, Samuel, 78, 100
Bass Avenue Cemetery, 8
Bat Creek, Tennessee, 2
Bateman, Dr. R. J., 160
Bates, Sam, 160
Baum, Louis, Family, 116
Bavaria, 5
Beale Street, 114, 150
Bearman, A. D., 139
Bearman, Eugene, 149
Bearman, Joseph, 138, 159
Bearman, Leo, Sr., 119, 121,

     147, 153, 179
Becker, Rabbi Arie, 181, 191,
     192
Becker, Leon, Family, 116
Beecher, Henry Ward, 32
Beerbohm, Max, 95
Bejach, Lois, 69, 105
Bejach, S., 115
Belz Corporation, 89, 90
Belz, Jack, 121, 153
Belz, M., 79
Belz, Philip, 89, 153, 180, 202
Belz, Sol, 79
Belzec, 172
Benjamin, Judah P., 42
Benny, Jack, 87
Benovitz, I., 77
Benovitz, S. D., 77
Benovitz, S. L., 100
Bensdorf Family, 79
Bensdorf, Herman, 164
Bergen Belsen, 171
Berger, Rabbi Herbert, 181
Berger, Leon, 117
Bernstein, Harry, 102
Bespalow, Eugene, 183
Beth El Emeth, 25, 26, 58, 117,
     151, 180
Beth Sholom, 118, 180, 181, 191,
     206
Bible Belt, 33, 208
Binstock, L., 79
Binswanger and Co., 85
Binswanger, Milton S., Sr., 85,
     102, 139, 146
Birmingham, 191
Bisno, Julius, 120, 153
Blacks, 42

Black and White Stores, 85
Blanchard, Jerred, 141
Bien's Dry Goods Store, 74
Block, D., Store, 18
Block, E. and L., Liquor Store, 22
Block, Ike, 85
Block, Jacob, 18
Block, Gronauer and Co., 22, 35
Block, Vera, 128
Blockman, Asher, 79
Blockman, H., 78
Blockman's Junk Store, 73
Blockman, M. D., 105
Blockman, Morris, 78
Blockman, William, 78
Blockson, Mary, 100
Bloom, Jacob, 9
Bloom, Mark, 27
Bloom, N., 24
Blue Laws, 48
Bluestein's Dry Goods Store, 74
Bluff City Chapter, B'nai B'rith Youth Organization for Girls, 121
Blumenfeld, H., 100
Blumenthal, H., 26
Blumenthal, J. D., 48
Bluthenthal, Jeanette, 171
B'nai B'rith Home, 119, 120, 136, 147, 150, 180
B'nai B'rith Organization, 27, 28, 50, 51, 53, 58, 97, 98, 125, 145, 157
B'nai B'rith Women, 120, 150
B'nai B'rith Youth Organization, 120, 121
B'nai B'rith Youth Organization for Girls, 121
B'nai Israel Congregation, 11, 24, 25, 27, 36, 52, 76
Bogatin, Irvin, 182
Bolivar, Tennessee, 24
Booth, Edwin, Theater, 30
Bornblum, Bert, 150
Bornblum, David, 150
Borod, Marx, 184
Boshwit, Abraham, 15
Boshwit, Avrome, 140, 146
Bower's Grocery Store, 73
Boy Scouts, 147, 148
Brain Trust, 123
Breckenridge, William C. P., 51
Bren, M. 26
Brenner, Aaron, 119, 120, 153
Brenner, Fred, Family, 116
Brenner, Henry, 126
Brenner, Isaac, 98
Bressler, Rabbi, 77
Brett, Jimmie, 182
Brode, Marvin, 149
Brode, Max, 77
Brodowsky, W., 77
Bronstein, M., 102
Brooks, Hattie, 136
Brown vs. Board of Education, 185
Brown, Arthur, Family, 116
Browning, Gordon, Governor, 105
Brum, Abe, 48
Bry's Department Store, 85, 138
Bry, Louis, 85
Bry, Nathan, 85
Buchanan, John P., 51
Burch, Lucius, 198

Buring, Nat, 133, 179
Buring, Nat, Packing Co., 133
Burson, Josephine,   119, 149,
    192, 193
Burson, Leo, 129, 183
Bush, President George, 130

Carrick, Emmaline, 152
Cash, Wilbur, 32
Catherine's Stout Shoppe, 184
Catholics, 2, 42
Catledge, Turner, 69, 70
Cerebral Palsy Association, 154
Chandler, Mayor Walter,   69,
    138, 180
Chase, Salmon P., 38
Cherry, Nathan, 98
Children of Israel Congregation,
    62, 125, 180
Christian Brothers College, 49
Christian Brothers High School,
    172
Christian Brothers University,
    148
Christian Century, 173
Christine School, 70
Christmas Parade, 19
Christmas Trees, 206
Christy's Minstrels, 13
Congress of Industrial Organiza-
    tions, 142
City Club, 96
City House Hotel, 48
Civil War, 3, 44, 54
Clement, Frank, 180, 190
Cleo Wrap, 150
Cleveland Orphans Asylum, 53

Cochran Hotel, 77
Coffey, Lula, 135
Cohen, Albert, Jr., 110
Cohen, H. A., 77
Cohen, Jake, 142
Cohen, I., 102
Cohen, Leiber, 77
Cohen's Loan Office, 114
Cohen, Rebecca, 141
Cohen, Robert, 100
Cohn, Bertrand, 156, 163, 164
Cohn, Fletcher Gans, 138
Cohn, H. B., 1-2
Cohn, Louise, 128
Cohn, Rosalee, 156, 164
Coleman, Sol, 21
Collins Chapel Hospital, 146
Commercial Appeal, 51, 69, 96,
    104, 108, 109, 116, 157, 160
Committee to Elect Roosevelt,
    138
Compton, A., 58
Concerts International, 202
Conservative Judaism, 180
Convent of the Good Shepherd,
    93
Cook, Everett, 140
Coolidge, Annie, 37
Cooper, Bernice, 196
Cooper Companies, 184
Cooper, Harry, 179
Cooper, Governor Prentice, 69
Cooper, Louis, 183
Cooper, Sam, 73, 130, 131
Cornell, Eric, 164
Coughlin, Father Charles, 155
Council of Social Agencies, 125,
    147

Credit Bureau of Memphis, 113
Croner, Jake, 77
Cross Cut Club, 122
Crowe, Sam, Salvage Store, 73
Crump, Edward Hull, xi, 69, 103, 104, 105, 107, 109, 142, 149, 160, 177
Cummings Elementary School, 108

Daily Appeal, 52, 56
Dandac, Julius, 24
Darmstadt, S., 51
Darrow, Clarence, 136
Davidson, Eli, 100
Davidson's Pool, 73
Davidson Sisters, 100
Davis, Cliff, 143
Debutante Ball, 116
de Hirsch, Baron Maurice, 76
Delugach, Gilbert, 153
Dempsey, Jack, 74
Depression, Great, 127, 128, 129, 134, 137, 141
Dermon, Dave, 115, 126
Des Moines Congregation, 78
Deutsche Bund, 155
Diamond Lodge #583, 50
Diamond, Ruth, 167, 169
Dichter, Mischa, 202
Diehl, Charles, 123
Displaced Persons Act, 111, 174
Dlugach, S., 78
Dogwood Village, 148

Engelberg, William, 129

Enlightenment, 4
Enrolled Militia, 44
Episcopalians, 2, 206
Epstein, Louis, 151
Epstein, Nathan, 108
Epstein, S. H., 78
Epstein, Theresa, 120
Epstein, William, 110
Eschman, Henry, 62
Esperanza Lodge, 50
Ettelson, Rabbi Harry W., 122, 126, 129, 136, 137, 179
Ettelson, Nell, 146
Ettingoff Family, 108
Euphrates Lodge of B'nai B'rith, 27, 42
Evans, Eli, 32, 178
Exelbierd, Joseph, 201

Fall of Second Temple, i
Farband Culture Center, 117
Farber Brothers, 113
Farber, Charles, 98
Faulkner, William, 165
Federal Reserve Bank, 130
Federation of Jewish Charities of Memphis, 53, 101, 102, 125, 129, 136
Feldman, F., 26
Federation of Jewish Welfare Agencies, 102
Feibelman, Herschel, 176, 193, 194
Felsenthal, Cecilia, 146
Felt, Frederika, 148
Felt, Jake, 78, 126, 137
Fibelman and Elson, 19

Finebaum, Dr. Ben T. Chapter of B'nai B'rith Youth Organization for Girls, 121

Fineshriber, Rabbi William, 98, 109, 112

Fisher, Bob, 152

Fisher, Mendel, 157

Fogelman, Avron, 208

Fogelman, Morris, 120, 150, 153

Foltz, H., 48

Foltz, Theodore, 24, 27

Ford, Henry, 111

Forrest, General Nathan Bedford, 35

Fort Sumter, 30

Fortas, Abe, 123, 124, 129, 136, 138

Fortas, Dr. Edward M. Chapter of B'nai B'rith Youth Organization for Girls, 121

Fox, Joseph, 120

Fortune Magazine, 155

Frank, Godfrey, 84

Frank, Henry, 110

Frank, Henry, The, 21

Frank, Leo, 107, 108

Frank, Julius and Anna, 164

Frank, Viola, 146

Frankfurt, 163

Frankfurter, Felix, 157

Frankland, A. E., 22, 27, 34, 35, 47, 58, 59

Franklin, F. 77

Franklin, Rabbi M., 77

Franklin, Sam M., 100

Frederick the Great, 4

Free Loan Society, 101

Freedman's Bureau, 45, 46

Freeman, Captain Maurice A., 35

Freudberg, Irving, 165

Fried, Stanley, 184

Friedberger, Anlage, 163

Friedlander, M., 18

Friedlander, Sam, 102

Friedman, Mrs. B., 77

Friedman, Estelle, 172

Friedman, Joel, 171

Friedman, Judah, 78

Friedman, Sophie Goldberger, 112, 138

French Revolution, 5

Front Street Theater, 202

Fruchter, Rabbi Alfred, 72, 151

Fruchter, Jeanette, 72, 151

Fuller, Reverend T. O., 160

Fund for Needy School Children, 196

Garber Ice Cream Co., 183

Garber, Jan, 183

Garber, Myron, 183

Galveston, 76

Gates, Elias, 91, 92, 98

Gates, Elias and Lehman Law Firm, 49, 91

Gates, Florence, 116

Gattman, Raye, 77, 138

Gensburger Brothers, 48

Gensburger, David, 58

George, Henry, Foundation, 106

Gerber, William, 69, 105, 138, 146, 153, 180

German Immigrants, 4, 6, 65, 71, 79

Gideon vs. Wainwright, 124
Glazer, Herbert, 154
Glickman, H., 77
Glueck, Dr. Nelson, 180
Goethe, 164
Gold, Mrs. Raphael, 117
Goldbaum, Miriam, 72, 129
Goldberg, Dr. Fred, 120, 153
Goldberg, J. Alexander, 19
Goldberger, David, 77
Goldberger, Emmanuel, 118
Goldberger, Gertrude, 118
Goldberger, Herman, 118
Goldberger, Herman, (1930s), 143
Goldberger, Dr. Joseph, 97
Goldberger, Leo, 117, 118, 127
Goldberger, Leopold, 77
Goldberger, Milton, 118, 126
Goldberger Printing Co., 118
Goldberger, Regina, 100, 118
Goldberger, Sam, 118
Goldman, H., 78
Goldman, I., 78
Goldsmith, A., 51
Goldsmith Civic Garden Center, 21
Goldsmith, Dora, 20
Goldsmith, E, O., 18
Goldsmith, Isaac, 19
Goldsmith, Jacob, 19, 20, 68
Goldsmith, Jack, 196, 197
Goldsmith, Jack, Jr., 183
Goldsmith, Louis, 50
Goldsmith, Mattie, 62
Goldsmith's, 19, 20, 196
Goldstein's Delicatessen, 73
Goldstein, Miriam, 135

Goldstein, Joseph, 102
Goltman, Dr. Max, 92
Goodman, Abe, 96, 105, 138
Goodman, Alice, 146
Goodman, Benjamin, Jr., 147, 160, 179, 182
Goodman, Estelle, 128
Goodman, Isabel, 182
Goodman, Rabbi Isadore, 180
Goodman, Joseph, 48
Goodman, Julius, 21, 84
Goodman, Pat, 146
Goodman, William, 22
Goodman, William, (1930s), 146
Gordon, Professor Cyrus, 2
Gottlieb, M., 51
Grafco, 130
Grant, Ulysses S., 38, 39, 40, 42, 43, 44
Greater Memphis Urban Development Corporation, 198
Green, Mr. and Mrs. A., 117
Greenblatt, Rabbi Nathan, 151
Greenhorns, 65
Greenlaw Opera House, 61
Green Family, 108
Grinspan, Mel, 153, 196, 197, 201
Gronauer, Herman, 21, 36, 44
Gronauer, Joseph, 49, 62
Gross, Emil, 35
Grossman, Rabbi Raphael, 202
Gruber, Anna, 171
Guardsmark, 200
Gurley, Congressman John Addison, 41

Haas, Jake, 89
Haas, Mildred, 179
Haase, Charles J., 97, 98, 102, 119
Haase, Gus, 50
Haase, Dr. Marcus, 96, 98, 110
Hadassah, 116, 117, 126, 148
Hadassah, Junior, 117
Hahn, Eva, 141
Haile, Andrew J., 37
Halle, A. Arthur, Sr., 140, 145, 182
Halle, A. Arthur, Jr., 201
Halle, Edwin W., 110
Halle, Louis, Family, 116
Halle, Phil A., Store, 140
Halle, Sol, 145
Halle, Solomon, 17
Halleck, Henry W., 41, 42
Hanauer, Louis, 36, 49, 61
Hanoch, N., 77
Hanover, Donna, 202
Hanover, J., 49
Hanover, J. Alan, 149
Hanover, Joseph, 111, 112, 138
Hanover, T. E., 74
Hanover's Shoe Store, 73
Hardwood Lumber Report, 207
Harpman Brothers, 84
Harpmann, Sig, 102
Harpmann, Sol, 28
Hart, David, 7
Hebrew Benevolent Society, 9, 26, 101
Hebrew Educational Institute, 37
Hebrew Immigrant Aid Society, 66, 76

Hebrew Language, 206
Hebrew Orphans Asylum, 51
Hebrew Relief Association, 53, 71
Hebrew Union College, 53, 66, 129, 180
Hebrew Watchman, 117, 157, 158
Herff, Herbert Foundation, 148
Herff, Herbert, 182
Herff Motor Co., 149
Herrmann, Belle, 80
Herrmann, Dr. Max, 93
Hertzberg, Arthur, 89
Hertzberg, Rabbi Arthur, 181
Herzberg Brothers, 49
Herzl, Theodore, 100
Hesse, Birdie, 62, 102
Hesse, Solomon, 28
Hexter, Avrome N., 110
Hexter, Mrs. George, 77
Heyman, Earl, 102
Higham, John, 23, 63, 111
Hildreth, Beatrice, 77
Hiller, Lucille, 116
Hirsch, D., 22
Hirsch, Eric, 114, 145
Hirsh, B. W., Jr., 140, 145
Hitler, Adolph, 155, 157, 164, 173, 191
Hobson Inn, 116
Hodges, Mary Magdalen, 93
Hohenberg Brothers Co., 131
Hohenberg, Elkan, 28
Hoffheimer, N., 28
Holocaust, 136, 160, 165, 172, 176, 201
Home Guards, 43
Hooks, Reverend Benjamin,

187, 196
Hooks, Ben, Breakfast Club, 196
Hooks, Frances, 148
Howard Association, The, 59, 60
Hull, Cordell, Secretary of State, 106, 137, 173
Humes High School, 130
Humko, 130
Hunt, Reverend Blair, 34
Hurlbut, General Stephen S., 39
Hurwitz, B., 79
Hutchison School, 156
Hyman, M., 78

Ickes, Harold, 123
Indianapolis Tree of Life Mutual Benefit Association, 58
Industrial Removal Office, 76
Ingram, Mayor William B., 193
Institute for Christian Clergy, 179
intermarriage, 24, 207
Interracial Committee, 126
Irish immigrants, 68
Isaacs, A., 77
Isaacs, Ignatz, 78
Isaacs, M. R., 48
Isaacs, S., 77
Isenberg Family, 79
Isenberg, Julie, 182
"Is Religion Necessary?" 136
Israel, i, 175, 206
Isserman, Dr. Ferdinand, 180, 189
Istrov, I., 100
Italian immigrants, 68
Italy, 4

Jacobs, Hortense, 128
Jacobson, Mildred, 116
Jaffe, Ray and Rose, 100
James Park, 63
Javits, Senator Jacob, 157
Jennings, Herbert, 140
Jewish community of Memphis, 2, 4, 72
Jewish Family Service, 147, 205, 207
Jewish Federation, 147, 148, 205, 206
Jewish Historical Society of Memphis and the Mid-South, 190
Jewish National Fund, 100, 136
Jewish Neighborhood House, 71, 101, 128, 135, 150, 171
Jewish Service Agency, 136
Jewish Spectator, 53
Jewish Student Union, 208
Jewish Welfare Board, 152
Jewish Welfare Fund, 107, 136, 146, 159, 170, 171, 181, 201
Jews and Christians, 28
Jews in the South, 27, 41
Johnson, Lady Bird, 192
Johnson, Lyndon Baines, 124, 191
Joseph II of Austria, 5
Judaeans, 3
Judah, Hart, 27
Just, Louis, 48

Kabakoff, Elias, 100
Kahn and Freiburg Dry Goods,

95
Kahn, Florence, 95
Kahn, Samuel, 96, 140
Kanarek, Israel, 153
Kanarek, Sol, 79
Kanarek, Zalke, 78
Kapell, Nathan, 78
Kapelow, Yetta, 171
Kaplan, Linda, 195
Kaplan, Morris, 108
Karchmer, Carl, 153
Karchmer, I. E., 154
Kaskel, Cesar, 41
Katz, Donna, 202
Katz, Eugene, 202
Katz, Grace, 195
Katz, Herman, 98
Katz, Jeanette, 181
Katz, Morris, 166
Katz, Nina, 146, 165, 166, 167
Katz Family, 108
Kaufman, Abe, Family, 116
Kaufman, Leah and Moishe, 169, 171
Keating, J. F., 77, 112
Kefauver, Estes, 103, 149
Kellerman, Lou, 116
Kelman, Meyer, 167, 169, 170
Kemker, Harry, 110
Kempner, Esther, 134
Kennedy, President John F., i, 185
Kennedy, Robert, 185, 198
Kerns, Julian, 116
Kibel, 167, 169
Kiersky, Elias, 110
Kilstein, Jacob, 167, 168, 169, 170, 171

King Cotton Products, 133
King, Reverend Martin Luther, Jr., 88, 185, 188, 189, 191
Kipper, Fannie and Dorothy, 135
Klein, George, 72
Knights and Ladies of Honor, 50
Kohlberg, Jacob, 57
Kohler, Kaufmann, 66
Kohler, P., 51
Koninsky, H., 22, 77
Kopald, S. L., Sr., 116
Kopald, S. L., Jr., 129, 130, 182
Koppman, Lionel, 32
Korean War, 177
Korones, Dr. Sheldon, 201
Kramer, Lewis, 99, 107
Kraus Cleaners, 147
Kremer, Lazard, 18, 28, 37
Kremer, Marjean, 195
Kremer, Sylvia, 135
Kriger, Rose Belz, Chapter of B'nai B'rith Youth Organization for Girls, 121
Kristallnacht, 158, 163, 172
Kuhn, M. A., 35
Kuhn, Fritz, 155
Ku Klux Klan, 109, 111, 123
Kutner, Rabbi Seymour, 151

Ladies Hebrew Benevolent Society, 26, 52
Landsman, 66
Langer, Jack, 180
Lansky Brothers, 149
Lansky's Store, 72
Laski, Dr. R. L., 28, 48, 49

Latura, WIld Bill, 104
Lautenberg, Senator Frank, 205
Lazarov, Joe, 153
Lazerowitz, Rosa, 120
Leavy, J. M. Tom, 43
Lee, General Robert E., 44
Lee, Seymour and Fannie, 21, 79
Lee, Will, 142
Leeser, Rabbi Isaac, 9, 40
Lehman and Co., 18
Lehman, Leopold, 48, 49
LeMoyne-Owen College, 195
Lemsky, Abe, 206, 207
Lemsky Fund, 206, 207
Leonard, Benny, 74
Lerner, Eugene, 165
Levi, Leo N., Hospital, 97
Levitch's Store, 72
Levin, Cantor Morris I., Chapter
    of B'nai B'rith Youth Organi-
    zation for Girls, 121
Levitz Family, 108
Levy, Abraham S., 22, 35
Levin, Solomon, 37
Levy, Charles, 18, 34
Levy, David, 9, 18, 24
Levy, David Asher, 138
Levy, Emanuel, 9, 58
Levy, Dr. Gilbert, 94, 110, 161
Levy, Hannah, 161
Levy, Jonas, 26
Levy, Cantor Joseph, 9
Levy, Jo and Ralph, 184
Levy, Joseph, 114
Levy, Leo, 114, 121, 164
Levy, Dr. Louis, 124, 125, 147
Levy, Matilda, 161
Levy, Moses, 18, 48

Levy, Pauline, Sewing Circle, 81,
    135
Levy, Samuel, 18
Levy's Drug Store, 73, 99
Levy's Ladies Toggery, 114, 164
Lewis, Audrey, 202
Lewis, Daniel, 85
Lewis Ford Co., 149
Lewis, Hubert, 202
Lewis, Jerry Lee, 149
Lewis, Joseph, 149
Lewis, Julius, 85, 171, 182
Lewis, Lawrence, 149
Lewis, Linda Burson, 202
Lewis, Moses, 68, 77, 85
Lewis, Selma, 195, 202
Lewis, Sol, Family, 116
Liberman, M. G., 113
Lichterman, Herbert, 113
Lichterman, Ira, 113, 140, 148
Lichterman, Lottie, 113, 148
Lichterman, Martin, 113
Lichterman Nature Center, 149
Lieberman, L., 19
Lightman, Jeanne, 202
Lightman, M. A., Sr., 114, 115,
    139, 146, 159
Lightman, Richard, 198, 202
Lincoln, Abraham, 14, 30, 38,
    41, 42
Lind, Jenny, 13
Lind, Jenny, Theater, 30
Lipman, A., 77
Lipman, Ida, 120, 182
Lipman, Ira, 200
Lipman's Loan Office, 114
Lipman, Sol, 154
Loeb and Holland, 19

Loeb, Adolph, 28
Loeb, Henry, Sr., 84
Loeb, Mayor Henry, Jr., 181, 187, 188
Loeb, William, 159
Loeb's Laundry, 84
Lodz, 167
Loewenberg, Ferdinand, 77
Loewenberg, Ruth, 148
Loewenberg, William, 113, 147, 148, 149, 161, 179
Loewenberg, William I., 148
Loewenthal, Dr. R., 49
Loskove, M., 78
Loskovitz Pool Room, 74
Lovenson, Samuel A., 110
Loventhal, Lee, 106
Lovers of Zion, 99
Lowenstein, B. and Brothers Co., 16, 48, 184
Lowenstein Brothers, 15, 18
Lowenstein, Elias, 16, 61
Lowenstein, J. H. and Brothers, 18, 59
Lowenstein, Marguerite, 116
Lowenstine, David, 43, 44, 49
Lowenstine, H. W., 49
Lucas, Louis, 199
Lynching, 104

McCarran, Senator Pat, 174
McKellar, Senator Kenneth, 106
McLain, William Tyler, 69
Magevney, Eugene, 2
Malco Theaters, 114, 198
Malkin, Sam, 115
Manis, Yetta Feinberg, 112

Mansfield, Richard, 95
Mann, Dr. Louis L., 179
Marcus, Rabbi Jacob Rader, 33
Margolin Hebrew Academy/Yeshiva of the South, 132
Margolin, Ben, 108, 132
Margolin, Joe, 108, 132
Margolin, Sam, 132, 151
Mark, Henry, 26
Markell, Joan, 148
Market Street School, 69, 70, 86
Marks, Henry, 22
Marks, Ruth, 170, 171
Marx and Bensdorf, 21, 97
Masons, 53
Maxon, Bishop James M., 160
Mayer, E., 19, 22
Mayer, Captain Max Halle, 144, 145
Meltzner, Aaron, 100
Memphis Academy of Arts, 147
Memphis Academy of Medicine, 94
Memphis and Charleston Railroad, 14
Memphis and Shelby County Human Relations Commission, 187
Memphis and Shelby County War and Welfare Fund Campaign, 146
Memphis Arbeiter Farband, 117
Memphis Avalanche, 62
Memphis Board of Education, 186
Memphis Board of Health, 54, 55, 57, 92, 96

Memphis Brooks Museum of Art, 125, 147

Memphis Chamber of Commerce, 130

Memphis Chapter B'nai B'rith Youth Organization, 121

Memphis Chicks, 133

Memphis Club, 50, 102

Memphis Committee on Community Relations, 186, 198

Memphis Community Chest, 85

Memphis Community Fund, 128, 129, 134, 147

Memphis Corporate Charter, 81

Memphis Cotton Carnival, 140

Memphis Cotton Exchange, 114

Memphis Council of Social Agencies, 96

Memphis Country Club, 207

Memphis Daily Appeal, 36

Memphis Daily Bulletin, 38

Memphis Eye, Ear, and Throat Hospital, 98

Memphis, founded, 1, 2

Memphis, fall of, 38

Memphis Goodwill Meeting, 134

Memphis Health Department, 92

Memphis Hebrew Academy, 132, 151

Memphis Hebrew Hospital and Relief Association, 57, 58

Memphis Hospital Medical School, 92

Memphis Hunt and Polo Club, 156

Memphis Jewish Community Center, 118, 152, 153, 154, 207

Memphis Jewish Federation, 120, 128, 205, 207

Memphis Jewish Foundation, 207

Memphis Jewish Home, 207

Memphis Law School, 132

Memphis Literacy Council, 166

Memphis Little Theater, 202

Memphis Lodge of Elks, 138

Memphis Medical College, 49

Memphis Mennerchor, 50

Memphis Mental Hygiene Agency, 190

Memphis Ministers Association, 187, 189

Memphis Ohio Railroad, 14

Memphis Parks Commission, 159

Memphis Pie Co., 73

Memphis Plough Community Fund, 87

Memphis Power and Light Co., 97

Memphis Refugee Committee, 156, 164

Memphis Riot of 1866, 45, 46

Memphis Rotary Club, 85, 87, 158

Memphis State University, 132, 133, 148, 185, 187

Memphis Symphony Orchestra, 125, 182

Memphis University School, 156

Memphis Volunteer Placement Committee, 195

Mengele, Dr. [Joseph], 169

Menke, Stella, 195

Menken Brothers Store, 17, 48
Menken, J. S., 28, 33, 62
Menken, Nathan D., 60
Menorah Institute, 71, 137, 145, 151
Merchants Credit Association, 113
Methodists, 2
Metro Memphis Shopping Center, 148
Meyer, Dr. Alphonse, Sr.,   93, 110
Meyer, Eulalie, 141
Meyerowitz, Benjamin, 77
Meyers, Angel S., 28
Mid-South Sight Conservation Association, 126
Mikveh, 78
Miles, Frank, 88
Miller, Bea, 202
Miller, L., 98
Miller, T., 100
Miller, William, 70
Milius, A. S., 22
Minor Grocery Store, 73
Minority Regional Purchasing Council, 198
"Miracle in Memphis, A," 93
Mitchell, John, 103, 149
Moneylenders, 7
Mook, Marjorie, 116
Mooney, C. P. J., 109
Morgenstern, Dr. Julian, 180
Morgenthau, H. and L., 22
Morningside Park, 156
Moss, Morrie and Lillian, 182
Morris, Louis, 140
Moskovitz, Herman, 100

Moskovitz, Jack, 100
Moskovitz's Grocery Store, 73
Mother Mary Euphrasia, 93
Motion Picture Theater Industry of Memphis and the Mid-South, 159
Myers, I. L. Paper Co., 139
Myers, Isaac, 139, 147
Myers, Mayer, 113, 139
Myers, Mayer Paper Co., 139

Napolean, 5
Nathan, Emil, 101
Nathan, James, Jr., 101
Nathan, Julius, 24, 27, 28
Nathan's Loans, 114
National Association for the Advancement of Colored People, 185, 187
National Conference of Christians and Jews, 122, 125, 134, 148, 160, 166, 190
National Cotton Council, 140
National Council of Churches of Christ in America, 160
National Council of Jewish Women, 134, 150, 164
National Mortgage Co., 132
National Origins Act, 111
Nayowitz, Rabbi Joseph, 151
Nazi(s), 155, 157, 165, 168
Nazi Refuge Fund Day, 159
Neo-Nazism, 208
Neumann, Robert G., 158
New Americans Club, 201
Newburger Cotton Co., 80
Newburger, Joseph, 80

New Deal, The, 177

New Orleans Crescent, 36

New Orleans Orphan Asylum Home, 53

New York Times, 69, 158

Nicholson Pavement, 54

Nineteenth Amendment, 112

Nineteenth Century Club, 122, 146

Notowitz, Max, 172

Novack, A., 117

Nylon Net Co., 149

Oak Hall, 20

Ochs, Mrs. Ike, 77

Okeon, Lester A., Chapter of B'nai B'rith Youth Organization for Girls, 121

Olim, Dr. Charles, 141

Olswanger, Berl, 182, 183

Olswing, Mr. and Mrs. Sam, 120

O'Mell, Sam, 78

Oppenheim, I., 115

Oppenheim, I. and S. Bejach, 84

Oppenheimer, Henry, 9

Organized Jewish Front Line Soldiers, 161

Orr, Marcus W. Print Room, 125

Orthodox Judaism, 89

Ottenheimer, Louis, 50

Overton, Mayor Watkins, 160

Owens, Father, 160

Padawer, M., 78, 79

Pale of Settlement, 64

Palestine, 136

Palmer, Attorney General Mitchell, 110

Panel of American Women, 196

Panic of 1819, 1

Parker, Dr. Joseph, 202

Passow, Rabbi Meyer, 181

Peabody Hotel, 90

Peddlers, 6, 7, 14, 15

Perel and Lowenstein, 120

Perel, Philip, 201

Peres and Micou, 10

Peres Colony, 137

Peres, Hardwig, 11, 100, 111, 122, 126, 137, 142, 146

Peres, Israel, 11, 62, 78, 79, 91, 100, 121

Peres, Israel H. Memorial Scholarship, 122, 123

Peres, Jacob, 9, 10, 21, 22, 24, 25, 40, 47, 49, 53, 76

Perlman, Frank, 98

Perlman, Itzhak, 202

Phagan, Mary, 107

Philharmonic Society, 30

Phillips, Anne, 108

Phoenix Boxing Arena, 74

Pi Tau Pi Fraternity, 102

Picard, Ralph, 138

Pierce, Harvey, 202

Pinch, The, 67, 68, 70, 71, 73, 76, 86, 93, 100, 127, 130

Pinstein, Aleck, 117

Plesofsky, Dr. Jacob, 181

Plough, Abe, 86, 87, 88, 123, 137, 146, 191, 208

Plough Foundation, 87

Plough, Inc., 86, 87, 88

Plough, Moses, Memorial Hay Fever Clinic, 125
pogroms, xii, 64
Poland, 166
Pope Pius VI, 5
Porter, Dr. D. T., 61
Postal, Bernard, 32
Presbyterians, 2
Presley, Elvis Aaron, 72, 149, 150, 185
Press Scimitar, 122, 136, 158, 160
Protestant Pastors Association, 160
Protocols of the Elders of Zion, 64, 111
Prussia, 5
Pump, Henrietta, 60
Putzel, M. L., 22

Race Relations Committee, 187, 188, 198
Ratner, Marvin, 198
Reconstruction, 45, 54, 104
Red Scare, 110
Reena Chapter, B'nai B'rith Youth Organization for Girls, 121
Reform Judaism, 25, 63, 66
Regina Health Center, 135
Reinach, H., 24
Republican Party of Tennessee, 129
Reudelheuber, Christine, 70
Revolutions of 1848, 6
Rex Club, 92, 98, 102, 116
Rex Ridgeway Club, 152
Reynolds, James, 88, 191

Rhodes College, 148
Rhodes, S. W., 59
Rice, Frank, 105
Ridblatt's Bakery, 73
Ridgeway Country Club, 98, 102
Ritterban, Amalia, 120
River City Chapter, B'nai B'rith Youth Organization for Girls, 121
Riverview Kansas Day Care Center, 148
Robinow, I. M., 157
Romans, 3
Romeo, Frank, Jr., 182
Roosevelt, Franklin Delano, 106, 123, 173
Rosen, Mr. and Mrs. H., 100
Rosen, Lester, 186, 187, 188, 193
Rosenbaum, Rebecca, 120
Rosenberg, Herbert, 73
Rosenblum Family, 108
Rosenblum, Julius, 98
Rosenblum, Raphael, 98
Rosenblum, Saul, 98
Rosenfield, Albert, 103
Rosenfield, William B., 111
Rosenheim, L., 50
Rosenheim, Samuel, 50, 77
Rosenthal, Mitchell, 101
Ross, Miriam, 152
Rothschild, Fannie, 8
Rothschild, Rabbi Jacob, 186
Rothstein, Sam, 98
Rudner, Dr. Henry, 93
Runaway House, 148, 154
Rushansky, Hyman, 117
Rushdie, Salmon, x

Russia, xii
Russian immigrants, new, 205
Russian Rendition, 110

Sacharin, Ben, 149
Sacharin's Fish Market, 73
Sachs, Ben, 102
St. Francis Hospital, 148
St. Joseph's Hospital, 53
St. Jude Children's Research Hospital, 148
St. Louis, The, 158
St. Mary's Episcopal Cathedral, 189
St. Patrick's Church, 160
Salky, Ethel, 135
Salky, Irvin, 198
Salky, Rose, 135
Salomon, Edward M., 138
Salon Circle, 100, 150
Salvation Army, 161
Samelson, Ike, 21, 84
Samfield, Rabbi Max, 53, 58, 62, 66, 77, 101, 119
Samuels Furniture Store, 74
Samuels, Helen, 180
Sarna, Jonathan, xi
Sarner, Rabbi Ferdinand, 58, 59
Sawrie's Boarding House, 116
Schaffer, Fagie, 72
Schaffer, Mr. and Mrs. H. G., 100
Schaffer, Mrs. H. I., 117
Schaffer, H. I., 78
Scharff, Aaron, 145, 184
Scharff, Abe, 147, 182
Schechter, H., 117

Schechter, Solomon, Day School, 206
Scheinberg, Jacob, 98, 117
Schering-Plough Corporation, 117
Scheuner, Harris, 182
Schiffman Family, 108
Schiller, 164
Schimmels, A. D., 51
Schirokauer, Dr. Arno, 156
Schlesinger, Sigmund, 37
Schlesinger's Dry Goods Store, 74
Schloss, Daniel, 18, 50
Schloss, Gilbert, 153
Schloss, Harry, 79
Schloss, Florence and Ollie, 116
Schloss, Samuel, 9, 18, 27
Schneider, A., 117
Schneider's Fruit Stand, 73
Schuster, Paul, 22, 49
Schutzbrief, 5
Schwab, A., 62
Schwab, William, 152
Schwartz, Paul, 154
Schwartzenberg, Hattie, 62
Scopes Trial, 136
Sebraning, I., 78
Sebraning Shoe Store, 73
Secession, 30, 31, 34
Seessel, Albert, 17
Seessel and Ashner, 84
Seessel, Arthur, 48
Seessel, Henry, 9, 16, 22, 28, 34, 47, 48
Seessel, Jane, 146, 202
Seidman, P. K., 183, 200
Seigel, Herbert, 110

Seiger, Rabbi Chaim, 202
Seligman, Fannie, 161
Seligman, Joseph, 108
Seligman, Leo, 162, 163, 181
Sephardim, 3, 6
Sewel, Mrs. Perry, 117
Shabbos goy, 72
Shainberg, Herbert, 153
Shainberg, Sam, 85
Shainberg's Store, 85, 196
Shankman, Aaron, 154
Shankman, Joe, 117
Shankman, Sam, 100, 126, 136, 183
Sharpe, Sam, 98
Shebs, S., 100
Shelby Graves Co., 35
Shendelman, Laizer, 67
Sherman, General William Tecumseh, 38, 39
Sherman Guards, 43
Siegel, Miriam, 135
Silberberg, Max, 98
Silver, Dr. Abba Hillel, 180
Simon, A., 62, 85, 126
Simon and Gwin Advertising Co., 133
Simon, Milton, 133
Simon, M., Dry Goods, 18, 24, 35
Simon, Selma, 195
Siskin the Tailor, 74
skinheads, 208
Slaton, Governor John, 108
Slavery, 32, 104
socialism, 65
Solomon, Haym, 7
Sondheim Family, 79

Sonny's Loan Office, 114
Sons of Israel, 99
Southern Christian Leadership Conference, 191
Southern Club, 28
Southern Law School, 132
Southern Leather Co., 113
Southern Tenant Farmers Union, 142
South Memphis Stockyards, 113
Southwestern College, 122, 156
Springarn, Dr. Marcus, 139
Springer, M., 77
Stadper, Dr. I., 100
Stampfer, Rabbi Elijah, 126, 151
Stanley, Carey, 202
Starks Family, 108
Starks, Reverend Henry, 87, 189
Statue of Liberty, xii
Steinberg, Mrs. Sam, 117
Steinberg, Samuel, 84, 126
Stern, Beatrice, 134
Stern, Harriet, 195
Stern, Dr. Neuton, 94, 141
Stern, Dr. Neuton, Chair of Cardiology at University of Tennessee Medical School, 95, 141
Stern, Dr. Thomas N., 94, 141, 201
Sternberg, Dave, 21, 79, 101, 102
Sternberg, I. and Sons, 84
Stevenson, Coke, 124
Strauss, Gaston D., 113
Strauss, Isaac, 35
Strauss, Joseph, 24
Strauss, Lehman, and Co., 18

Stuyvesant, Governor Peter, 4, 28, 205
Summit Club, 187
Suzore's Theater, 73
Sugarmon, Russell, 198
Sykes, Mrs. Frank, 152
Synagogue Council of America, 160

Talmud Torah, 77, 129, 181
Tannenbaum, Frances and Blema, 135
Tannenbaum, N., 70
Taubenblatt, Sam, 145
Taubenblatt's Delicatessen, 74
Taxing District of Memphis, 61
Taxon, Rabbi Morris, 129, 137
Temple Israel, 9, 66, 103, 109, 110, 112, 118, 129, 131, 137, 147, 159, 179, 180, 188, 200, 201
Tendler, Dr. Morton, 181
Tennessee Hotel, 165, 171
Tennessee Mental Health Convention, 190
Tennessee Society for Prevention of Cruelty to Animals and Children, 53, 62
Tennessee State Supreme Court, 10
Third United States Colored Heavy Artillery, 45
Thompson, Russell, 199
Tobey, Mayor Frank, 180
Tobias, Bertha, 116
Tomlinson, H. T., 28
Touro, Judah, 9

Tribunaski, 167
Truman, President Harry S., 174
Tuckahoe Lane, 156
Tumanskaya, Mme. Valentina, 89
Turner, Jesse, 198
Tuska, Rabbi Simon, 24, 32, 36, 37, 40, 50, 52, 53
Tuska, Simon, Lodge, 28

United Bedding Co., 89
United Charities of Memphis, 53
United Hebrew Relief Association, 28
United Palestine Appeal, 126
United Way, 120, 130, 148, 154
Unity Lodge, 50
University of Memphis, 132, 148, 208
University of Tennessee Medical School, 92
Urbanization, 177
Urban League, 186

Vendig, Sol, 28
Vienna, 5
Vietnam, 185

Wainman, Charles, 119
Waldauer, Abe, 102, 105, 106, 138, 145, 146, 183
Waldauer, Dorothy, 106, 107, 135
Walker, John, 24
Walsh Family, 73, 73, 127

Walter the Tinner, 73
War on Poverty, 193
Warhaftig, H., 101
Warren, Earl, 124
Washer, Harry, 121, 144
Washer Post of Jewish War Veterans, 144
Washington, Booker T. Minority Development, 148
Washington, George, ii, x
Washington Rifle Co., 35
Wax, Helen, 179, 190
Wax, Rabbi James, 179, 180, 182, 186, 187, 188, 189, 190, 191, 197
Weil, Trude, 183
Weinberg, Lew, 133
Weinberg, S., 78
Weinberg's, 133
Weinman, Louis, 79
Weinberg, Marilyn, 196
Weinreich, Frieda, 168, 169
Weinreich, Sam, 168, 170, 171
Weintraub, Sam, 144
Weiss, A., 77
Weiss, D., 79
Weiss, Dora, 100
Weiss, Evelyn, 92
Weiss, Harry, 110
Weiss, Mary, 100
Weiss, Miriam, Chapter of B'nai B'rith Youth Organization for Girls, 121
Weiss's Saloon, 74
Wener, Sy, 153
Wexler, Louise, 52
White Paper, 137
White Supremacy, 104

Who's Who of Clubwomen of Tennessee, 138
Willing Hands Sewing Circle, 80
Willis, A. W., 198
Wilson, President Woodrow, 110
Winchester, James, 9
Winchester, Marcus, 9
Wingfield, Dr. Marshall, 180
Wise, Rabbi Isaac Mayer, 24, 27, 41, 66
Wise, Rabbi Stephen S., 136, 137, 146, 156, 157, 173
Witkowsky, Joseph, 21
Wolf, Charles, 120
Wolf, Frederick, 36
Wolf, Harry, 129
Wolf, Herbert, Joanne, and Louise, 200
Wolf, M., 79
Wolf, Tobias, 22
Wolff, Mr. and Mrs. Harry S., 120
Wolfson, Louis, 124
Woolf, Leonard, 176
Workers Council of Jewish Neighborhood House, 128
Workmen's Circle, 98
World War I, 110, 173
World War II, 143, 144, 152, 153, 176
Wright, H., 26
Wruble, Diane Leach, 187
Wruble, Dr. Lawrence, 187
Wurzburg, Abe, 86, 147
Wurzburg Brothers, 86
Wurzburg, Jocelyn, 196
Wurzburg, Reggie, 86

Wurtzburger, Leo, 103, 116, 150

Yale University, 142
Yellow Fever, 54, 61, 104
Yellow Fever Fund, 78
Yeshiva of the South, 152
Yiddish, 4, 64, 67, 72, 98, 99
Young Judaean Club, 118
Young Men's Christian Association, 147, 148, 152
Young Men's Hebrew Association, 51, 92, 102, 152
Young Men's Hebrew Relief Organization, 129
Yulee, David, 42

Zellner Shoe Co., 18
Zimmerman, Otto, 51, 62
Zimmerman's Dry Goods Store, 74
Zionism, 65, 99, 100, 118, 146, 156
Zionist Council, 137
Zionist District of Memphis, 125
Zionist Youth Council, 119
Zito's Restaurant, 74
Zuckerman, Pinchas, 202
Zwechenbaum, S., 79
Zweifel, D., 48